OXFORD STUDENT TEXTS

Series Editor: Steven Croft

William Congreve

The Way of the World

Edited by Diane Maybank

UNIVERSITY PRESS

Great Clarendon Street, Oxford OX2 6DP, United Kingdom

Oxford University Press is a department of the University of Oxford.
It furthers the University's objective of excellence in research, scholarship,
and education by publishing worldwide

Oxford is a registered trade mark of Oxford University Press
in the UK and in certain other countries

© Oxford University Press 2014

The moral rights of the author have been asserted

First published 2014

All rights reserved. No part of this publication may be reproduced,
stored in a retrieval system, or transmitted, in any form or by any means,
without the prior permission in writing of Oxford University Press,
or as expressly permitted by law, or under terms agreed with the appropriate
reprographics rights organization. Enquiries concerning reproduction
outside the scope of the above should be sent to the Rights Department,
Oxford University Press, at the address above

You must not circulate this book in any other binding or cover
and you must impose this same condition on any acquirer

British Library Cataloguing in Publication Data

Data available

ISBN: 978-0-19-839344-3

1 3 5 7 9 10 8 6 4 2

Typeset by PDQ Digital Media Solutions Ltd

Printed in Great Britain by CPI Group (UK) Ltd., Croydon, CR0 4YY

Paper used in the production of this book is a natural, recyclable product made from
wood grown in sustainable forests. The manufacturing process conforms to the
environmental regulations of the country of origin.

The publishers would like to thank the following for permission to reproduce
photographs:

Pages 4, 7, 184: National Portrait Gallery, London; page 10: British Museum, London,
UK/The Bridgeman Art Library; page 15: 2000 New Mermaids edition of The Way of
the World, ed. Brian Gibbons, A&C Black, London; page 170: Private Collection/The
Bridgeman Art Library; page 181: Image Asset Management Ltd/Alamy; page 191:
Photostage; page 206: Shakespeare Theatre Company, photo by Carol Rosegg;
page 219: Mander and Mitchenson, University of Bristol/ArenaPAL

Contents

Acknowledgements iv

Foreword vi

William Congreve in Context 1
A life of William Congreve 2
1700: England on the cusp of change 8
Congreve's detractors and his defence of comedy 12

The Way of the World 15

Notes 123

Interpretations 166
Restoration comedy 166
Spectacle and intimacy: Inside a 'tennis court theatre' 170
Who were Congreve's audience? 173
Sources and literary references for *The Way of the World* 176
Casting and characters 178
What women want in *The Way of the World* (and what they get) 193
Making drama out of unpromising material: Money and the law 197
Language and style 201
Critical views 210

Essay Questions 213

Chronology 215

Further Reading 220

Glossary 224

Appendix 1 Congreve's London 229

Appendix 2 Ideas for studying the play in the classroom 231

Appendix 3 Comparative texts 233

Acknowledgements

The text of the play is taken from *William Congreve: The Way of the World and Other Plays*, edited by Eric S. Rump (Penguin Classics, 2006).

Acknowledgements from Diane Maybank

My thanks go to Steven Croft for his positive encouragement and to Jan Doorly for her careful editing and excellent professional advice at all stages of this project. In the course of preparing this edition I have consulted several biographies of Congreve and read many scholarly reviews of *The Way of the World*. I have acknowledged these sources in the Further Reading section of this edition and remain indebted to their authors for ideas and insights that have helped me in fully appreciating the complexities of this challenging and far-sighted comedy. Debates about *The Way of the World* continue to remind us of Congreve's relevance to matters concerning women, personal freedom and public responsibility. Recent productions of the play have shown how much great dialogue and witty repartee matter to a good evening's entertainment at the theatre. I hope this edition will assist readers in their quest to understand one of the defining plays of the early eighteenth century.

This book is dedicated to Paul Miller: 'And gladly wolde he lerne and gladly teche'.

Editors

Steven Croft, the series editor, holds degrees from Leeds and Sheffield universities. He has taught at secondary and tertiary level and headed the Department of English and Humanities in a tertiary college. He has 25 years' examining experience at A level and is currently a Principal Examiner for English. He has written several books on teaching English at A level, and his publications for Oxford University Press include *Exploring Literature*, *Success in AQA Language and Literature* and *Exploring Language and Literature*.

Diane Maybank attended the universities of Kent, Cambridge and London where she studied English Literature as an undergraduate and Film Studies as a postgraduate. She has been teaching English and Media Studies for over 30 years in schools and colleges in France, New Zealand and the UK. Until 2011 she taught in the English and Media Department at a sixth form college.

Foreword

Oxford Student Texts, under the founding editorship of Victor Lee, have established a reputation for presenting literary texts to students in both a scholarly and an accessible way. The new editions aim to build on this successful approach. They have been written to help students, particularly those studying English literature for AS or A level, to develop an increased understanding of their texts. Each volume in the series, which covers a selection of key poetry and drama texts, consists of four main sections which link together to provide an integrated approach to the study of the text.

The first part provides important background information about the writer, his or her times and the factors that played an important part in shaping the work. This discussion sets the work in context and explores some key contextual factors.

This section is followed by the poetry or play itself. The text is presented without accompanying notes so that students can engage with it on their own terms without the influence of secondary ideas. To encourage this approach, the Notes are placed in the third section, immediately following the text. The Notes provide explanations of particular words, phrases, images, allusions and so forth, to help students gain a full understanding of the text. They also raise questions or highlight particular issues or ideas which are important to consider when arriving at interpretations.

The fourth section, Interpretations, goes on to discuss a range of issues in more detail. This involves an examination of the influence of contextual factors as well as looking at such aspects as language and style, and various critical views or interpretations. A range of activities for students to carry out, together with discussions as to how these might be approached, are integrated into this section.

At the end of each volume there is a selection of Essay Questions, a Chronology, and a Further Reading list.

We hope you enjoy reading this text and working with these supporting materials, and wish you every success in your studies.

Steven Croft   *Series Editor*

William Congreve in Context

A story persists that following *The Way of the World*'s disappointing first night, William Congreve felt his audience's indifference so keenly that he marched on stage and berated them for being fools and philistines. The story is true in spirit if not in fact. Had Congreve misjudged the prevailing mood, which called for plays with clear moral and emotional purpose? No; he had simply chosen not to pander to it and suffered the consequences.

Everything about the situation at Lincoln's Inn Fields theatre in 1700 had urged the writing of a popular play. The company to which he had pledged loyalty was almost bankrupt. The Italian dancers, hired to attract big audiences and cash in on the taste for light entertainment, had cost a small fortune. The theatre's location was not central enough to guarantee safe travel, and the auditorium was a third the size of its rival at Drury Lane. Public campaigns against the immorality of the London stage were putting off newly won audiences, especially women. There were simply not enough customers to support two theatres, and the smaller one was losing out.

Congreve, meanwhile, was intellectually and creatively engrossed in dramaturgy (dramatic composition and representation, see Glossary page 224) and committed to writing great parts for his ageing company of actors. The audience were of secondary interest – unless you were in the auditorium, where the play's distinctive London setting would have left you in no doubt that you were the target for its attack on greed, sexual infidelity and family politics.

Major events (such as a new play by a celebrated playwright) that coincide with the turn of a century are usually invested with special significance. With hindsight, does *The Way of the World* express the spirit of a society at a key point in its history? Does the play read the national mood, reflect upon it deeply, and articulate it?

The play masters, surpasses even, the best features of Restoration comedy – the genre associated since the 1660s with the Stuart kings. By 1700 they were out of power and thoroughly discredited. Restoration comedy's rakes (see Glossary) and loose women, with their cynical behaviour and sexually explicit wit, were out of tune with the new order rapidly establishing itself under the constitutional monarchs William and Mary, who reigned together from 1689. Congreve's characters find their vices challenged by strong Whig (see Glossary) values: good sense, restraint, judgement – values somewhat softened by sensibility, but firmly backed by the rule of law.

The Way of the World has had many obstacles to surmount in its 300-year history. It was beset by revisions, adaptations, bowdlerization (see Glossary) or plain indifference; the establishment, both judicial and theatrical, attempted to 'protect' the public from Congreve's honest appraisal of a world of hypocrites and power players, where the stakes are reputation, property and sexual possession.

Today we might still question why Congreve wrote opening scenes so baffling they were more satisfying to read than to watch. They still present a tricky first hurdle for directors.

Congreve wrote no more plays after 1700 and left the theatre scene altogether within a few years. He had written five major plays before his thirtieth birthday, the majority of which were highly successful. The 60 years that followed witnessed the rise in popularity of rather mediocre sentimental comedy (see Glossary), until Oliver Goldsmith (c.1730–1774) and Richard Brinsley Sheridan (1751–1816) emerged as Congreve's theatrical heirs. Like him, they had been shaped by childhood experiences in Ireland. His were the plays they turned to first when they sought to renew and revive the satiric tradition with more benevolent (see Glossary) wit and candid emotions. In Congreve they found a playwright worth emulating for his brilliant dialogue, probing honesty and witty appraisal of men and women engaged in finding a morally and intellectually rigorous mode of living in spite of the ways of the world.

A life of William Congreve

William Congreve was born in Bardsey, a village north of Leeds in West Yorkshire, on 24 January 1670 to parents William (1637–1708) and Mary (c. 1636–1715). Theirs was a wealthy family with royalist (see Glossary) loyalties. He spent his formative years in Ireland, where his army-officer father was posted in 1674. The family settled in Kilkenny in County Kildare in 1681 when his father joined the Duke of Ormond's regiment as a lieutenant in the Irish army.

In 1682 young William entered the highly prestigious Kilkenny College. By all accounts this was an excellent school and Congreve's lifelong love of classical literature began here. From 1686 he continued his studies at Trinity College, Dublin. Here he met the writer Jonathan Swift (1667–1745), with whom he enjoyed a lifelong friendship. He became a regular visitor to the city theatres, including the famous Smock Alley.

In 1688 most of the staff and students at Trinity left for England. The college closed the following year owing to the uncertain and dangerous political situation occasioned by the struggle for the succession to the English throne (see page 9). As the pro-Catholic policies of James II (1633–1701) were enforced in Ireland, Congreve's father lost his commission and the family returned to their main residence at Stretton in Staffordshire. By 1691 William of Orange had defeated James II's army in Ireland and established Protestantism as a political power there. In the period of reasonable stability that followed, Congreve's father returned to Ireland to become land agent for Richard Boyle, the Earl of Cork.

In 1691 Congreve was entered by his father as a law student at the Middle Temple in London, where he 'studied' for the next four years. (Although indifferent to a career in law, he showed his appreciation of what it can do to support a civilized society in *The Way of the World*.) Congreve's passion for writing soon emerged and he joined the company of like-minded wits and writers at Will's Coffee House in Covent Garden. John Dryden (1631–1700), England's foremost literary figure, became a particular friend, mentor and advocate.

In 1692 Congreve published a fashionable romance, *Incognita: or, Love and Duty reconcil'd*, which he had written in his student days. His reputation among London's literary elite grew rapidly. He was soon contributing verses and assisting Dryden with his translations of satires by Juvenal and Persius, and his *Examen Poeticum*, published in 1693.

Portrait of William Congreve from the studio of Sir Godfrey Kneller, 1709

Congreve's career as a playwright could not have started in a more brilliant fashion. *The Old Bachelor* was praised by critics and adored by audiences when it premièred at the Theatre Royal, Drury Lane in March 1693. It enjoyed an unprecedented 14-day run and remained in the company's repertoire for over a century.

Within a year, and still only 23, he had written his second play and begun an intriguing relationship with Anne Bracegirdle (c. 1674–1748), one of the most celebrated actors of the age. Congreve had created the role of Araminta in *The Old Bachelor* for Bracegirdle, but we can only speculate about his love for her; in the absence of facts, questions about their relationship remain unresolved.

She had a fearsome reputation for chastity, so perhaps it was a case of unrequited love. Was she the model for the witty, exasperating and elusive Millamant? Why did the relationship end? Why did he leave her a paltry £200 in his will? What we do know is that he wrote some memorable leading parts for her: Araminta, Cynthia, Angelica, Almira and Millamant. How much his feelings for Bracegirdle are reflected in these roles can never be determined.

The Double Dealer, his second play, had its première at Drury Lane in December 1693. Despite a royal command performance attended by Queen Mary, it was not a success. Congreve, who was always deeply sensitive to the reception of his work, felt slighted and discouraged. However, his third play, *Love for Love*, repeated his first success when it opened at the new theatre in Lincoln's Inn Fields in April 1695, enjoying a 13-night run.

Why the change in venue? The United Company, in residence at Drury Lane, was a deeply unhappy and dissatisfied group of players, restive under the mercurial management of Christopher Rich (1647–1714). Divisions in the company came to a head when actors Thomas Betterton (1635–1710) and Elizabeth Barry (1658–1713) walked out and formed a new company with some of Drury Lane's star players, including Bracegirdle. They applied for a performance licence and from 1695 to 1705 performed in the refurbished Lisle's tennis court at Lincoln's Inn Fields.

The actors' cooperative that took shape there was unique; actors became shareholders and even patent-holders (see Glossary). Congreve and fellow playwright Sir John Vanbrugh (1664–1726) became co-managers. Congreve's support for this new venture went so far as to offer to write a play a year for the company, and he invested money in the theatre.

The year 1695 was a highly successful one for Congreve, whose literary reputation now brought him public commissions. He was appointed to the first of a number of political sinecures (see Glossary), becoming commissioner for licensing hackney coaches. Through his Whig connections he was able to observe closely how party officials governed. He admired the way they consolidated power through brokering deals, making legal contracts and securing finances. He showed how such methods and principles could rein in a disorderly family like the Wishforts in *The Way of the World*.

In February 1697 Congreve's only tragedy, *The Mourning Bride*, was staged to great acclaim. *The Way of the World* premièred in March 1700. His greatest play marked the end of his career as a dramatist; it was not well received or even understood by audiences, and probably achieved no more than a six-night run. To a playwright of Congreve's fame and stature, this was a humiliation and a rejection of the gifts and insights he had to offer.

Although aged only 30, Congreve became a somewhat reclusive figure, reluctant to make new friends and despondent about the theatre and life in general. By 1695 his health had begun to trouble him; he made regular visits to spa towns to take the waters for fatigue, dyspepsia and gout. For a man of letters it must have been particularly difficult to cope with the other ailment that afflicted him, the threat of blindness, caused by cataracts as early as 1710.

He spent time in the company of Bracegirdle, attending her performances. They had been neighbours since the mid-1690s. They rode out and dined together almost every day, keeping the town gossips guessing about the exact nature of their friendship. After about ten years the relationship seems to have dwindled away. Around 1702 or 1703 Bracegirdle was introduced to Congreve's cousin Robert Leke, third Earl of Scarsdale (1654–1707), and it appears that she eventually transferred her affections to him.

Congreve's collection of sinecures continued to grow, making him financially secure. He was appointed Customs Collector at Poole, Dorset (1700–1702), Commissioner for Wine Licences (1705–1714) and Under-Searcher for Customs in the Pool of London. In 1714 he was offered the secretaryship of the island of Jamaica at £700 per annum. Royalties from his plays and publishing ventures provided additional revenue. With the support of his friend and publisher Jacob Tonson (1655/6–1763) he prepared a collected edition of his *Works* in 1710. He continued to live in fairly humble style in lodgings with Edward and Frances Porter (Frances was Bracegirdle's sister) in Surrey Street near the Strand.

Some time before 1714, Congreve began a relationship with Lady Henrietta Godolphin (1681–1733). She was the eldest daughter of the Duke and Duchess of Marlborough and married to Francis Godolphin (1678–1766). She and Congreve embarked on a discreet but deeply felt love affair that lasted until Congreve's death. They were inseparable, a situation tolerated by Henrietta's husband and accepted in their circle of friends and acquaintances.

A life of William Congreve

Lady Henrietta Godolphin, in a mezzotint version of a portrait by Sir Godfrey Kneller

A daughter, Mary (who died in 1764), born to Henrietta in November 1723 was almost certainly Congreve's. She was given the title Lady Mary Godolphin and accepted as a legitimate daughter within one of England's wealthiest families. This was not the cynical husband-wife-lover triangle of Restoration comedy; it was never exposed, never ridiculed, always discreetly conducted by all parties.

In September 1728 Congreve was involved in a carriage accident and may have sustained an internal injury that was never treated. He was already in poor health and this accident probably hastened his death. He died in his Surrey Street lodgings on 19 January 1729. Henrietta arranged for his funeral service and burial in Westminster Abbey. She set up his memorial plaque and wrote a loving epitaph.

Congreve died a relatively rich man. He had invested prudently in South Sea stock, which yielded £10,000 for his estate, most of which he left to Henrietta. He made her husband the executor of his will, thus avoiding scandal.

His will stipulated that neither Henrietta's present nor any future husband should have any control over her inheritance. It seems he wanted to ensure that his illegitimate daughter would inherit his estate in due course. It was agreed that Henrietta would use some of the £10,000 to purchase a set of diamonds for Mary; Congreve's initials would be engraved on the back of each one. Thus we see Congreve depending on the clear and reliable nature of the law to accommodate the messy realities of his personal life. The diamonds suggest a desire to live on remembered, albeit in code, in his daughter's life.

In due course Mary married the Duke of Leeds and inherited the mysteriously engraved diamonds. Can we recognize in the *deed of trust* in *The Way of the World* (V.595) the kind of judgement that safeguards reputation and puts social difficulties to rights, as was achieved by Congreve's will?

Congreve's friends and fellow writers in the Kit-Cat Club (see Glossary) respected his intellect, artistic powers and warmth of spirit. His letters show that he remained loyal and generous to his intimate circle of friends, not all of whom were from the London coffee houses and grand country mansions of England. He showed equal loyalty towards humble friends of little renown, such as school friends made in Ireland.

In a well-documented age, Congreve presents an elusive figure to his biographers as he disguised or concealed some of the key relationships in his life, especially those with women. He seems to have been unable to avoid the necessity for secrecy and deception in his personal life; to the author of *The Way of the World*, this must have been a vexing compromise.

1700: England on the cusp of change

The Stuart monarchs, Charles II (who died in 1685) and his successor James II reigned over a people increasingly at odds with their values. England's growing mercantile class was creating most of the nation's wealth and driving new ideas. It rejected aristocratic values and absolute monarchy, demanding a stronger voice for itself in Parliament to reflect its importance to the economy and England's standing in the world as a trading nation.

The reign of James II plunged the country into turmoil, and civil war became a possibility again. He had converted to the Catholic faith and did not hesitate to use powers that he believed were bestowed on him by God; rebellion against him was crushed, bloodily if need be. Parliament was prorogued (suspended) for an indefinite term and the rule of law was also set aside. When James's queen, his second wife Mary (1658–1718), gave birth to a son in June 1688, the prospect of rule by a Catholic dynasty loomed, causing widespread alarm.

The Dutch Prince William of Orange was married to James's elder daughter Mary (from his first marriage); the couple were cousins, and both were Protestant. A group of English noblemen invited William to move against the king in order to protect Mary's claim to the throne, now threatened by the royal birth. He 'invaded' England on 5 November 1688; people rallied to his cause and James fled the country without engaging in full battle. His flight amounted to abdication.

William's troops reached London by mid-December, where he was invited by a number of leading Whigs and Tories (see Glossary) to hold a Convention Parliament (see Glossary), which met on 22 January 1689. Protestant rule in England was duly secured. In the same year William and Mary were crowned in Westminster Abbey and ascended the throne as joint constitutional monarchs.

Their powers were circumscribed by a Bill of Rights. From now on, no monarch would be allowed to set aside the law or maintain a standing army in peacetime. Parliament was required to meet regularly and could not be prorogued indefinitely. The largely bloodless 'Glorious Revolution', which began in 1688 and was resolved within a year, was widely welcomed in England; a period of stability and prosperity followed. The country found a new confidence and sense of purpose, especially among its merchant classes. When the former king James II died in 1701, the Act of Settlement secured the Hanoverian succession (see Glossary) to ensure that there were designated Protestant heirs to the English throne.

William Congreve in Context

Engraving depicting the ceremonial presentation of the Bill of Rights to William and Mary

By 1700 the new social order heralded by the Glorious Revolution was vigorously asserting its identity and expressing itself in language, manners, and values. Money and property, underpinned by contract law rather than inheritance, were what counted in London. This was a complex and challenging society, busy shaping and defining itself. Skill and cunning were required to negotiate the path to prosperity and security. After a century that had seen the excesses of civil war, absolutism and libertinism (see Glossary), there was a new caution about expressing emotions and feelings in public. Congreve examines the ways in which these forces shaping the national character were highly relevant to personal matters such as finding a marriage partner. The relationship between Mirabell and Millamant reveals how the personal and the political converge.

The Way of the World is a deeply felt response to the changing values of the age. The Wishfort and Fainall households are flawed by egotism and vulnerable to the tyrannical wielding of power by senior members. These households need to be reordered so that their disruptive influences are curbed and excessive appetites are reined in; it's possible to see the state of England shown in microcosm here. Good order can be restored by plain speaking, the safeguarding of women's freedoms, and respect for property rights. These values can be secured through the rule of law and by the consent of the governed; all are important Whig ideals. The revolution of 1688 was 'Glorious' because it was achieved by negotiated settlement; *The Way of the World* endorses this principle of consent over coercion.

Powers conferred on a parent like Lady Wishfort or a husband like Fainall need to be justified, not simply taken for granted, or tyranny might ensue. If the private citizen is protected, all will be well in the realm. So Millamant is wary of choosing a husband and tests Mirabell to the limit, seeking assurances that he will not turn into a tyrant after their union is inscribed in law. Mirabell intends to govern her, but by consent not force. If bad marriages like the Fainalls' cannot be prevented, the situation can be retrieved by a *deed of trust* (V.595) that empowers the woman because it ensures she has some control over the purse strings.

Theories of human nature

Two English philosophers, Thomas Hobbes (1588–1679) and John Locke (1632–1704), put forward highly influential theories about human nature, language and government. Their ideas were strongly debated during the second half of the seventeenth century and we can see their influence in *The Way of the World*.

It is clear that many characters in the play are driven by uncontrolled appetite. In *Leviathan*, published in 1651, Hobbes proposed that appetite is the strongest driving force in human behaviour. Left to ourselves, in what he called a 'state of nature', competitive greed would make our lives 'solitary, poor, nasty, brutish, and short'. We form civil societies to avoid this misery. To ensure the continuance of a just society we need an agreed set of assumptions, and contracts upheld by law.

Hobbes believed that complete obedience to an absolute ruler such as a king was needed to control the competing factions in society. But he argued for individual rights as well, equality before God, and a political order representative of the will of the people. He urged members of society to give up some freedoms in exchange for the protection of a 'social contract' between rulers and subjects.

Locke published his *Essay Concerning Human Understanding* and *Two Treatises of Government* in 1689. He believed that ownership of property, civil society and legitimate government prosper only when people are ruled by consent; any government that assumes power without the people's consent can be legitimately overthrown. Locke also believed that language is not simply an imitation of objects in the external world but a reflection of the mind that produces it. We should therefore be on our guard against false wits like Witwoud and Petulant, whose language masks reality, fostering an indifference to its 'truth'.

The Wishfort family in the play is the analogue (see Glossary) of the state; it is conflicted because of an arbitrary ruling about an inheritance. It is vulnerable because it has no natural male heirs and so attracts the attentions of opportunists like Fainall. It is riven by a generational power struggle in which sexual instincts play a major role, however much they are disguised beneath modish manners.

In practice, the family structures and political systems that constitute civilized society are never ideal. They are full of fudged principles, compromise and pragmatism; this is exactly what we feel has been necessary to achieve a reasonable outcome for all parties at the end of *The Way of the World*.

Congreve's detractors and his defence of comedy

In 1698 Jeremy Collier (1650–1726) published *A Short View of the Immorality and Profaneness of the English Stage*. His arguments were well received and they strengthened public hostility towards plays that dealt frankly with sex and adultery. He singled out the drama of Vanbrugh and Congreve as being particularly offensive to common

Congreve's detractors and his defence of comedy

decency. Collier's work was read by people who had never been to the theatre but were subsequently left in no doubt that Puritan (see Glossary) and merchant-class values were ridiculed there.

Collier maintained that the purpose of drama was to teach morality and to maintain the status quo. Simplistic as these views may seem, they appealed to middle-class taste by providing a thundering critique of Restoration comedy, the drama of a now discredited past.

Congreve was so incensed that he wrote a reply: *Amendments of Mr Collier's False and Imperfect Citations* (1698). But no writer, however intelligent, can mount a point-for-point argument against unreasoned bigotry, and Congreve failed to convince. His intervention only harmed his reputation.

His attempted rebuttal of Collier, however, tells us what Congreve believed comedy should be. He takes the following precepts from Aristotle's *Poetics*.

- Comedy should represent on stage the worst kind of people, and their manners should betray their vice.
- Wrongdoing should be exposed in the most ridiculous way.
- Laughter should be the weapon that exposes vice.
- Good people will heed the warnings of folly and be instructed how to avoid it.

He makes some further points about the interpretation of comedy.

- The morality of a speech or action can only be determined by observing it in context.
- There is no intention to ridicule God if biblical language is directed against secular people or situations.
- The views expressed by a character should not be mistaken for those of the writer.
- The purpose of satire is to expose folly, not to celebrate it.
- Words do not have a fixed meaning; good writers explore their shades of meaning.
- The audience needs to be actively involved in the process of interpretation, which requires intellectual and emotional effort.

William Congreve in Context

In *The Way of the World*, the lustful hypocrite Lady Wishfort is the owner of a copy of Collier's *Short View of the Stage* (III.63–64); does she represent Congreve's opinion of the typical Collier supporter? Congreve was too subtle a playwright to be overtly moralistic, and he does accept sexual competition in his characters as natural. Did this leave him open to the charge of immorality?

Today, it seems less shocking for Congreve's characters to express their views and show their passions frankly on stage. He is acknowledged to be a creator of great parts for actors who have a good ear for his finely tuned, rhythmic dialogue. Theatre professionals can bring out the play's meaning for modern audiences, who find his vision neither artificial nor heartless. Coming to the play for the first time, it is best to accept that the complex web of relationships is implied rather than clarified in the play's opening scenes.

Above all, the world Congreve creates isn't farce or fantasy but shows his characters seeking human happiness and keenly arguing for the kind of society that, provided its members pay their dues, will be worthy of them.

THE
Way of the World,
A
COMEDY.

As it is ACTED

AT THE

Theatre in *Lincoln's-Inn-Fields*,

BY

His Majesty's Servants.

Written by Mr. *CONGREVE*.

Audire est Operæ pretium, procedere recte
Qui mœchis non vultis ——   Hor. Sat. 2. l. 1.
—— *Metuat doti deprensa.* ——   Ibid.

LONDON:

Printed for *Jacob Tonson*, within *Gray's-Inn-Gate* next
Gray's-Inn-Lane. 1700.

Dedication

To the Right Honourable Ralph Earl of Mountague etc.
My Lord,
Whether the world will arraign me of vanity or not, that I have presumed to dedicate this comedy to your Lordship, I am yet in doubt: though it may be it is some degree of vanity even to doubt of it. One who has at any time had the honour of your Lordship's conversation, cannot be supposed to think very meanly of that which he would prefer to your perusal; yet it were to incur the imputation of too much sufficiency to pretend to such a merit as might abide the test of your Lordship's censure.

Whatever value may be wanting to this play while yet it is mine, will be sufficiently made up to it when it is once become your Lordship's; and it is my security that I cannot have overrated it more by my dedication than your Lordship will dignify it by your patronage.

That it succeeded on the stage was almost beyond my expectation; for but little of it was prepared for that general taste which seems now to be predominant in the palates of our audience.

Those characters which are meant to be ridiculous in most of our comedies are of fools so gross that, in my humble opinion, they should rather disturb than divert the well-natured and reflecting part of an audience; they are rather objects of charity than contempt; and instead of moving our mirth, they ought very often to excite our compassion.

The Way of the World

This reflection moved me to design some characters which should appear ridiculous not so much through a natural folly (which is incorrigible, and therefore not proper for the stage) as through an affected wit; a wit, which at the same time that it is affected, is also false. As there is some difficulty in the formation of a character of this nature, so there is some hazard which attends the progress of its success upon the stage. For many come to a play so over-charged with criticism that they very often let fly their censure, when through their rashness they have mistaken their aim. This I had occasion lately to observe; for this play had been acted two or three days, before some of these hasty judges could find the leisure to distinguish betwixt the character of a Witwoud and a Truewit.

I must beg your Lordship's pardon for this digression from the true course of this epistle; but that it may not seem altogether impertinent, I beg that I may plead the occasion of it, in part of that excuse of which I stand in need for recommending this comedy to your protection. It is only by the countenance of your Lordship, and the few so qualified, that such who write with care and pains can hope to be distinguished, for the prostituted name of poet promiscuously levels all that bear it.

Terence, the most correct writer in the world, had a Scipio and a Lelius, if not to assist him, at least to support him in his reputation; and notwithstanding his extraordinary merit, it may be their countenance was not more than necessary.

The purity of his style, the delicacy of his turns, and the justness of his characters, were all of them beauties which the greater part of his audience were incapable of tasting; some of the coarsest strokes of Plautus, so severally censured by Horace, were more likely to affect the multitude; such who come with expectation to laugh out the last act of a play,

Dedication

and are better entertained with two or three unseasonable jests, than with the artful solution of the fable.

As Terence excelled in his performances, so had he great advantages to encourage his undertakings; for he built most on the foundations of Menander: his plots were generally modelled, and his characters ready drawn to his hand. He copied Menander; and Menander had no less light in the formation of his characters from the observations of Theophrastus, of whom he was a disciple; and Theophrastus it is known was not only the disciple but the immediate successor of Aristotle, the first and greatest judge of poetry. These were great models to design by; and the further advantage which Terence possessed, towards giving his plays the due ornaments of purity of style, and justness of manners, was not less considerable from the freedom of conversation which was permitted him with Lelius and Scipio, two of the greatest and most polite men of his age. And indeed, the privilege of such a conversation is the only certain means of attaining to the perfection of dialogue.

If it has happened in any part of this comedy, that I have gained a turn of style, or expression more correct, or at least more corrigible than in those which I have formerly written, I must, with equal pride and gratitude, ascribe it to the honour of your Lordship's admitting me into your conversation, and that of a society where everybody else was so well worthy of you, in your retirement last summer from the town, for it was immediately after that this comedy was written. If I have failed in my performance, it is only to be regretted, where there were so many not inferior either to a Scipio or a Lelius, that there should be one wanting equal to the capacity of a Terence.

If I am not mistaken, poetry is almost the only art which has not yet laid claim to your Lordship's patronage. Architecture, and painting, to the great honour of our country, have flourished under your influence and protection. In the mean time, poetry, the eldest sister of all arts, and parent of most, seems to have resigned her birthright by having neglected to pay her duty to your Lordship, and by permitting others of a later extraction to prepossess that place in your esteem to which none can pretend a better title. Poetry, in its nature, is sacred to the good and great; the relation between them is reciprocal, and they are ever propitious to it. It is the privilege of poetry to address to them, and it is their prerogative alone to give it protection.

This received maxim is a general apology for all writers who consecrate their labours to great men. But I could wish at this time that this address were exempted from the common pretence of all dedications; and that, as I can distinguish your Lordship even among the most deserving, so this offering might become remarkable by some particular instance of respect, which should assure your Lordship that I am, with all due sense of your extreme worthiness and humanity,

>MY LORD,
>Your Lordship's most obedient
>and most obliged humble servant,
>WILL. CONGREVE.

Prologue

Spoken by Mr Betterton

Of those few fools, who with ill stars are cursed,
Sure scribbling fools, called poets, fare the worst;
For they're a sort of fools which Fortune makes,
And after she has made 'em fools, forsakes.
With Nature's oafs 'tis quite a diff'rent case,   5
For Fortune favours all her idiot race;
In her own nest the cuckoo eggs we find,
O'er which she broods to hatch the changeling kind.
No portion for her own she has to spare,
So much she dotes on her adopted care.   10
   Poets are bubbles, by the town drawn in,
Suffered at first some trifling stakes to win;
But what unequal hazards do they run!
Each time they write, they venture all they've won;
The squire that's buttered still, is sure to be undone.   15
This author, heretofore, has found your favour,
But pleads no merit from his past behaviour.
To build on that might prove a vain presumption,
Should grants to poets made admit resumption;
And in Parnassus he must lose his seat,   20
If that be found a forfeited estate.
   He owns, with toil he wrought the following scenes,
But if they're naught ne'er spare him for his pains;
Damn him the more; have no commiseration
For dullness on mature deliberation.   25
He swears he'll not resent one hissed-off scene,
Nor, like those peevish wits, his play maintain,
Who, to assert their sense, your taste arraign.
Some plot we think he has, and some new thought;
Some humour too, no farce; but that's a fault.   30

The Way of the World

Satire, he thinks, you ought not to expect;
For so reformed a town who dares correct?
To please, this time, has been his sole pretence;
He'll not instruct, lest it should give offence.
Should he by chance a knave or fool expose,   35
That hurts none here, sure here are none of those.
In short, our play, shall (with your leave to show it)
Give you one instance of a passive poet.
Who to your judgments yields all resignation;
So save or damn, after your own discretion.   40

The Characters of the Play

Fainall, *in love with* Mrs Marwood
Mirabell, *in love with* Mrs Millamant
Witwoud, } *followers of* }
Petulant, } Mrs Millamant }
Sir Wilfull Witwoud, *half-brother to* Witwoud, *and nephew to* Lady Wishfort
Waitwell, *servant to* Mirabell

Lady Wishfort, *enemy to* Mirabell, *for having falsely pretended love to her*
Mrs Millamant, *a fine lady, niece to* Lady Wishfort, *and loves* Mirabell
Mrs Marwood, *friend to* Mr Fainall, *and likes* Mirabell
Mrs Fainall, *daughter to* Lady Wishfort, *and wife to* Fainall, *formerly friend to* Mirabell
Foible, *woman to* Lady Wishfort
Mincing, *woman to* Mrs Millamant

Dancers, Footmen, and Attendants.

The scene
LONDON
The time equal to that of the presentation.

Act I

A chocolate-house

[*Mirabell and Fainall rising from cards. Betty waiting*]

MIRABELL   You are a fortunate man, Mr Fainall.
FAINALL   Have we done?
MIRABELL   What you please. I'll play on to entertain you.
FAINALL   No, I'll give you your revenge another time, when you are not so indifferent; you are thinking of something else now, and play too negligently. The coldness of a losing gamester lessens the pleasure of the winner. I'd no more play with a man that slighted his ill fortune, than I'd make love to a woman who undervalued the loss of her reputation.
MIRABELL   You have a taste extremely delicate, and are for refining on your pleasures.
FAINALL   Prithee, why so reserved? Something has put you out of humour.
MIRABELL   Not at all. I happen to be grave today, and you are gay; that's all.
FAINALL   Confess, Millamant and you quarrelled last night after I left you; my fair cousin has some humours that would tempt the patience of a Stoic. What, some coxcomb came in and was well received by her, while you were by?
MIRABELL   Witwoud and Petulant, and what was worse, her aunt, your wife's mother, my evil genius; or to sum up all in her own name, my old Lady Wishfort came in.
FAINALL   Oh there it is then – she has a lasting passion for you, and with reason. – What, then my wife was there?
MIRABELL   Yes, and Mrs Marwood, and three or four more whom I never saw before. Seeing me, they all put on their

The Way of the World

grave faces, whispered one another; then complained aloud of the vapours, and after fell into a profound silence.
FAINALL They had a mind to be rid of you.
MIRABELL For which reason I resolved not to stir. At last the good old lady broke through her painful taciturnity with an invective against long visits. I would not have understood her, but Millamant joining in the argument, I rose and with a constrained smile told her, I thought nothing was so easy as to know when a visit began to be troublesome. She reddened and I withdrew, without expecting her reply.
FAINALL You were to blame to resent what she spoke only in compliance with her aunt.
MIRABELL She is more mistress of herself than to be under the necessity of such a resignation.
FAINALL What? Though half her fortune depends upon her marrying with my lady's approbation?
MIRABELL I was then in such a humour that I should have been better pleased if she had been less discreet.
FAINALL Now I remember, I wonder not they were weary of you; last night was one of their cabal nights; they have 'em three times a week, and meet by turns at one another's apartments, where they come together like the coroner's inquest, to sit upon the murdered reputations of the week. You and I are excluded; and it was once proposed that all the male sex should be excepted; but somebody moved that to avoid scandal there might be one man of the community; upon which motion Witwoud and Petulant were enrolled members.
MIRABELL And who may have been the foundress of this sect? My Lady Wishfort, I warrant, who publishes her detestation of mankind, and full of the vigour of fifty-five, declares for a friend and ratafia, and let posterity shift for itself, she'll breed no more.

FAINALL   The discovery of your sham addresses to her, to conceal your love to her niece, has provoked this separation. Had you dissembled better, things might have continued in the state of nature.

MIRABELL   I did as much as man could, with any reasonable conscience; I proceeded to the very last act of flattery with her, and was guilty of a song in her commendation. Nay, I got a friend to put her into a lampoon, and compliment her with the imputation of an affair with a young fellow, which I carried so far that I told her the malicious town took notice that she had grown fat of a sudden; and when she lay in of a dropsy, persuaded her she was reported to be in labour. The devil's in't, if an old woman is to be flattered further, unless a man should endeavour downright personally to debauch her; and that my virtue forbad me. But for the discovery of that amour I am indebted to your friend, or your wife's friend, Mrs Marwood.

FAINALL   What should provoke her to be your enemy, without she has made you advances which you have slighted? Women do not easily forgive omissions of that nature.

MIRABELL   She was always civil to me till of late. I confess I am not one of those coxcombs who are apt to interpret a woman's good manners to her prejudice, and think that she who does not refuse 'em everything, can refuse 'em nothing.

FAINALL   You are a gallant man, Mirabell; and though you may have cruelty enough not to satisfy a lady's longing, you have too much generosity not to be tender of her honour. Yet you speak with an indifference which seems to be affected, and confesses you are conscious of a negligence.

MIRABELL   You pursue the argument with a distrust that

seems to be unaffected, and confesses you are conscious of a concern for which the lady is more indebted to you than your wife.
FAINALL Fie, fie, friend, if you grow censorious I must leave you. – I'll look upon the gamesters in the next room.
MIRABELL Who are they?
FAINALL Petulant and Witwoud. [*To Betty*] Bring me some chocolate.
 [*Exit*]
MIRABELL Betty, what says your clock?
BETTY Turned of the last canonical hour, sir.
 [*Exit*]
MIRABELL How pertinently the jade answers me! [*Looking on his watch*] Ha? almost one o'clock! Oh, y'are come –
 [*Enter a servant*]
Well, is the grand affair over? You have been something tedious.
SERVANT Sir, there's such coupling at Pancras that they stand behind one another, as 'twere in a country dance. Ours was the last couple to lead up, and no hopes appearing of dispatch, besides the parson growing hoarse, we were afraid his lungs would have failed before it came to our turn; so we drove round to Duke's Place, and there they were riveted in a trice.
MIRABELL So, so, you are sure they are married.
SERVANT Married and bedded, sir; I am witness.
MIRABELL Have you the certificate?
SERVANT Here it is, sir.
MIRABELL Has the tailor brought Waitwell's clothes home, and the new liveries?
SERVANT Yes, sir.
MIRABELL That's well. Do you go home again, d'ye hear, and adjourn the consummation till farther order; bid Waitwell shake his ears, and Dame Partlet rustle up her

feathers, and meet me at one o'clock by Rosamond's Pond, that I may see her before she returns to her lady; and as you tender your ears, be secret.

[*Exit servant*]
[*Re-enter Fainall*]

FAINALL Joy of your success, Mirabell; you look pleased.

MIRABELL Ay; I have been engaged in a matter of some sort of mirth, which is not yet ripe for discovery. I am glad this is not a cabal night. I wonder, Fainall, that you who are married, and of consequence should be discreet, will suffer your wife to be of such a party.

FAINALL Faith, I am not jealous. Besides, most who are engaged are women and relations; and for the men, they are of a kind too contemptible to give scandal.

MIRABELL I am of another opinion. The greater the coxcomb, always the more the scandal; for a woman who is not a fool can have but one reason for associating with a man that is.

FAINALL Are you jealous as often as you see Witwoud entertained by Millamant?

MIRABELL Of her understanding I am, if not of her person.

FAINALL You do her wrong; for to give her her due, she has wit.

MIRABELL She has beauty enough to make any man think so, and complaisance enough not to contradict him who shall tell her so.

FAINALL For a passionate lover, methinks you are a man somewhat too discerning in the failings of your mistress.

MIRABELL And for a discerning man, somewhat too passionate a lover; for I like her with all her faults; nay, like her for her faults. Her follies are so natural, or so artful, that they become her; and those affectations which in another woman would be odious, serve but to make her more agreeable. I'll tell thee, Fainall, she once

The Way of the World

used me with that insolence, that in revenge I took her to pieces; sifted her, and separated her failings; I studied 'em, and got 'em by rote. The catalogue was so large that I was not without hopes one day or other to hate her heartily: to which end I so used myself to think of 'em that at length, contrary to my design and expectation, they gave me every hour less and less disturbance; till in a few days it became habitual to me to remember 'em without being displeased. They are now grown as familiar to me as my own frailties; and in all probability, in a little time longer I shall like 'em as well.

FAINALL Marry her, marry her; be half as well acquainted with her charms as you are with her defects, and my life on't, you are your own man again.

MIRABELL Say you so?

FAINALL Ay, ay, I have experience; I have a wife, and so forth.

  [Enter Messenger]

MESSENGER Is one Squire Witwoud here?

BETTY Yes; what's your business?

MESSENGER I have a letter for him, from his brother Sir Wilfull, which I am charged to deliver into his own hands.

BETTY He's in the next room, friend; that way.

  [Exit Messenger]

MIRABELL What, is the chief of that noble family in town, Sir Wilfull Witwoud?

FAINALL He is expected today. Do you know him?

MIRABELL I have seen him. He promises to be an extraordinary person; I think you have the honour to be related to him.

FAINALL Yes; he is half-brother to this Witwoud by a former wife, who was sister to my Lady Wishfort, my wife's mother. If you marry Millamant, you must call cousins too.

MIRABELL I had rather be his relation than his acquaintance.
FAINALL He comes to town in order to equip himself for travel.
MIRABELL For travel! Why, the man that I mean is above forty.
FAINALL No matter for that; 'tis for the honour of England, that all Europe should know we have blockheads of all ages.
MIRABELL I wonder there is not an act of parliament to save the credit of the nation, and prohibit the exportation of fools.
FAINALL By no means, 'tis better as 'tis; 'tis better to trade with a little loss than to be quite eaten up with being overstocked.
MIRABELL Pray, are the follies of this knight-errant and those of the squire his brother anything related?
FAINALL Not at all; Witwoud grows by the knight, like a medlar grafted on a crab. One will melt in your mouth, and t'other set your teeth on edge; one is all pulp, and the other all core.
MIRABELL So one will be rotten before he be ripe, and the other will be rotten without ever being ripe at all.
FAINALL Sir Wilfull is an odd mixture of bashfulness and obstinacy. – But when he's drunk, he's as loving as the monster in *The Tempest*, and much after the same manner. To give the t'other his due, he has something of good nature and does not always want wit.
MIRABELL Not always; but as often as his memory fails him, and his commonplace of comparisons. He is a fool with a good memory and some few scraps of other folks' wit. He is one whose conversation can never be approved, yet it is now and then to be endured. He has indeed one good quality, he is not exceptious; for he so passionately

affects the reputation of understanding raillery, that he will construe an affront into a jest, and call downright rudeness and ill language, satire and fire.

FAINALL   If you have a mind to finish his picture, you have an opportunity to do it at full length. Behold the original!

[*Enter Witwoud*]

WITWOUD   Afford me your compassion, my dears! Pity me, Fainall, Mirabell, pity me!

MIRABELL   I do from my soul.

FAINALL   Why, what's the matter?

WITWOUD   No letters for me, Betty?

BETTY   Did not the messenger bring you one but now, sir?

WITWOUD   Ay, but no other?

BETTY   No, sir.

WITWOUD   That's hard, that's very hard. – A messenger, a mule, a beast of burden, he has brought me a letter from the fool my brother, as heavy as a panegyric in a funeral sermon, or a copy of commendatory verses from one poet to another. And what's worse, 'tis as sure a forerunner of the author as an epistle dedicatory.

MIRABELL   A fool, and your brother, Witwoud!

WITWOUD   Ay, ay, my half-brother. My half-brother he is, no nearer upon honour.

MIRABELL   Then 'tis possible he may be but half a fool.

WITWOUD   Good, good, Mirabell, *le drôle!* Good, good, hang him, don't let's talk of him. – Fainall, how does your lady? Gad, I say anything in the world to get this fellow out of my head. I beg pardon that I should ask a man of pleasure and the town, a question at once so foreign and domestic. But I talk like an old maid at a marriage, I don't know what I say; but she's the best woman in the world.

FAINALL   'Tis well you don't know what you say, or else your commendation would go near to make me either vain or jealous.

WITWOUD No man in town lives well with a wife but Fainall. Your judgment, Mirabell?

MIRABELL You had better step and ask his wife, if you would be credibly informed.

WITWOUD Mirabell.

MIRABELL Ay.

WITWOUD My dear, I ask ten thousand pardons. – Gad, I have forgot what I was going to say to you.

MIRABELL I thank you heartily, heartily.

WITWOUD No, but prithee excuse me; my memory is such a memory.

MIRABELL Have a care of such apologies, Witwoud; for I never knew a fool but he affected to complain either of the spleen or his memory.

FAINALL What have you done with Petulant?

WITWOUD He's reckoning his money – my money it was. I have no luck today.

FAINALL You may allow him to win of you at play, for you are sure to be too hard for him at repartee; since you monopolize the wit that is between you, the fortune must be his of course.

MIRABELL I don't find that Petulant confesses the superiority of wit to be your talent, Witwoud.

WITWOUD Come, come, you are malicious now, and would breed debates. – Petulant's my friend, and a very honest fellow, and a very pretty fellow, and has a smattering – faith and troth, a pretty deal of an odd sort of a small wit; nay, I'll do him justice. I'm his friend, I won't wrong him neither. – And if he had but any judgment in the world, – he would not be altogether contemptible. Come come, don't detract from the merits of my friend.

FAINALL You don't take your friend to be over-nicely bred?

WITWOUD No, no, hang him, the rogue has no manners at

The Way of the World

all, that I must own. – No more breeding than a bum-baily, that I grant you. – 'Tis pity, faith; the fellow has fire and life.
MIRABELL   What, courage?
WITWOUD   Hum, faith, I don't know as to that; I can't say as to that. – Yes, faith, in a controversy he'll contradict anybody.
MIRABELL   Though 'twere a man whom he feared, or a woman whom he loved.
WITWOUD   Well, well, he does not always think before he speaks; we have all our failings. You are too hard upon him, you are, faith. Let me excuse him; I can defend most of his faults, except one or two; one he has, that's the truth on't; if he were my brother, I could not acquit him. – That, indeed, I could wish were otherwise.
MIRABELL   Ay, marry, what's that, Witwoud?
WITWOUD   O, pardon me. – Expose the infirmities of my friend? – No, my dear, excuse me there.
FAINALL   What, I warrant he's unsincere, or 'tis some such trifle.
WITWOUD   No, no, what if he be? 'Tis no matter for that, his wit will excuse that. A wit should no more be sincere than a woman constant; one argues a decay of parts, as t'other of beauty.
MIRABELL   Maybe you think him too positive?
WITWOUD   No, no, his being positive is an incentive to argument, and keeps up conversation.
FAINALL   Too illiterate?
WITWOUD   That! that's his happiness; his want of learning gives him the more opportunities to show his natural parts.
MIRABELL   He wants words.
WITWOUD   Ay, but I like him for that now; for his want of words gives me the pleasure very often to explain his meaning.

FAINALL He's impudent.
WITWOUD No, that's not it.
MIRABELL Vain.
WITWOUD No.
MIRABELL What, he speaks unseasonable truths sometimes, because he has not wit enough to invent an evasion?
WITWOUD Truths! Ha, ha, ha! No, no, since you will have it, – I mean he never speaks truth at all, – that's all. He will lie like a chambermaid, or a woman of quality's porter. Now that is a fault.
  [*Enter Coachman*]
COACHMAN Is Master Petulant here, mistress?
BETTY Yes.
COACHMAN Three gentlewomen in the coach would speak with him.
FAINALL O brave Petulant; three!
BETTY I'll tell him.
COACHMAN You must bring two dishes of chocolate and a glass of cinnamon-water.
  [*Exit Betty and Coachman*]
WITWOUD That should be for two fasting strumpets, and a bawd troubled with wind. Now you may know what the three are.
MIRABELL You are very free with your friend's acquaintance.
WITWOUD Ay, ay, friendship without freedom is as dull as love without enjoyment, or wine without toasting. But to tell you a secret, these are trulls that he allows coach-hire, and something more, by the week, to call on him once a day at public places.
MIRABELL How!
WITWOUD You shall see he won't go to 'em because there's no more company here to take notice of him. – Why this is nothing to what he used to do; before he found out this way, I have known him call for himself.

The Way of the World

FAINALL Call for himself? What dost thou mean?
WITWOUD Mean, why he would slip you out of this chocolate-house, just when you had been talking to him; as soon as your back was turned – whip, he was gone. Then trip to his lodging, clap on a hood and scarf and mask, slap into a hackney-coach, and drive hither to the door again in a trice, where he would send in for himself, that I mean, call for himself, wait for himself, nay, and what's more, not finding himself, sometimes leave a letter for himself.
MIRABELL I confess this is something extraordinary. – I believe he waits for himself now, he is so long a-coming. Oh, I ask his pardon.
   [*Enter Petulant*]
BETTY Sir, the coach stays.
PETULANT Well, well, I come. – 'Sbud, a man had as good be a professed midwife as a professed whoremaster, at this rate! To be knocked up and raised at all hours, and in all places. Pox on 'em, I won't come. – D'ye hear, tell 'em I won't come. – Let 'em snivel and cry their hearts out.
FAINALL You are very cruel, Petulant.
PETULANT All's one, let it pass. – I have a humour to be cruel.
MIRABELL I hope they are not persons of condition that you use at this rate.
PETULANT Condition! Condition's a dried fig, if I am not in humour. – By this hand, if they were your – a – a – your what-d'ye-call-'ems themselves, they must wait or rub off, if I want appetite.
MIRABELL What-d'ye-call-'ems! What are they, Witwoud?
WITWOUD Empresses, my dear; by your what-d'ye-call-'ems he means Sultana queens.
PETULANT Ay, Roxolanas.
MIRABELL Cry you mercy.

FAINALL Witwoud says they are –
PETULANT What does he say th'are?
WITWOUD I? Fine ladies, I say.
PETULANT Pass on, Witwoud. – Hearkee, by this light his relations: two co-heiresses his cousins, and an old aunt that loves caterwauling better than a conventicle.
WITWOUD Ha, ha, ha! I had a mind to see how the rogue would come off. – Ha, ha, ha! Gad, I can't be angry with him, if he said they were my mother and my sisters.
MIRABELL No!
WITWOUD No; the rogue's wit and readiness of invention charm me; dear Petulant!
BETTY They are gone, sir, in great anger.
PETULANT Enough, let 'em trundle. Anger helps complexion, saves paint.
FAINALL This continence is all dissembled; this is in order to have something to brag of the next time he makes court to Millamant, and swear he has abandoned the whole sex for her sake.
MIRABELL Have you not left your impudent pretensions there yet? I shall cut your throat sometime or other, Petulant, about that business.
PETULANT Ay, ay, let that pass. – There are other throats to be cut –
MIRABELL Meaning mine, sir?
PETULANT Not I – I mean nobody – I know nothing. But there are uncles and nephews in the world, and they may be rivals – what then? All's one for that.
MIRABELL How! Hearkee Petulant, come hither. – Explain, or I shall call your interpreter.
PETULANT Explain! I know nothing. – Why, you have an uncle, have you not, lately come to town, and lodges by my Lady Wishfort's?
MIRABELL True.

The Way of the World

PETULANT Why, that's enough. – You and he are not friends; and if he should marry and have a child, you may be disinherited, ha?

MIRABELL Where hast thou stumbled upon all this truth?

PETULANT All's one for that; why then, say I know something.

MIRABELL Come, thou art an honest fellow, Petulant, and shalt make love to my mistress, thou shalt faith. What hast thou heard of my uncle?

PETULANT I? Nothing I. If throats are to be cut, let swords clash. Snug's the word; I shrug and am silent.

MIRABELL O raillery, raillery. Come, I know thou art in the women's secrets. – What, you're a cabalist; I know you stayed at Millamant's last night, after I went. Was there any mention made of my uncle, or me? Tell me. If thou hadst but good nature equal to thy wit, Petulant, Tony Witwoud, who is now thy competitor in fame, would show as dim by thee as a dead whiting's eye by a pearl of orient; he would no more be seen by thee than Mercury is by the sun. Come, I'm sure thou wilt tell me.

PETULANT If I do, will you grant me common sense then, for the future?

MIRABELL Faith, I'll do what I can for thee; and I'll pray that heaven may grant it thee in the meantime.

PETULANT Well, hearkee.

[*Mirabell and Petulant talk apart*]

FAINALL Petulant and you both will find Mirabell as warm a rival as a lover.

WITWOUD Pshaw! pshaw! That she laughs at Petulant is plain. And for my part, but that it is almost a fashion to admire her, I should. – Hearkee, to tell you a secret, but let it go no further; between friends, I shall never break my heart for her.

FAINALL How!

WITWOUD She's handsome; but she's a sort of an uncertain woman.
FAINALL I thought you had died for her.
WITWOUD Umh – no –
FAINALL She has wit.
WITWOUD 'Tis what she will hardly allow anybody else. Now, demme, I should hate that, if she were as handsome as Cleopatra. Mirabell is not so sure of her as he thinks for.
FAINALL Why do you think so?
WITWOUD We stayed pretty late there last night, and heard something of an uncle to Mirabell, who is lately come to town, – and is between him and the best part of his estate. Mirabell and he are at some distance, as my Lady Wishfort has been told; and you know she hates Mirabell worse than a Quaker hates a parrot, or than a fishmonger hates a hard frost. Whether this uncle has seen Mrs Millamant or not, I cannot say; but there were items of such a treaty being in embryo, and if it should come to life, poor Mirabell would be in some sort unfortunately fobbed, i'faith.
FAINALL 'Tis impossible Millamant should hearken to it.
WITWOUD Faith, my dear, I can't tell; she's a woman, and a kind of a humorist.
MIRABELL And this is the sum of what you could collect last night?
PETULANT The quintessence. Maybe Witwoud knows more; he stayed longer. – Besides, they never mind him; they say anything before him.
MIRABELL I thought you had been the greatest favourite.
PETULANT Ay, *tête à tête*, but not in public, because I make remarks.
MIRABELL Do you?
PETULANT Ay, ay, pox, I'm malicious, man. Now he's soft

The Way of the World

you know; they are not in awe of him. – The fellow's well-bred; he's what you call a – what-d'ye-call-'em. A fine gentleman, but he's silly withal.

MIRABELL   I thank you, I know as much as my curiosity requires. – Fainall, are you for the Mall?

FAINALL   Ay, I'll take a turn before dinner.

WITWOUD   Ay, we'll all walk in the park; the ladies talked of being there.

MIRABELL   I thought you were obliged to watch for your brother Sir Wilfull's arrival.

WITWOUD   No, no, he comes to his aunt's, my Lady Wishfort. Pox on him, I shall be troubled with him too; what shall I do with the fool?

PETULANT   Beg him for his estate, that I may beg you afterwards; and so have but one trouble with you both.

WITWOUD   O rare Petulant! Thou art as quick as a fire in a frosty morning; thou shalt to the Mall with us, and we'll be very severe.

PETULANT   Enough, I'm in a humour to be severe.

MIRABELL   Are you? Pray then walk by yourselves: let not us be accessory to your putting the ladies out of countenance with your senseless ribaldry, which you roar out aloud as often as they pass by you; and when you have made a handsome woman blush, then you think you have been severe.

PETULANT   What, what? Then let 'em either show their innocence by not understanding what they hear, or else show their discretion by not hearing what they would not be thought to understand.

MIRABELL   But hast not thou then sense enough to know that thou ought'st to be most ashamed thyself, when thou hast put another out of countenance?

PETULANT   Not I, by this hand. – I always take blushing either for a sign of guilt, or ill breeding.

MIRABELL   I confess you ought to think so. You are in the right, that you may plead the error of your judgment in defence of your practice.

> Where modesty's ill manners, 'tis but fit
> That impudence and malice pass for wit.

[*Exeunt*]

Act II

St James's Park

[Enter Mrs Fainall and Mrs Marwood]

MRS FAINALL   Ay, ay, dear Marwood, if we will be happy, we must find the means in ourselves, and among ourselves. Men are ever in extremes; either doting or averse. While they are lovers, if they have fire and sense, their jealousies are insupportable; and when they cease to love, (we ought to think at least) they loathe; they look upon us with horror and distaste; they meet us like the ghosts of what we were, and as such, fly from us.

MRS MARWOOD   True, 'tis an unhappy circumstance of life, that love should ever die before us; and that the man so often should outlive the lover. But say what you will, 'tis better to be left than never to have been loved. To pass our youth in dull indifference, to refuse the sweets of life because they once must leave us, is as preposterous as to wish to have been born old, because we one day must be old. For my part, my youth may wear and waste, but it shall never rust in my possession.

MRS FAINALL   Then it seems you dissemble an aversion to mankind, only in compliance with my mother's humour.

MRS MARWOOD   Certainly. To be free, I have no taste of those insipid dry discourses with which our sex of force must entertain themselves, apart from men. We may affect endearments to each other, profess eternal friendships, and seem to dote like lovers; but 'tis not in our natures long to persevere. Love will resume his empire in our breasts, and every heart, or soon or late, receive and readmit him as its lawful tyrant.

MRS FAINALL   Bless me, how have I been deceived! Why

you profess a libertine!

MRS MARWOOD You see my friendship by my freedom. Come, be as sincere, acknowledge that your sentiments agree with mine.

MRS FAINALL Never.

MRS MARWOOD You hate mankind?

MRS FAINALL Heartily, inveterately.

MRS MARWOOD Your husband?

MRS FAINALL Most transcendently; ay, though I say it, meritoriously.

MRS MARWOOD Give me your hand upon it.

MRS FAINALL There.

MRS MARWOOD I join with you; what I have said has been to try you.

MRS FAINALL Is it possible? Dost thou hate those vipers, men?

MRS MARWOOD I have done hating 'em, and am now come to despise 'em; the next thing I have to do, is eternally to forget 'em.

MRS FAINALL There spoke the spirit of an Amazon, a Penthesilea.

MRS MARWOOD And yet I am thinking sometimes to carry my aversion further.

MRS FAINALL How?

MRS MARWOOD Faith, by marrying; if I could but find one that loved me very well and would be thoroughly sensible of ill usage, I think I should do myself the violence of undergoing the ceremony.

MRS FAINALL You would not make him a cuckold?

MRS MARWOOD No; but I'd make him believe I did, and that's as bad.

MRS FAINALL Why, had not you as good do it?

MRS MARWOOD Oh, if he should ever discover it, he would then know the worst, and be out of his pain; but I would

The Way of the World

have him ever to continue upon the rack of fear and jealousy.
MRS FAINALL Ingenious mischief! Would thou wert married to Mirabell.
MRS MARWOOD Would I were.
MRS FAINALL You change colour.
MRS MARWOOD Because I hate him.
MRS FAINALL So do I; but I can hear him named. But what reason have you to hate him in particular?
MRS MARWOOD I never loved him; he is, and always was, insufferably proud.
MRS FAINALL By the reason you give for your aversion, one would think it dissembled; for you have laid a fault to his charge of which his enemies must acquit him.
MRS MARWOOD Oh, then it seems you are one of his favourable enemies. Methinks you look a little pale, and now you flush again.
MRS FAINALL Do I? I think I am a little sick o' the sudden.
MRS MARWOOD What ails you?
MRS FAINALL My husband. Don't you see him? He turned short upon me unawares, and has almost overcome me.
 [*Enter Fainall and Mirabell*]
MRS MARWOOD Ha, ha, ha; he comes opportunely for you.
MRS FAINALL For you, for he has brought Mirabell with him.
FAINALL My dear.
MRS FAINALL My soul.
FAINALL You don't look well today, child.
MRS FAINALL D'ye think so?
MIRABELL He is the only man that does, madam.
MRS FAINALL The only man that would tell me so at least; and the only man from whom I could hear it without mortification.
FAINALL Oh, my dear, I am satisfied of your tenderness;

Act II

I know you cannot resent anything from me; especially what is an effect of my concern.

MRS FAINALL Mr Mirabell, my mother interrupted you in a pleasant relation last night; I would fain hear it out.

MIRABELL The persons concerned in that affair have yet a tolerable reputation. – I am afraid Mr Fainall will be censorious.

MRS FAINALL He has a humour more prevailing than his curiosity and will willingly dispense with the hearing of one scandalous story, to avoid giving an occasion to make another by being seen to walk with his wife. This way Mr Mirabell, and I dare promise you will oblige us both.

[*Exeunt Mrs Fainall and Mirabell*]

FAINALL Excellent creature! Well sure if I should live to be rid of my wife, I should be a miserable man.

MRS MARWOOD Ay!

FAINALL For having only that one hope, the accomplishment of it, of consequence, must put an end to all my hopes; and what a wretch is he who must survive his hopes! Nothing remains when that day comes but to sit down and weep like Alexander, when he wanted other worlds to conquer.

MRS MARWOOD Will you not follow 'em?

FAINALL Faith, I think not.

MRS MARWOOD Pray let us; I have a reason.

FAINALL You are not jealous?

MRS MARWOOD Of whom?

FAINALL Of Mirabell.

MRS MARWOOD If I am, is it inconsistent with my love to you that I am tender of your honour?

FAINALL You would intimate then, as if there were a fellow-feeling between my wife and him.

MRS MARWOOD I think she does not hate him to that degree she would be thought.

The Way of the World

FAINALL But he, I fear, is too insensible.
MRS MARWOOD It may be you are deceived.
FAINALL It may be so. I do now begin to apprehend it.
MRS MARWOOD What?
FAINALL That I have been deceived madam, and you are false.
MRS MARWOOD That I am false! What mean you?
FAINALL To let you know I see through all your little arts. – Come, you both love him, and both have equally dissembled your aversion. Your mutual jealousies of one another have made you clash till you have both struck fire. I have seen the warm confession reddening on your cheeks and sparkling from your eyes.
MRS MARWOOD You do me wrong.
FAINALL I do not. – 'Twas for my ease to oversee and wilfully neglect the gross advances made him by my wife; that by permitting her to be engaged, I might continue unsuspected in my pleasures, and take you oftener to my arms in full security. But could you think, because the nodding husband would not wake, that e'er the watchful lover slept?
MRS MARWOOD And wherewithal can you reproach me?
FAINALL With infidelity, with loving of another, with love of Mirabell.
MRS MARWOOD 'Tis false. I challenge you to show an instance that can confirm your groundless accusation. I hate him.
FAINALL And wherefore do you hate him? He is insensible, and your resentment follows his neglect. An instance? The injuries you have done him are a proof: your interposing in his love. What cause had you to make discoveries of his pretended passion? To undeceive the credulous aunt, and be the officious obstacle of his match with Millamant?
MRS MARWOOD My obligations to my lady urged me; I had

professed a friendship to her, and could not see her easy nature so abused by that dissembler.

FAINALL What, was it conscience then? Professed a friendship! O the pious friendships of the female sex!

MRS MARWOOD More tender, more sincere, and more enduring than all the vain and empty vows of men, whether professing love to us, or mutual faith to one another.

FAINALL Ha, ha, ha! You are my wife's friend too.

MRS MARWOOD Shame and ingratitude! Do you reproach me? You, you upbraid me! Have I been false to her, through strict fidelity to you, and sacrificed my friendship to keep my love inviolate? And have you the baseness to charge me with the guilt, unmindful of the merit! To you it should be meritorious that I have been vicious. And do you reflect that guilt upon me, which should lie buried in your bosom?

FAINALL You misinterpret my reproof. I meant but to remind you of the slight account you once could make of strictest ties, when set in competition with your love to me.

MRS MARWOOD 'Tis false, you urged it with deliberate malice. – 'Twas spoke in scorn, and I never will forgive it.

FAINALL Your guilt, not your resentment, begets your rage. If yet you loved, you could forgive a jealousy; but you are stung to find you are discovered.

MRS MARWOOD It shall be all discovered. You too shall be discovered; be sure you shall. I can but be exposed. – If I do it myself, I shall prevent your baseness.

FAINALL Why, what will you do?

MRS MARWOOD Disclose it to your wife; own what has passed between us.

FAINALL Frenzy!

MRS MARWOOD By all my wrongs I'll do't. – I'll publish to

The Way of the World

the world the injuries you have done me, both in my fame and fortune. With both I trusted you, you bankrupt in honour, as indigent of wealth.

FAINALL Your fame I have preserved. Your fortune has been bestowed as the prodigality of your love would have it, in pleasures which we both have shared. Yet had not you been false, I had ere this repaid it. 'Tis true! Had you permitted Mirabell with Millamant to have stolen their marriage, my lady had been incensed beyond all means of reconcilement; Millamant had forfeited the moiety of her fortune, which then would have descended to my wife. – And wherefore did I marry, but to make lawful prize of a rich widow's wealth, and squander it on love and you?

MRS MARWOOD Deceit and frivolous pretence.

FAINALL Death, am I not married? What's pretence? Am I not imprisoned, fettered? Have I not a wife? Nay a wife that was a widow, a young widow, a handsome widow; and would be again a widow, but that I have a heart of proof, and something of a constitution to bustle through the ways of wedlock and this world. Will you yet be reconciled to truth and me?

MRS MARWOOD Impossible. Truth and you are inconsistent. – I hate you, and shall for ever.

FAINALL For loving you?

MRS MARWOOD I loathe the name of love after such usage; and next to the guilt with which you would asperse me, I scorn you most. Farewell.

FAINALL Nay, we must not part thus.

MRS MARWOOD Let me go.

FAINALL Come, I'm sorry.

MRS MARWOOD I care not – let me go. – Break my hands, do. – I'd leave 'em to get loose.

FAINALL I would not hurt you for the world. Have I no other hold to keep you here?

Act II

MRS MARWOOD   Well, I have deserved it all.
FAINALL   You know I love you.
MRS MARWOOD   Poor dissembling! Oh, that – well, it is not yet –
FAINALL   What? What is it not? What is it not yet? It is not yet too late –
MRS MARWOOD   No, it is not yet too late – I have that comfort.
FAINALL   It is to love another.
MRS MARWOOD   But not to loathe, detest, abhor mankind, myself and the whole treacherous world.
FAINALL   Nay, this is extravagance. – Come, I ask your pardon. – No tears. – I was to blame; I could not love you and be easy in my doubts. – Pray, forbear. – I believe you; I'm convinced I've done you wrong, and any way, every way will make amends. I'll hate my wife yet more, damn her. – I'll part with her, rob her of all she's worth, and we'll retire somewhere, anywhere, to another world. I'll marry thee; be pacified. – 'Sdeath, they come; hide your face, your tears. – You have a mask; wear it a moment. This way, this way. Be persuaded.
   [*Exeunt*]
   [*Enter Mirabell and Mrs Fainall*]
MRS FAINALL   They are here yet.
MIRABELL   They are turning into the other walk.
MRS FAINALL   While I only hated my husband, I could bear to see him; but since I have despised him, he's too offensive.
MIRABELL   Oh, you should hate with prudence.
MRS FAINALL   Yes, for I have loved with indiscretion.
MIRABELL   You should have just so much disgust for your husband as may be sufficient to make you relish your lover.
MRS FAINALL   You have been the cause that I have loved

49

The Way of the World

without bounds, and would you set limits to that aversion of which you have been the occasion? Why did you make me marry this man?

MIRABELL Why do we daily commit disagreeable and dangerous actions? To save that idol, reputation. If the familiarities of our loves had produced that consequence of which you were apprehensive, where could you have fixed a father's name with credit, but on a husband? I knew Fainall to be a man lavish of his morals, an interested and professing friend, a false and a designing lover; yet one whose wit and outward fair behaviour have gained a reputation with the town enough to make that woman stand excused who has suffered herself to be won by his addresses. A better man ought not to have been sacrificed to the occasion; a worse had not answered to the purpose. When you are weary of him, you know your remedy.

MRS FAINALL I ought to stand in some degree of credit with you, Mirabell.

MIRABELL In justice to you, I have made you privy to my whole design, and put it in your power to ruin or advance my fortune.

MRS FAINALL Whom have you instructed to represent your pretended uncle?

MIRABELL Waitwell, my servant.

MRS FAINALL He is an humble servant to Foible, my mother's woman, and may win her to your interest.

MIRABELL Care is taken for that – she is won and worn by this time. They were married this morning.

MRS FAINALL Who?

MIRABELL Waitwell and Foible. I would not tempt my servant to betray me by trusting him too far. If your mother, in hopes to ruin me, should consent to marry my pretended uncle, he might, like Mosca in *The Fox*, stand upon terms; so I made him sure beforehand.

Act II

MRS FAINALL   So, if my poor mother is caught in a contract, you will discover the imposture betimes, and release her by producing a certificate of her gallant's former marriage.

MIRABELL   Yes, upon condition she consent to my marriage with her niece, and surrender the moiety of her fortune in her possession.

MRS FAINALL   She talked last night of endeavouring at a match between Millamant and your uncle.

MIRABELL   That was by Foible's direction, and my instruction, that she might seem to carry it more privately.

MRS FAINALL   Well, I have an opinion of your success, for I believe my lady will do anything to get a husband; and when she has this, which you have provided for her, I suppose she will submit to anything to get rid of him.

MIRABELL   Yes, I think the good lady would marry anything that resembled a man, though 'twere no more than what a butler could pinch out of a napkin.

MRS FAINALL   Female frailty! We must all come to it, if we live to be old and feel the craving of a false appetite when the true is decayed.

MIRABELL   An old woman's appetite is depraved like that of a girl. – 'Tis the green sickness of a second childhood, and, like the faint offer of a latter spring, serves but to usher in the fall, and withers in an affected bloom.

MRS FAINALL   Here's your mistress.

[*Enter Millamant, Witwoud, and Mincing*]

MIRABELL   Here she comes, i'faith, full sail, with her fan spread and her streamers out, and a shoal of fools for tenders. – Ha, no, I cry her mercy.

MRS FAINALL   I see but one poor empty sculler, and he tows her woman after him.

MIRABELL   You seem to be unattended, madam. You used to have the *beau monde* throng after you, and a flock of gay, fine perukes hovering round you.

The Way of the World

WITWOUD   Like moths about a candle. – I had like to have lost my comparison for want of breath.
MILLAMANT   Oh, I have denied myself airs today. I have walked as fast through the crowd –
WITWOUD   As a favourite in disgrace, and with as few followers.
MILLAMANT   Dear Mr Witwoud, truce with your similitudes; for I am as sick of 'em –
WITWOUD   As a physician of a good air. – I cannot help it madam, though 'tis against myself.
MILLAMANT   Yet again! Mincing, stand between me and his wit.
WITWOUD   Do, Mrs Mincing, like a screen before a great fire. I confess I do blaze today; I am too bright.
MRS FAINALL   But dear Millamant, why were you so long?
MILLAMANT   Long! Lord, have I not made violent haste? I have asked every living thing I met for you; I have enquired after you as after a new fashion.
WITWOUD   Madam, truce with your similitudes. No, you met her husband, and did not ask him for her.
MIRABELL   By your leave, Witwoud, that were like enquiring after an old fashion, to ask a husband for his wife.
WITWOUD   Hum, a hit, a hit, a palpable hit, I confess it.
MRS FAINALL   You were dressed before I came abroad.
MILLAMANT   Ay, that's true. – Oh, but then I had – Mincing, what had I? Why was I so long?
MINCING   Oh mem, your la'ship stayed to peruse a pecquet of letters.
MILLAMANT   Oh, ay, letters – I had letters – I am persecuted with letters – I hate letters. Nobody knows how to write letters, and yet one has 'em, one does not know why. They serve one to pin up one's hair.
WITWOUD   Is that the way? Pray madam, do you pin up your hair with all your letters? I find I must keep copies.

MILLAMANT Only with those in verse, Mr Witwoud. I never pin up my hair with prose. I fancy one's hair would not curl if it were pinned up with prose. I think I tried once, Mincing.
MINCING O mem, I shall never forget it.
MILLAMANT Ay, poor Mincing tift and tift all the morning.
MINCING Till I had the cremp in my fingers I'll vow, mem. And all to no purpose. But when your la'ship pins it up with poetry, it sits so pleasant the next day as anything, and is so pure and so crips.
WITWOUD Indeed, so crips?
MINCING You're such a critic Mr Witwoud.
MILLAMANT Mirabell, did not you take exceptions last night? Oh, ay, and went away. – Now I think on't, I'm angry. – No, now I think on't I'm pleased, for I believe I gave you some pain.
MIRABELL Does that please you?
MILLAMANT Infinitely; I love to give pain.
MIRABELL You would affect a cruelty which is not in your nature; your true vanity is in the power of pleasing.
MILLAMANT Oh, I ask your pardon for that. One's cruelty is one's power, and when one parts with one's cruelty, one parts with one's power; and when one has parted with that, I fancy one's old and ugly.
MIRABELL Ay, ay, suffer your cruelty to ruin the object of your power, to destroy your lover – and then how vain, how lost a thing you'll be! Nay, 'tis true: you are no longer handsome when you've lost your lover; your beauty dies upon the instant. For beauty is the lover's gift; 'tis he bestows your charms, your glass is all a cheat. The ugly and the old, whom the looking-glass mortifies, yet after commendation can be flattered by it, and discover beauties in it; for that reflects our praises, rather than your face.

MILLAMANT   Oh, the vanity of these men! Fainall, d'ye hear him? If they did not commend us, we were not handsome! Now you must know they could not commend one, if one was not handsome. Beauty the lover's gift – Lord, what is a lover, that it can give? Why, one makes lovers as fast as one pleases, and they live as long as one pleases, and they die as soon as one pleases; and then, if one pleases, one makes more.

WITWOUD   Very pretty. Why, you make no more of making of lovers, madam, than of making so many card-matches.

MILLAMANT   One no more owes one's beauty to a lover, than one's wit to an echo. They can but reflect what we look and say; vain empty things if we are silent or unseen, and want a being.

MIRABELL   Yet to those two vain empty things you owe two of the greatest pleasures of your life.

MILLAMANT   How so?

MIRABELL   To your lover you owe the pleasure of hearing yourselves praised; and to an echo the pleasure of hearing yourselves talk.

WITWOUD   But I know a lady that loves talking so incessantly, she won't give an echo fair play; she has that everlasting rotation of tongue, that an echo must wait till she dies before it can catch her last words.

MILLAMANT   Oh, fiction! Fainall, let us leave these men.

MIRABELL [*aside to Mrs Fainall*]   Draw off Witwoud.

MRS FAINALL   Immediately. – I have a word or two for Mr Witwoud.

MIRABELL   I would beg a little private audience too –
   [*Exit Witwoud and Mrs Fainall*]
You had the tyranny to deny me last night, though you knew I came to impart a secret to you that concerned my love.

MILLAMANT   You saw I was engaged.

MIRABELL Unkind. You had the leisure to entertain a herd of fools; things who visit you from their excessive idleness, bestowing on your easiness that time which is the encumbrance of their lives. How can you find delight in such society? It is impossible they should admire you; they are not capable. Or if they were, it should be to you as a mortification; for sure, to please a fool is some degree of folly.

MILLAMANT I please myself. – Besides, sometimes to converse with fools is for my health.

MIRABELL Your health! Is there a worse disease than the conversation of fools?

MILLAMANT Yes, the vapours; fools are physics for it, next to assafoetida.

MIRABELL You are not in a course of fools?

MILLAMANT Mirabell, if you persist in this offensive freedom you'll displease me. – I think I must resolve, after all, not to have you; we shan't agree.

MIRABELL Not in our physic, it may be.

MILLAMANT And yet our distemper in all likelihood will be the same; for we shall be sick of one another. I shan't endure to be reprimanded, nor instructed; 'tis so dull to act always by advice, and so tedious to be told of one's faults – I can't bear it. Well, I won't have you Mirabell – I'm resolved – I think – you may go. Ha, ha, ha! What would you give that you could help loving me?

MIRABELL I would give something that you did not know I could not help it.

MILLAMANT Come, don't look grave then. Well, what do you say to me?

MIRABELL I say that a man may as soon make a friend by his wit, or a fortune by his honesty, as win a woman with plain dealing and sincerity.

MILLAMANT Sententious Mirabell! Prithee, don't look

The Way of the World

with that violent and inflexible wise face, like Solomon at the dividing of the child in an old tapestry hanging.

MIRABELL   You are merry, madam, but I would persuade you for one moment to be serious.

MILLAMANT   What, with that face? No, if you keep your countenance, 'tis impossible I should hold mine. Well, after all, there is something very moving in a love-sick face. Ha, ha, ha! – Well, I won't laugh; don't be peevish. Heigho! Now I'll be melancholy, as melancholy as a watch-light. Well, Mirabell, if ever you will win me, woo me now. – Nay, if you are so tedious, fare you well; I see they are walking away.

MIRABELL   Can you not find in the variety of your disposition one moment –

MILLAMANT   To hear you tell me that Foible's married, and your plot like to speed? – No.

MIRABELL   But how came you to know it?

MILLAMANT   Unless by the help of the devil, you can't imagine; unless she should tell me herself. Which of the two it may have been, I will leave you to consider; and when you have done thinking of that, think of me.
   [*Exit*]

MIRABELL   I have something more – gone! Think of you? To think of a whirlwind, though 'twere in a whirlwind, were a case of more steady contemplation; a very tranquillity of mind and mansion. A fellow that lives in a windmill has not a more whimsical dwelling than the heart of a man that is lodged in a woman. There is no point of the compass to which they cannot turn, and by which they are not turned; and by one as well as another, for motion, not method is their occupation. To know this, and yet continue to be in love, is to be made wise from the dictates of reason, and yet persevere to play the fool by the force of instinct. – Oh, here come my pair of turtles. – What, billing so sweetly? Is not Valentine's day over with you yet?

[*Enter Waitwell and Foible*]

Sirrah Waitwell, why sure you think you were married for your own recreation, and not for my conveniency.

WAITWELL Your pardon, sir. With submission, we have indeed been solacing in lawful delights; but still with an eye to business, sir. I have instructed her as well as I could. If she can take your directions as readily as my instructions, sir, your affairs are in a prosperous way.

MIRABELL Give you joy, Mrs Foible.

FOIBLE Oh las, sir, I'm so ashamed. – I'm afraid my lady has been in a thousand inquietudes for me. But I protest, sir, I made as much haste as I could.

WAITWELL That she did indeed, sir. It was my fault that she did not make more.

MIRABELL That I believe.

FOIBLE But I told my lady as you instructed me, sir: that I had a prospect of seeing Sir Rowland your uncle, and that I would put her ladyship's picture in my pocket to show him; which I'll be sure to say has made him so enamoured of her beauty, that he burns with impatience to lie at her ladyship's feet and worship the original.

MIRABELL Excellent Foible! Matrimony has made you eloquent in love.

WAITWELL I think she has profited, sir. I think so.

FOIBLE You have seen Madam Millamant, sir?

MIRABELL Yes.

FOIBLE I told her, sir, because I did not know that you might find an opportunity; she had so much company last night.

MIRABELL Your diligence will merit more. In the meantime –

[*Gives money*]

The Way of the World

FOIBLE   Oh dear sir, your humble servant. 530
WAITWELL   Spouse.
MIRABELL   Stand off, sir, not a penny – Go on and prosper, Foible; the lease shall be made good and the farm stocked, if we succeed.
FOIBLE   I don't question your generosity, sir; and you need 535 not doubt of success. If you have no more commands, sir, I'll be gone; I'm sure my lady is at her toilet, and can't dress till I come. [*Looking out*] Oh dear, I'm sure that was Mrs Marwood that went by in a mask; if she has seen me with you I'm sure she'll tell my lady. I'll make haste home 540 and prevent her. Your servant, sir. B'w'y, Waitwell.
   [*Exit Foible*]
WAITWELL   Sir Rowland, if you please. The jade's so pert upon her preferment she forgets herself.
MIRABELL   Come sir, will you endeavour to forget yourself, and transform into Sir Rowland? 545
WAITWELL   Why sir, it will be impossible I should remember myself – Married, knighted, and attended all in one day! 'Tis enough to make any man forget himself. The difficulty will be how to recover my acquaintance and familiarity with my former self, and fall from my transformation to 550 a reformation into Waitwell. Nay, I shan't be quite the same Waitwell, neither – for now I remember me, I am married, and can't be my own man again.

   Ay there's the grief; that's the sad change of life;
   To lose my title, and yet keep my wife. 555
   [*Exeunt*]

Act III

A Room in Lady Wishfort's House

[*Lady Wishfort at her toilet, Peg waiting*]
LADY WISHFORT   Merciful, no news of Foible yet?
PEG   No, madam.
LADY WISHFORT   I have no more patience. – If I have not fretted myself till I am pale again, there's no veracity in me. Fetch me the red – the red, do you hear, sweet-heart? An errant ash colour, as I'm a person. Look you how this wench stirs! Why dost thou not fetch me a little red? Did'st thou not hear me, mopus?
PEG   The red ratifia does your ladyship mean, or the cherry brandy?
LADY WISHFORT   Ratifia, fool? No, fool. Not the ratifia, fool – grant me patience! I mean the Spanish paper, idiot; complexion, darling. Paint, paint, paint; dost thou understand that, changeling, dangling thy hands like bobbins before thee? Why dost thou not stir, puppet? thou wooden thing upon wires!
PEG   Lord, madam, your ladyship is so impatient – I cannot come at the paint, madam; Mrs Foible has locked it up, and carried the key with her.
LADY WISHFORT   A pox take you both – fetch me the cherry brandy then. [*Exit Peg*] I'm as pale and as faint, I look like Mrs Qualmsick, the curate's wife, that's always breeding. Wench, come, come, wench, what art thou doing? Sipping? Tasting? Save thee, dost thou not know the bottle?
   [*Enter Peg with a bottle and china cup*]
PEG   Madam, I was looking for a cup.
LADY WISHFORT   A cup, save thee, and what a cup hast thou brought! Dost thou take me for a fairy, to drink out of an

The Way of the World

acorn? Why didst thou not bring thy thimble? Hast thou ne'er a brass thimble clinking in thy pocket with a bit of nutmeg? I warrant thee. Come, fill, fill. So – again. [*One knocks.*] See who that is. Set down the bottle first. Here, here, under the table. – What, wouldst thou go with the bottle in thy hand like a tapster? As I'm a person, this wench has lived in an inn upon the road before she came to me, like Maritornes the Asturian in *Don Quixote*. No Foible yet?

PEG   No, madam, Mrs Marwood.

LADY WISHFORT   Oh, Marwood, let her come in. Come in, good Marwood.

[*Enter Mrs Marwood*]

MRS MARWOOD   I'm surprised to find your ladyship in *dishabilie* at this time of day.

LADY WISHFORT   Foible's a lost thing; has been abroad since morning, and never heard of since.

MRS MARWOOD   I saw her but now, as I came masked through the park, in conference with Mirabell.

LADY WISHFORT   With Mirabell! You call my blood into my face with mentioning that traitor. She durst not have the confidence. I sent her to negotiate an affair in which, if I'm detected, I'm undone. If that wheedling villain has wrought upon Foible to detect me, I'm ruined. Oh my dear friend, I'm a wretch of wretches if I'm detected.

MRS MARWOOD   Oh madam, you cannot suspect Mrs Foible's integrity.

LADY WISHFORT   Oh, he carries poison in his tongue that would corrupt integrity itself. If she has given him an opportunity, she has as good as put her integrity into his hands. Ah, dear Marwood, what's integrity to an opportunity? Hark! I hear her. – Go, you thing, and send her in. [*Exit Peg*] Dear friend, retire into my closet, that I may examine her with more freedom. – You'll pardon me, dear friend; I can make bold with you. – There are books over the chimney – Quarles and Prynne, and the *Short View of the Stage*, with Bunyan's works, to entertain you.

[*Exit Mrs Marwood*]

[*Enter Foible*]

O Foible, where hast thou been? What hast thou been doing?

FOIBLE   Madam, I have seen the party.

LADY WISHFORT   But what hast thou done?

FOIBLE   Nay, 'tis your ladyship has done, and are to do; I have only promised. But a man so enamoured – so transported! Well, here it is, all that is left; all that is not kissed away. Well, if worshipping of pictures be a sin, poor Sir Rowland, I say.

LADY WISHFORT   The miniature has been counted like. – But hast thou not betrayed me, Foible? Hast thou not detected me to that faithless Mirabell? What hadst thou to do with him in the park? Answer me, he has got nothing out of thee?

FOIBLE [*aside*]   So, the devil has been beforehand with me. What shall I say? – Alas, madam, could I help it, if I met that confident thing? Was I in fault? If you had heard how he used me, and all upon your ladyship's account, I'm sure you would not suspect my fidelity. Nay, if that had been the worst, I could have borne; but he had a fling at your ladyship too, and then I could not hold, but i'faith I gave him his own.

LADY WISHFORT   Me? What did the filthy fellow say?

FOIBLE   Oh madam, 'tis a shame to say what he said, with his taunts and his fleers, tossing up his nose. 'Humh!' says he, 'what, you are a-hatching some plot,' says he, 'you are so early abroad, or catering,' says he, 'ferreting for some disbanded officer, I warrant. Half-pay is but thin subsistence,' says he. 'Well, what pension does your lady

The Way of the World

propose? Let me see,' says he. 'What, she must come down pretty deep, now she's superannuated,' says he, 'and –'
LADY WISHFORT   Ods my life, I'll have him, I'll have him murdered. I'll have him poisoned. Where does he eat? I'll marry a drawer to have him poisoned in his wine. I'll send for Robin from Locket's immediately.
FOIBLE   Poison him? Poisoning's too good for him. Starve him madam, starve him; marry Sir Rowland and get him disinherited. Oh, you would bless yourself to hear what he said.
LADY WISHFORT   A villain! 'Superannuated!'
FOIBLE   'Humh,' says he, 'I hear you are laying designs against me too,' says he, 'and Mrs Millamant is to marry my uncle' (he does not suspect a word of your ladyship); 'but,' says he, 'I'll fit you for that, I warrant you,' says he. 'I'll hamper you for that,' says he, 'you and your old frippery too,' says he, 'I'll handle you –'
LADY WISHFORT   Audacious villain! 'handle' me, would he durst! – 'Frippery? old frippery!' Was there ever such a foul-mouthed fellow? I'll be married tomorrow, I'll be contracted tonight.
FOIBLE   The sooner the better, madam.
LADY WISHFORT   Will Sir Rowland be here, say'st thou? When, Foible?
FOIBLE   Incontinently, madam. No new sheriff's wife expects the return of her husband after knighthood with that impatience in which Sir Rowland burns for the dear hour of kissing your ladyship's hands after dinner.
LADY WISHFORT   'Frippery! Superannuated frippery!' I'll frippery the villain; I'll reduce him to frippery and rags! A tatterdemalion! –I hope to see him hung with tatters, like a Long Lane penthouse or a gibbet thief. A slander-mouthed railer: I warrant the spend-thrift prodigal's in debt as much as the million lottery, or the whole court

upon a birthday. I'll spoil his credit with his tailor. Yes, he shall have my niece with her fortune, he shall.

FOIBLE He! I hope to see him lodge in Ludgate first, and angle into Blackfriars for brass farthings with an old mitten.

LADY WISHFORT Ay dear Foible; thank thee for that, dear Foible. He has put me out of all patience. I shall never recompose my features to receive Sir Rowland with any economy of face. This wretch has fretted me that I am absolutely decayed. Look, Foible.

FOIBLE Your ladyship has frowned a little too rashly, indeed, madam. There are some cracks discernible in the white varnish.

LADY WISHFORT Let me see the glass. – Cracks, say'st thou? Why I am arrantly flayed; I look like an old peeled wall. Thou must repair me Foible, before Sir Rowland comes, or I shall never keep up to my picture.

FOIBLE I warrant you, madam; a little art once made your picture like you, and now a little of the same art must make you like your picture. Your picture must sit for you, madam.

LADY WISHFORT But art thou sure Sir Rowland will not fail to come? Or will a' not fail when he does come? Will he be importunate, Foible, and push? For if he should not be importunate, I shall never break decorums. I shall die with confusion, if I am forced to advance. – Oh no, I can never advance. – I shall swoon if he should expect advances. No, I hope Sir Rowland is better bred than to put a lady to the necessity of breaking her forms. I won't be too coy neither. – I won't give him despair – but a little disdain is not amiss; a little scorn is alluring.

FOIBLE A little scorn becomes your ladyship.

LADY WISHFORT Yes, but tenderness becomes me best – a sort of a dyingness. You see that picture has a sort of a –

The Way of the World

ha, Foible? A swimminess in the eyes. Yes, I'll look so. – My niece affects it, but she wants features. Is Sir Rowland handsome? Let my toilet be removed – I'll dress above. I'll receive Sir Rowland here. Is he handsome? Don't answer me. I won't know; I'll be surprised. I'll be taken by surprise.

FOIBLE By storm, madam. Sir Rowland's a brisk man.

LADY WISHFORT Is he! Oh, then he'll importune, if he's a brisk man. I shall save decorums if Sir Rowland importunes. I have a mortal terror at the apprehension of offending against decorums. Nothing but importunity can surmount decorums. Oh, I'm glad he's a brisk man. Let my things be removed, good Foible.
[*Exit*]
[*Enter Mrs Fainall*]

MRS FAINALL Oh Foible, I have been in a fright, lest I should come too late. That devil Marwood saw you in the park with Mirabell, and I'm afraid will discover it to my lady.

FOIBLE Discover what, madam?

MRS FAINALL Nay, nay, put not on that strange face. I am privy to the whole design, and know that Waitwell, to whom thou wert this morning married, is to personate Mirabell's uncle, and as such, winning my lady, to involve her in those difficulties from which Mirabell only must release her, by his making his conditions to have my cousin and her fortune left to her own disposal.

FOIBLE O dear madam, I beg your pardon. It was not my confidence in your ladyship that was deficient; but I thought the former good correspondence between your ladyship and Mr Mirabell might have hindered his communicating this secret.

MRS FAINALL Dear Foible, forget that.

FOIBLE O dear madam, Mr Mirabell is such a sweet

winning gentleman – but your ladyship is the pattern of generosity. Sweet lady, to be so good! Mr Mirabell cannot choose but be grateful. I find your ladyship has his heart still. Now, madam, I can safely tell your ladyship our success. Mrs Marwood had told my lady, but I warrant I managed myself. I turned it all for the better. I told my lady that Mr Mirabell railed at her. I laid horrid things to his charge, I'll vow; and my lady is so incensed, that she'll be contracted to Sir Rowland tonight, she says. I warrant I worked her up, that he may have her for asking for, as they say of a Welsh maidenhead.

MRS FAINALL O rare Foible!

FOIBLE Madam, I beg your ladyship to acquaint Mr Mirabell of his success. I would be seen as little as possible to speak to him. Besides, I believe Madam Marwood watches me. – She has a month's mind, but I know Mr Mirabell can't abide her. [*Enter Footman*] John, remove my lady's toilet. Madam, your servant. My lady is so impatient, I fear she'll come for me if I stay.

MRS FAINALL I'll go with you up the back stairs, lest I should meet her.

[*Exeunt*]
[*Enter Mrs Marwood*]

MRS MARWOOD Indeed Mrs Engine, is it thus with you? Are you become a go-between of this importance? Yes, I shall watch you. Why this wench is the *passe-partout*, a very master key to everybody's strong-box. My friend Fainall, have you carried it so swimmingly? I thought there was something in it; but it seems it's over with you. Your loathing is not from a want of appetite then, but from a surfeit. Else you could never be so cool to fall from a principal to be an assistant; to procure for him! 'A pattern of generosity,' that I confess. Well, Mr Fainall, you have met with your match. – O man, man! Woman, woman!

The Way of the World

The devil's an ass; if I were a painter, I would draw him like an idiot, a driveller, with a bib and bells. Man should have his head and horns, and woman the rest of him. Poor simple fiend! 'Madam Marwood has a month's mind, but he can't abide her.' – 'Twere better for him you had not been his confessor in that affair, without you could have kept his counsel closer. I shall not prove another pattern of generosity and stalk for him, till he takes his stand to aim at a fortune. He has not obliged me to that with those excesses of himself; and now I'll have none of him. Here comes the good lady, panting ripe; with a heart full of hope, and a head full of care, like any chemist upon the day of projection.

[*Enter Lady Wishfort*]

LADY WISHFORT   O dear Marwood, what shall I say for this rude forgetfulness? But my dear friend is all goodness.

MRS MARWOOD   No apologies, dear madam. I have been very well entertained.

LADY WISHFORT   As I'm a person, I am in a very chaos to think I should so forget myself. – But I have such an olio of affairs really I know not what to do. [*Calls*] Foible! I expect my nephew, Sir Wilfull, every moment too – why, Foible! He means to travel for improvement.

MRS MARWOOD   Methinks Sir Wilfull should rather think of marrying than travelling at his years. I hear he is turned of forty.

LADY WISHFORT   Oh, he's in less danger of being spoiled by his travels. I am against my nephew's marrying too young. It will be time enough when he comes back and has acquired discretion to choose for himself.

MRS MARWOOD   Methinks Mrs Millamant and he would make a very fit match. He may travel afterwards. 'Tis a thing very usual with young gentlemen.

LADY WISHFORT   I promise you I have thought on't; and

since 'tis your judgment, I'll think on't again, I assure you
I will; I value your judgment extremely. On my word, I'll
propose it.
  [*Enter Foible*]
Come, come Foible, I had forgot my nephew will be here
before dinner. I must make haste.
FOIBLE   Mr Witwoud and Mr Petulant are come to dine
with your ladyship.
LADY WISHFORT   Oh dear, I can't appear till I'm dressed.
Dear Marwood, shall I be free with you again, and beg
you to entertain 'em? I'll make all imaginable haste. Dear
friend, excuse me.
  [*Exit Lady Wishfort and Foible*]
  [*Enter Millamant and Mincing*]
MILLAMANT   Sure never anything was so unbred as that
odious man. – Marwood, your servant.
MRS MARWOOD   You have a colour; what's the matter?
MILLAMANT   That horrid fellow, Petulant, has provoked
me into a flame. I have broke my fan – Mincing, lend me
yours; is not all the powder out of my hair?
MRS MARWOOD   No. What has he done?
MILLAMANT   Nay, he has done nothing; he has only talked
– nay, he has said nothing neither; but he has contradicted
everything that has been said. For my part, I thought
Witwoud and he would have quarrelled.
MINCING   I vow mem, I thought once they would have fit.
MILLAMANT   Well, 'tis a lamentable thing, I'll swear, that
one has not the liberty of choosing one's acquaintance as
one does one's clothes.
MRS MARWOOD   If we had the liberty, we should be as weary
of one set of acquaintance, though never so good, as we
are of one suit, though never so fine. A fool and a doily
stuff would now and then find days of grace, and be worn
for variety.

The Way of the World

MILLAMANT   I could consent to wear 'em, if they would wear alike, but fools never wear out – they are such *drap-du-Berry* things, without one could give 'em to one's chambermaid after a day or two.

MRS MARWOOD   'Twere better so indeed. Or what think you of the play-house? A fine gay glossy fool should be given there, like a new masking habit, after the masquerade is over, and we have done with the disguise. For a fool's visit is always a disguise, and never admitted by a woman of wit but to blind her affair with a lover of sense. If you would but appear bare-faced now, and own Mirabell, you might as easily put off Petulant and Witwoud as your hood and scarf. And indeed 'tis time, for the town has found it; the secret is grown too big for the pretence. 'Tis like Mrs Primly's great belly; she may lace it down before, but it burnishes on her hips. Indeed, Millamant, you can no more conceal it than my Lady Strammel can her face, that goodly face, which in defiance of her Rhenish-wine tea, will not be comprehended in a mask.

MILLAMANT   I'll take my death, Marwood, you are more censorious than a decayed beauty, or a discarded toast; Mincing, tell the men they may come up. My aunt is not dressing; their folly is less provoking than your malice. [*Exit Mincing*] 'The town has found it.' What has it found? That Mirabell loves me is no more a secret than it is a secret that you discovered it to my aunt, or than the reason why you discovered it is a secret.

MRS MARWOOD   You are nettled.

MILLAMANT   You're mistaken. Ridiculous!

MRS MARWOOD   Indeed my dear, you'll tear another fan if you don't mitigate those violent airs.

MILLAMANT   Oh silly! Ha, ha, ha! I could laugh immoderately. Poor Mirabell! His constancy to me has quite destroyed his complaisance for all the world beside.

Act III

I swear, I never enjoined it him to be so coy. – If I had the vanity to think he would obey me, I would command him to show more gallantry. – 'Tis hardly well bred to be so particular on one hand, and so insensible on the other. But I despair to prevail, and so let him follow his own way. Ha, ha, ha. Pardon me, dear creature, I must laugh, ha, ha, ha, though I grant you 'tis a little barbarous, ha, ha, ha.

MRS MARWOOD What pity 'tis, so much fine raillery, and delivered with so significant gesture, should be so unhappily directed to miscarry.

MILLAMANT Ha? Dear creature, I ask your pardon – I swear I did not mind you.

MRS MARWOOD Mr Mirabell and you both may think it a thing impossible, when I shall tell him, by telling you –

MILLAMANT Oh dear, what? For it is the same thing if I hear it, ha, ha, ha.

MRS MARWOOD That I detest him, hate him, madam.

MILLAMANT Oh madam, why so do I – and yet the creature loves me, ha, ha, ha. How can one forbear laughing to think of it. – I am a sybil if I am not amazed to think what he can see in me. I'll take my death, I think you are handsomer – and within a year or two as young. If you could but stay for me, I should overtake you – but that cannot be. Well, that thought makes me melancholy. – Now I'll be sad.

MRS MARWOOD Your merry note may be changed sooner than you think.

MILLAMANT D'ye say so? Then I'm resolved I'll have a song to keep up my spirits.

  [*Enter Mincing*]

MINCING The gentlemen stay but to comb, madam, and will wait on you.

MILLAMANT Desire Mrs –, that is in the next room, to sing

the song I would have learned yesterday. You shall hear it madam – not that there's any great matter in it, but 'tis agreeable to my humour.

[*Set by Mr John Eccles, and sung by Mrs Hodgson*]
(Song)
I
Love's but the frailty of the mind, 360
When 'tis not with ambition joined;
A sickly flame, which if not fed, expires;
And feeding, wastes in self-consuming fires.
II
'Tis not to wound a wanton boy
Or am'rous youth, that gives the joy; 365
But 'tis the glory to have pierced a swain,
For whom inferior beauties sighed in vain.
III
Then I alone the conquest prize,
When I insult a rival's eyes;
If there's delight in love, 'tis when I see 370
That heart which others bleed for, bleed for me.

[*Enter Petulant and Witwoud*]
MILLAMANT Is your animosity composed, gentlemen?
WITWOUD Raillery, raillery, madam; we have no animosity.
– We hit off a little wit now and then, but no animosity.
– The falling out of wits is like the falling out of lovers; 375
we agree in the main, like treble and bass. Ha, Petulant?
PETULANT Ay, in the main – but when I have a humour to contradict.
WITWOUD Ay, when he has a humour to contradict, then I contradict too. What, I know my cue. Then we contradict 380
one another like two battledores; for contradictions beget one another like Jews.

PETULANT If he says black's black, if I have a humour to say 'tis blue, let that pass; all's one for that. If I have a humour to prove it, it must be granted.

WITWOUD Not positively must – but it may, it may.

PETULANT Yes, it positively must, upon proof positive.

WITWOUD Ay, upon proof positive it must; but upon proof presumptive it only may. That's a logical distinction now, madam.

MRS MARWOOD I perceive your debates are of importance and very learnedly handled.

PETULANT Importance is one thing, and learning's another; but a debate's a debate, that I assert.

WITWOUD Petulant's an enemy to learning; he relies altogether on his parts.

PETULANT No, I'm no enemy to learning; it hurts not me.

MRS MARWOOD That's a sign indeed it's no enemy to you.

PETULANT No, no, it's no enemy to anybody but them that have it.

MILLAMANT Well, an illiterate man's my aversion. I wonder at the impudence of any illiterate man to offer to make love.

WITWOUD That I confess I wonder at too.

MILLAMANT Ah! to marry an ignorant that can hardly read or write.

PETULANT Why should a man be ever the further from being married though he can't read, any more than he is from being hanged? The Ordinary's paid for setting the psalm, and the parish priest for reading the ceremony. And for the rest which is to follow in both cases, a man may do it without book – so all's one for that.

MILLAMANT D'ye hear the creature? Lord, here's company; I'll be gone.

[*Exeunt Millamant and Mincing*]

The Way of the World

WITWOUD In the name of Bartlemew and his fair, what have we here?

MRS MARWOOD 'Tis your brother, I fancy. Don't you know him?

WITWOUD Not I. – Yes, I think it is he. – I've almost forgot him; I have not seen him since the Revolution.

[*Enter Sir Wilfull Witwoud in a country riding habit, and Servant to Lady Wishfort*]

SERVANT Sir, my lady's dressing. Here's company, if you please to walk in, in the mean time.

SIR WILFULL Dressing! What, it's but morning here, I warrant with you, in London; we should count it towards afternoon in our parts, down in Shropshire. Why then, belike my aunt han't dined yet – ha, friend?

SERVANT Your aunt, sir?

SIR WILFULL My aunt, sir, yes my aunt, sir, and your lady, sir; your lady is my aunt, sir. – Why, what, dost thou not know me, friend? Why then send somebody here that does. How long hast thou lived with thy lady, fellow, ha?

SERVANT A week, sir; longer than anybody in the house, except my lady's woman.

SIR WILFULL Why then, belike thou dost not know thy lady if thou seest her, ha, friend?

SERVANT Why truly, sir, I cannot safely swear to her face in a morning, before she is dressed. 'Tis like I may give a shrewd guess at her by this time.

SIR WILFULL Well, prithee try what thou canst do; if thou canst not guess, enquire her out, dost hear fellow? And tell her, her nephew, Sir Wilfull Witwoud, is in the house.

SERVANT I shall, sir.

SIR WILFULL Hold ye, hear me, friend; a word with you in your ear. Prithee who are these gallants?

SERVANT Really sir, I can't tell; here come so many here, 'tis hard to know 'em all.

[Exit Servant]

SIR WILFULL   Oons, this fellow knows less than a starling; I don't think a' knows his own name.

MRS MARWOOD   Mr Witwoud, your brother is not behindhand in forgetfulness; I fancy he has forgot you too.

WITWOUD   I hope so. – The devil take him that remembers first, I say.

SIR WILFULL   Save you, gentlemen and lady.

MRS MARWOOD   For shame, Mr Witwoud; why won't you speak to him? – And you, sir.

WITWOUD   Petulant, speak.

PETULANT   And you, sir.

SIR WILFULL   No offence, I hope.
[Salutes Mrs Marwood]

MRS MARWOOD   No sure, sir.

WITWOUD   This is a vile dog, I see that already. No offence! Ha, ha, ha! To him, to him, Petulant; smoke him.

PETULANT   It seems as if you had come a journey, sir, hem, hem.
[Surveying him round]

SIR WILFULL   Very likely, sir, that it may seem so.

PETULANT   No offence, I hope, sir.

WITWOUD   Smoke the boots, the boots, Petulant, the boots. Ha, ha, ha.

SIR WILFULL   Maybe not, sir; thereafter as 'tis meant, sir.

PETULANT   Sir, I presume upon the information of your boots.

SIR WILFULL   Why, 'tis like you may, sir. If you are not satisfied with the information of my boots, sir, if you will step to the stable, you may enquire further of my horse, sir.

PETULANT   Your horse, sir! Your horse is an ass, sir!

SIR WILFULL   Do you speak by way of offence, sir?

The Way of the World

MRS MARWOOD   The gentleman's merry, that's all, sir. [*Aside*] 'Slife, we shall have a quarrel betwixt an horse and an ass, before they find one another out. [*Aloud*] You must not take anything amiss from your friends, sir. You are among your friends here, though it may be you don't know it. If I am not mistaken, you are Sir Wilfull Witwoud.

SIR WILFULL   Right, lady; I am Sir Wilfull Witwoud, so I write myself; no offence to anybody, I hope; and nephew to the Lady Wishfort of this mansion.

MRS MARWOOD   Don't you know this gentleman, sir?

SIR WILFULL   Hum! What, sure 'tis not – yea, by'r lady, but 'tis. – 'S'heart, I know not whether 'tis or no – yea but 'tis by the Rekin. Brother Anthony! What Tony, i'faith! What, dost thou not know me? By'r Lady, nor I thee, thou art so becravatted, and beperiwigged. – 'S'heart, why dost not speak? Art thou o'erjoyed?

WITWOUD   Odso, brother, is it you? Your servant, brother.

SIR WILFULL   Your servant! Why, yours, sir. Your servant again, 's'heart, and your friend and servant to that, and a (*puff*) and a flapdragon for your service, sir; and a hare's foot, and a hare's scut for your service, sir, an you be so cold and so courtly!

WITWOUD   No offence, I hope, brother.

SIR WILFULL   'S'heart, sir, but there is, and much offence. – A pox, is this your Inns o' Court breeding, not to know your friends and your relations, your elders, and your betters?

WITWOUD   Why, brother Wilfull of Salop, you may be as short as a Shrewsbury cake, if you please. But I tell you, 'tis not modish to know relations in town. You think you're in the country, where great lubberly brothers slabber and kiss one another when they meet, like a call of serjeants. – 'Tis not the fashion here; 'tis not indeed, dear brother.

Act III

SIR WILFULL   The fashion's a fool; and you're a fop, dear brother. 'S'heart, I've suspected this. – By'r Lady I conjectured you were a fop, since you began to change the style of your letters, and write in a scrap of paper gilt round the edges, no broader than a subpoena. I might expect this, when you left off 'Honoured Brother', and 'hoping you are in good health', and so forth, to begin with a 'Rat me, knight, I'm so sick of a last night's debauch' – ods heart, and then tell a familiar tale of a cock and a bull, and a whore and a bottle, and so conclude. – You could write news before you were out of your time, when you lived with honest Pumplenose the attorney of Furnival's Inn; you could entreat to be remembered then to your friends round the Rekin. We could have gazettes then, and *Dawk's Letter*, and the weekly bill, till of late days.

PETULANT   'Slife, Witwoud, were you ever an attorney's clerk? Of the family of the Furnivals? Ha, ha, ha!

WITWOUD   Ay, ay, but that was for a while. Not long, not long; pshaw, I was not in my own power then. An orphan, and this fellow was my guardian; ay, ay, I was glad to consent to that man to come to London. He had the disposal of me then. If I had not agreed to that, I might have been bound 'prentice to a felt-maker in Shrewsbury; this fellow would have bound me to a maker of felts.

SIR WILFULL   'S'heart, and better than to be bound to a maker of fops, where, I suppose, you have served your time; and now you may set up for yourself.

MRS MARWOOD   You intend to travel, sir, as I'm informed.

SIR WILFULL   Belike I may, madam. I may chance to sail upon the salt seas, if my mind hold.

PETULANT   And the wind serve.

SIR WILFULL   Serve or not serve, I shan't ask licence of you, sir; nor the weather-cock your companion. I direct my discourse to the lady, sir. 'Tis like my aunt may have told

The Way of the World

you, madam. – Yes, I have settled my concerns, I may say now, and am minded to see foreign parts. If an how that the peace holds, whereby, that is, taxes abate.

MRS MARWOOD I thought you had designed for France at all adventures.

SIR WILFULL I can't tell that; 'tis like I may, and 'tis like I may not. I am somewhat dainty in making a resolution, because when I make it I keep it. I don't stand shill I, shall I, then; if I say't, I'll do't. But I have thoughts to tarry a small matter in town, to learn somewhat of your lingo first, before I cross the seas. I'd gladly have a spice of your French, as they say, whereby to hold discourse in foreign countries.

MRS MARWOOD Here is an academy in town for that use.

SIR WILFULL There is? 'Tis like there may.

MRS MARWOOD No doubt you will return very much improved.

WITWOUD Yes, refined, like a Dutch skipper from a whale-fishing.

[*Enter Lady Wishfort and Fainall*]

LADY WISHFORT Nephew, you are welcome.

SIR WILFULL Aunt, your servant.

FAINALL Sir Wilfull, your most faithful servant.

SIR WILFULL Cousin Fainall, give me your hand.

LADY WISHFORT Cousin Witwoud, your servant; Mr Petulant, your servant. – Nephew, you are welcome again. Will you drink anything after your journey, nephew, before you eat? Dinner's almost ready.

SIR WILFULL I'm very well, I thank you, aunt; however, I thank you for your courteous offer. 'S'heart, I was afraid you would have been in the fashion too, and have remembered to have forgot your relations. Here's your cousin Tony, belike I mayn't call him brother for fear of offence.

LADY WISHFORT   Oh he's a rallier, nephew – my cousin's a wit, and your great wits always rally their best friends to choose. When you have been abroad, nephew, you'll understand raillery better.
  [*Fainall and Mrs Marwood talk apart*]
SIR WILFULL   Why then let him hold his tongue in the meantime, and rail when that day comes.
  [*Enter Mincing*]
MINCING   Mem, I come to acquaint your la'ship that dinner is impatient.
SIR WILFULL   Impatient? Why then belike it won't stay till I pull off my boots. Sweetheart, can you help me to a pair of slippers? – My man's with his horses, I warrant.
LADY WISHFORT   Fie, fie, nephew, you would not pull off your boots here. – Go down into the hall; dinner shall stay for you. – My nephew's a little unbred; you'll pardon him, madam. – Gentlemen, will you walk? Marwood?
MRS MARWOOD   I'll follow you, madam, before Sir Wilfull is ready.
  [*Manent Mrs Marwood and Fainall*]
FAINALL   Why then, Foible's a bawd, an errant, rank, matchmaking bawd. And I it seems am a husband, a rank husband; and my wife a very arrant, rank wife, – all in the way of the world. 'Sdeath, to be an anticipated cuckold, a cuckold in embryo! Sure I was born with budding antlers like a young satyr, or a citizen's child. 'Sdeath to be out-witted, to be out-jilted, – out-matrimonied! If I had kept my speed like a stag, 'twere somewhat, but to crawl after, with my horns, like a snail, and out-stripped by my wife – 'tis scurvy wedlock.
MRS MARWOOD   Then shake it off. You have often wished for an opportunity to part, and now you have it. But first prevent their plot; the half of Millamant's fortune is too considerable to be parted with, to a foe, to Mirabell.

FAINALL Damn him! that had been mine – had you not made that fond discovery. That had been forfeited, had they been married. My wife had added lustre to my horns by that increase of fortune; I could have worn 'em tipped with gold, though my forehead had been furnished like a deputy-lieutenant's hall.

MRS MARWOOD They may prove a cap of maintenance to you still, if you can away with your wife. And she's no worse than when you had her – I dare swear she had given up her game before she was married.

FAINALL Hum! That may be. – She might throw up her cards; but I'll be hanged if she did not put Pam in her pocket.

MRS MARWOOD You married her to keep you; and if you can contrive to have her keep you better than you expected, why should you not keep her longer than you intended?

FAINALL The means, the means.

MRS MARWOOD Discover to my lady your wife's conduct; threaten to part with her. – My lady loves her, and will come to any composition to save her reputation. Take the opportunity of breaking it, just upon the discovery of this imposture. My lady will be enraged beyond bounds, and sacrifice niece and fortune and all at that conjuncture. And let me alone to keep her warm; if she should flag in her part, I will not fail to prompt her.

FAINALL Faith, this has an appearance.

MRS MARWOOD I'm sorry I hinted to my lady to endeavour a match between Millamant and Sir Wilfull; that may be an obstacle.

FAINALL Oh, for that matter leave me to manage him; I'll disable him for that. He will drink like a Dane; after dinner, I'll set his hand in.

MRS MARWOOD Well, how do you stand affected towards your lady?

Act III

FAINALL Why, faith, I'm thinking of it. – Let me see – I am married already, so that's over. – My wife has played the jade with me; well, that's over too. – I never loved her, or if I had, why that would have been over too by this time. – Jealous of her I cannot be, for I am certain; so there's an end of jealousy. Weary of her I am, and shall be. – No, there's no end of that; no, no, that were too much to hope. Thus far concerning my repose. Now for my reputation. – As to my own, I married not for it; so that's out of the question. – And as to my part in my wife's – why she had parted with hers before; so bringing none to me, she can take none from me. 'Tis against all rule of play that I should lose to one who has not wherewithal to stake.

MRS MARWOOD Besides, you forget, marriage is honourable.

FAINALL Hum! Faith, and that's well thought on; marriage is honourable as you say; and if so, wherefore should cuckoldom be a discredit, being derived from so honourable a root?

MRS MARWOOD Nay I know not; if the root be honourable, why not the branches?

FAINALL So, so; why this point's clear. – Well, how do we proceed?

MRS MARWOOD I will contrive a letter which shall be delivered to my lady at the time when that rascal who is to act Sir Rowland is with her. It shall come as from an unknown hand – for the less I appear to know of the truth, the better I can play the incendiary. Besides, I would not have Foible provoked if I could help it, because you know she knows some passages. Nay, I expect all will come out; but let the mine be sprung first, and then I care not if I'm discovered.

FAINALL If the worst come to the worst, I'll turn my wife to grass. – I have already a deed of settlement of the best

part of her estate, which I wheedled out of her; and that
you shall partake at least. 680
MRS MARWOOD I hope you are convinced that I hate
Mirabell now; you'll be no more jealous?
FAINALL Jealous, no – by this kiss. Let husbands be jealous;
but let the lover still believe. Or if he doubt, let it be only
to endear his pleasure and prepare the joy that follows, 685
when he proves his mistress true. But let husbands' doubts
convert to endless jealousy; or if they have belief, let it
corrupt to superstition and blind credulity. I am single,
and will herd no more with 'em. True, I wear the badge;
but I'll disown the order. And since I take my leave of 690
'em, I care not if I leave 'em a common motto to their
common crest.

> All husbands must or pain or shame endure;
> The wise too jealous are, fools too secure.

[*Exeunt*]

Act IV

Scene continues

[*Enter Lady Wishfort and Foible*]
LADY WISHFORT   Is Sir Rowland coming, say'st thou, Foible? and are things in order?
FOIBLE   Yes, madam. I have put wax-lights in the sconces, and placed the footmen in a row in the hall, in their best liveries, with the coachman and postilion to fill up the equipage.
LADY WISHFORT   Have you pullvilled the coachman and postilion, that they may not stink of the stable when Sir Rowland comes by?
FOIBLE   Yes, madam.
LADY WISHFORT   And are the dancers and the music ready, that he may be entertained in all points with correspondence to his passion?
FOIBLE   All is ready, madam.
LADY WISHFORT   And – well – and how do I look, Foible?
FOIBLE   Most killing well, madam.
LADY WISHFORT   Well, and how shall I receive him? In what figure shall I give his heart the first impression? There is a great deal in the first impression. Shall I sit? No, I won't sit – I'll walk; ay, I'll walk from the door upon his entrance, and then turn full upon him. – No, that will be too sudden. I'll lie – ay, I'll lie down. – I'll receive him in my little dressing-room; there's a couch – yes, yes, I'll give the first impression on a couch. – I won't lie neither, but loll and lean upon one elbow, with one foot a little dangling off, jogging in a thoughtful way. – Yes – and then as soon as he appears, start, ay, start and be surprised, and rise to meet him in a pretty disorder. – Yes – oh, nothing is more alluring than a levée from a couch

The Way of the World

in some confusion. – It shows the foot to advantage, and furnishes with blushes and re-composing airs beyond comparison. Hark! There's a coach.
FOIBLE 'Tis he, madam.
LADY WISHFORT Oh dear, has my nephew made his addresses to Millamant? I ordered him.
FOIBLE Sir Wilfull is set in to drinking, madam, in the parlour.
LADY WISHFORT Ods my life, I'll send him to her. Call her down, Foible; bring her hither. I'll send him as I go. – When they are together, then come to me, Foible, that I may not be too long alone with Sir Rowland.
    [*Exit*]
    [*Enter Millamant, and Mrs Fainall*]
FOIBLE Madam, I stayed here to tell your ladyship that Mr Mirabell has waited this half hour for an opportunity to talk with you, though my lady's orders were to leave you and Sir Wilfull together. Shall I tell Mr Mirabell that you are at leisure?
MILLAMANT No – what would the dear man have? I am thoughtful, and would amuse myself – bid him come another time.

> *There never yet was woman made,*
> *Nor shall, but to be curs'd.*

    [*Repeating and walking about*]
    That's hard!
MRS FAINALL You are very fond of Sir John Suckling today, Millamant, and the poets.
MILLAMANT He? Ay, and filthy verses; so I am.
FOIBLE Sir Wilfull is coming, madam. Shall I send Mr Mirabell away?
MILLAMANT Ay, if you please, Foible, send him away – or

send him hither – just as you will, dear Foible. I think I'll see him; shall I? Ay, let the wretch come.

Thyrsis a youth of the inspir'd train –

[*Repeating*]
Dear Fainall, entertain Sir Wilfull. – Thou hast philosophy to undergo a fool, thou art married and hast patience. – I would confer with my own thoughts.

MRS FAINALL   I am obliged to you, that you would make me your proxy in this affair; but I have business of my own.
[*Enter Sir Wilfull*]
O Sir Wilfull, you are come at the critical instant. There's your mistress up to the ears in love and contemplation; pursue your point, now or never.

SIR WILFULL   Yes; my aunt would have it so. – I would gladly have been encouraged with a bottle or two, because I'm somewhat wary at first, before I am acquainted. – But I hope after a time, I shall break my mind – that is, upon further acquaintance. – So for the present, cousin, I'll take my leave. – If so be you'll be so kind to make my excuse, I'll return to my company – [*This while Millamant walks about repeating to herself*]

MRS FAINALL   Oh fie, Sir Wilfull! What, you must not be daunted.

SIR WILFULL   Daunted, no, that's not it, it is not so much for that – for if so be that I set on't, I'll do't. But only for the present, 'tis sufficient till further acquaintance, that's all – your servant.

MRS FAINALL   Nay, I'll swear you shall never lose so favourable an opportunity, if I can help it. I'll leave you together and lock the door.
[*Exit*]

SIR WILFULL   Nay, nay cousin – I have forgot my gloves.

The Way of the World

– What d'ye do? 'S'heart, a' has locked the door indeed, I think. – Nay, cousin Fainall, open the door. – Pshaw, what a vixen trick is this? – Nay, now a' has seen me too. – Cousin, I made bold to pass through as it were. – I think this door's enchanted. –

MILLAMANT   [*repeating*]

> *I prithee spare me, gentle boy,*
> *Press me no more for that slight toy.*

SIR WILFULL   Anan? Cousin, your servant.
MILLAMANT   *That foolish trifle of a heart* – Sir Wilfull!
SIR WILFULL   Yes – your servant. No offence I hope, cousin.
MILLAMANT   [*repeating*]

> *I swear it will not do its part,*
> *Tho' thou dost thine, employ'st the power and art.*

Natural, easy Suckling!

SIR WILFULL   Anan? Suckling? No such suckling neither, cousin, nor stripling; I thank heaven, I'm no minor.
MILLAMANT   Ah rustic! ruder than Gothic.
SIR WILFULL   Well, well, I shall understand your lingo one of these days, cousin; in the meanwhile, I must answer in plain English.
MILLAMANT   Have you any business with me, Sir Wilfull?
SIR WILFULL   Not at present, cousin. – Yes, I made bold to see, to come and know if that how you were disposed to fetch a walk this evening, if so be that I might not be troublesome, I would have sought a walk with you.
MILLAMANT   A walk? What then?
SIR WILFULL   Nay, nothing – only for the walk's sake, that's all –
MILLAMANT   I nauseate walking; 'tis a country diversion, I

loathe the country and everything that relates to it.
SIR WILFULL   Indeed! Hah! Look ye, look ye, you do? Nay, 'tis like you may. – Here are choice of pastimes here in town, as plays and the like; that must be confessed indeed.
MILLAMANT   Ah, *l'étourdie!* I hate the town too.
SIR WILFULL   Dear heart, that's much. – Hah! that you should hate 'em both! Hah! 'tis like you may; there are some can't relish the town, and others can't away with the country. – 'Tis like you may be one of those, cousin.
MILLAMANT   Ha, ha, ha. Yes, 'tis like I may. – You have nothing further to say to me?
SIR WILFULL   Not at present, cousin. – 'Tis like when I have an opportunity to be more private, I may break my mind in some measure. – I conjecture you partly guess – however, that's as time shall try; but spare to speak and spare to speed, as they say.
MILLAMANT   If it is of no great importance, Sir Wilfull, you will oblige me to leave me; I have just now a little business –
SIR WILFULL   Enough, enough, cousin; yes, yes, all a case – when you're disposed, when you're disposed. Now's as well as another time; and another time as well as now. All's one for that. – Yes, yes, if your concerns call you, there's no haste; it will keep cold, as they say. – Cousin, your servant. – I think this door's locked.
MILLAMANT   You may go this way, sir.
SIR WILFULL   Your servant; then with your leave I'll return to my company.
   [*Exit*]
MILLAMANT   Ay, ay; ha, ha, ha!

Like Phoebus sung the no less am'rous boy.

[*Enter Mirabell*]

MIRABELL   – *Like Daphne she as lovely and as coy.* Do you lock yourself up from me, to make my search more curious? Or is this pretty artifice contrived, to signify that here the chase must end and my pursuit be crowned, for you can fly no further –

MILLAMANT   Vanity! No – I'll fly and be followed to the last moment. Though I am upon the very verge of matrimony, I expect you should solicit me as much as if I were wavering at the grate of a monastery, with one foot over the threshold. I'll be solicited to the very last, nay and afterwards.

MIRABELL   What, after the last?

MILLAMANT   Oh, I should think I was poor and had nothing to bestow, if I were reduced to an inglorious ease, and freed from the agreeable fatigues of solicitation.

MIRABELL   But do not you know that when favours are conferred upon instant and tedious solicitation, that they diminish in their value, and that both the giver loses the grace, and the receiver lessens his pleasure?

MILLAMANT   It may be in things of common application, but never sure in love. Oh, I hate a lover that can dare to think he draws a moment's air independent on the bounty of his mistress. There is not so impudent a thing in nature as the saucy look of an assured man, confident of success. The pedantic arrogance of a very husband has not so pragmatical an air. Ah! I'll never marry, unless I am first made sure of my will and pleasure.

MIRABELL   Would you have 'em both before marriage? Or will you be contented with the first now, and stay for the other till after grace?

MILLAMANT   Ah, don't be impertinent. – My dear liberty, shall I leave thee? My faithful solitude, my darling contemplation, must I bid you then adieu? ay-h adieu, my morning thoughts, agreeable wakings, indolent slumbers, all ye *douceurs*, ye *sommeils du matin*, adieu. – I can't do't, 'tis more than impossible. – Positively Mirabell, I'll lie a-bed in a morning as long as I please.

MIRABELL Then I'll get up in a morning as early as I please.

MILLAMANT Ah, idle creature, get up when you will – and d'ye hear, I won't be called names after I'm married; positively I won't be called names.

MIRABELL Names!

MILLAMANT Ay, as wife, spouse, my dear, joy, jewel, love, sweetheart and the rest of that nauseous cant in which men and their wives are so fulsomely familiar; I shall never bear that. – Good Mirabell, don't let us be familiar or fond, nor kiss before folks, like my Lady Fadler and Sir Francis; nor go to Hyde Park together the first Sunday in a new chariot, to provoke eyes and whispers, and then never to be seen there together again, as if we were proud of one another the first week, and ashamed of one another for ever after. Let us never visit together, nor go to a play together, but let us be very strange and well-bred; let us be as strange as if we had been married a great while, and as well bred as if we were not married at all.

MIRABELL Have you any more conditions to offer? Hitherto your demands are pretty reasonable.

MILLAMANT Trifles. – As liberty to pay and receive visits to and from whom I please; to write and receive letters, without interrogatories or wry faces on your part. To wear what I please, and choose conversation with regard only to my own taste; to have no obligation upon me to converse with wits that I don't like, because they are your acquaintance, or to be intimate with fools, because they may be your relations. Come to dinner when I please; dine in my dressing-room when I'm out of humour, without giving a reason. To have my closet inviolate; to be sole empress of my tea-table, which you must never presume to approach without first asking leave. And lastly, wherever I am, you shall always knock at the door before you come in. These articles subscribed, if I continue to endure you a little longer, I may by degrees dwindle into a wife.

MIRABELL Your bill of fare is something advanced in this latter account. Well, have I liberty to offer conditions – that when you are dwindled into a wife, I may not be beyond measure enlarged into a husband?

MILLAMANT You have free leave; propose your utmost, speak and spare not.

MIRABELL I thank you. *Inprimis* then, I covenant that your acquaintance be general; that you admit no sworn confidante, or intimate of your own sex; no she-friend to screen her affairs under your countenance and tempt you to make trial of a mutual secrecy. No decoy-duck to wheedle you a fop, scrambling to the play in a mask; then bring you home in a pretended fright, when you think you shall be found out – and rail at me for missing the play, and disappointing the frolic, which you had to pick me up and prove my constancy.

MILLAMANT Detestable *inprimis*! I go to the play in a mask!

MIRABELL *Item*, I article that you continue to like your own face, as long as I shall. And while it passes current with me, that you endeavour not to new coin it. To which end, together with all vizards for the day, I prohibit all masks for the night, made of oiled skins and I know not what – hog's-bones, hare's-gall, pig-water, and the marrow of a roasted cat. In short, I forbid all commerce with the gentlewoman in what-d'ye-call-it Court. *Item*, I shut my doors against all bawds with baskets, and penny-worths of muslin, china, fans, atlases, etc, etc. – *Item*, when you shall be breeding –

MILLAMANT Ah! Name it not.

MIRABELL   Which may be presumed, with a blessing on our endeavours –
MILLAMANT   Odious endeavours!
MIRABELL   I denounce against all strait-lacing, squeezing for a shape, till you mould my boy's head like a sugar-loaf; and instead of a man-child, make me the father to a crooked billet. Lastly, to the dominion of the tea-table I submit – but with proviso that you exceed not in your province, but restrain yourself to native and simple tea-table drinks, as tea, chocolate and coffee. As likewise to genuine and authorized tea-table talk, such as mending of fashions, spoiling reputations, railing at absent friends, and so forth; but that on no account you encroach upon the men's prerogative, and presume to drink healths, or toast fellows; for prevention of which, I banish all foreign forces, all auxiliaries to the tea-table, as orange-brandy, all aniseed, cinnamon, citron and Barbadoes waters, together with ratifia and the most noble spirit of clary. But for cowslip wine, poppy-water and all dormitives, those I allow. – These provisos admitted, in other things I may prove a tractable and complying husband.
MILLAMANT   Oh horrid provisos! Filthy strong waters! I toast fellows, odious men! I hate your odious provisos.
MIRABELL   Then we're agreed. Shall I kiss your hand upon the contract? And here comes one to be a witness to the sealing of the deed.
   [*Enter Mrs Fainall*]
MILLAMANT   Fainall, what shall I do? Shall I have him? I think I must have him.
MRS FAINALL   Ay, ay, take him, take him, what should you do?
MILLAMANT   Well then – I'll take my death I'm in a horrid fright. – Fainall, I shall never say it. – Well – I think – I'll endure you.

The Way of the World

MRS FAINALL   Fie, fie, have him, have him, and tell him so in plain terms; for I am sure you have a mind to him.

MILLAMANT   Are you? I think I have – and the horrid man looks as if he thought so too. – Well, you ridiculous thing you, I'll have you. – I won't be kissed, nor I won't be thanked. – Here, kiss my hand though. – So, hold your tongue now, and don't say a word.

MRS FAINALL   Mirabell, there's a necessity for your obedience; you have neither time to talk nor stay. My mother is coming; and in my conscience if she should see you, would fall into fits, and maybe not recover time enough to return to Sir Rowland, who as Foible tells me is in a fair way to succeed. Therefore spare your ecstasies for another occasion, and slip down the backstairs, where Foible waits to consult you.

MILLAMANT   Ay, go, go. In the meantime I suppose you have said something to please me.

MIRABELL   I am all obedience.

[*Exit Mirabell*]

MRS FAINALL   Yonder Sir Wilfull's drunk, and so noisy that my mother has been forced to leave Sir Rowland to appease him; but he answers her only with singing and drinking. What they have done by this time I know not, but Petulant and he were upon quarrelling as I came by.

MILLAMANT   Well, if Mirabell should not make a good husband, I am a lost thing – for I find I love him violently.

MRS FAINALL   So it seems, when you mind not what's said to you. – If you doubt him, you had best take up with Sir Wilfull.

MILLAMANT   How can you name that superannuated lubber, foh!

[*Enter Witwoud from drinking*]

MRS FAINALL   So, is the fray made up, that you have left 'em?

Act IV

WITWOUD Left 'em? I could stay no longer. – I have laughed like ten christenings – I am tipsy with laughing. – If I had stayed any longer I should have burst – I must have been let out and pieced in the sides like an unsized camlet. Yes, yes, the fray is composed; my lady came in like a *noli prosequi* and stopped their proceedings.

MILLAMANT What was the dispute?

WITWOUD That's the jest, there was no dispute, they could neither of 'em speak for rage, and so fell a-sputtering at one another like two roasting apples.

[*Enter Petulant drunk*]

Now Petulant, all's over, all's well? Gad, my head begins to whim it about – why dost thou not speak? Thou art both as drunk and as mute as a fish.

PETULANT Look you, Mrs Millamant, if you can love me, dear nymph – say it – and that's the conclusion. – Pass on, or pass off – that's all.

WITWOUD Thou hast uttered volumes, folios, in less than decimo sexto, my dear Lacedemonian. Sirrah Petulant, thou art an epitomizer of words.

PETULANT Witwoud, – you are an annihilator of sense.

WITWOUD Thou art a retailer of phrases, and dost deal in remnants of remnants, like a maker of pincushions – thou art in truth (metaphorically speaking) a speaker of shorthand.

PETULANT Thou art (without a figure) just one half of an ass, and Baldwin yonder, thy half-brother, is the rest. – A gemini of asses split would make just four of you.

WITWOUD Thou dost bite, my dear mustard-seed; kiss me for that.

PETULANT Stand off. – I'll kiss no more males. – I have kissed your twin yonder in a humour of reconcilation, till he [*hiccup*] rises upon my stomach like a radish.

MILLAMANT Eh, filthy creature – what was the quarrel?

PETULANT   There was no quarrel – there might have been a quarrel.
WITWOUD   If there had been words enow between 'em to have expressed provocation, they had gone together by the ears like a pair of castanets.
PETULANT   You were the quarrel.
MILLAMANT   Me!
PETULANT   If I have a humour to quarrel, I can make less matters conclude premises. – If you are not handsome, what then, if I have a humour to prove it? If I shall have my reward, say so; if not, fight for your face the next time yourself – I'll go sleep.
WITWOUD   Do, wrap thyself up like a wood-louse and dream revenge; and hear me, if thou canst learn to write by tomorrow morning, pen me a challenge. – I'll carry it for thee.
PETULANT   Carry your mistress's monkey a spider – go flea dogs, and read romances – I'll go to bed to my maid.
   [*Exit*]
MRS FAINALL   He's horridly drunk – how came you all in this pickle?
WITWOUD   A plot, a plot, to get rid of the knight, – your husband's advice; but he sneaked off.
   [*Enter Lady Wishfort and Sir Wilfull drunk*]
LADY WISHFORT   Out upon't, out upon't, at years of discretion, and comport yourself at this rantipole rate.
SIR WILFULL   No offence, aunt.
LADY WISHFORT   Offence? As I'm a person, I'm ashamed of you. – Fogh! how you stink of wine! D'ye think my niece will ever endure such a borachio! you're an absolute borachio.
SIR WILFULL   Borachio!
LADY WISHFORT   At a time when you should commence an amour and put your best foot foremost –

Act IV

SIR WILFULL 'S'heart, an you grutch me your liquor, make a bill. – Give me more drink, and take my purse.
[*Sings*]

> Prithee fill me the glass
> Till it laugh in my face, 380
> With ale that is potent and mellow;
> He that whines for a lass,
> Is an ignorant ass,
> For a bumper has not its fellow.

But if you would have me marry my cousin, – say the word, and I'll do't. – Wilfull will do't, that's the word – Willfull will do't; that's my crest – my motto I have forgot. 385

LADY WISHFORT My nephew's a little overtaken, cousin – but 'tis with drinking your health. – O' my word you are obliged to him. 390

SIR WILFULL *In vino veritas* aunt. – If I drunk your health today cousin – I am a borachio. But if you have a mind to be married, say the word, and send for the piper, Wilfull will do't. If not, dust it away, and let's have t'other round – Tony! Ods-heart, where's Tony? Tony's an honest fellow, 395 but he spits after a bumper, and that's a fault.
[*Sings*]

> We'll drink, and we'll never ha' done, boys,
> Put the glass then around with the sun, boys,
> Let Apollo's example invite us;
> For he's drunk every night, 400
> And that makes him so bright,
> That he's able next morning to light us.

The sun's a good pimple, an honest soaker, he has a cellar at your Antipodes. If I travel, aunt, I touch at your

93

Antipodes – your Antipodes are a good rascally sort of topsy-turvy fellows. – If I had a bumper, I'd stand upon my head and drink a health to 'em. – A match or no match, cousin with the hard name? Aunt, Wilfull will do't; if she has her maidenhead, let her look to't, – if she has not, let her keep her own counsel in the meantime, and cry out at the nine months' end.

MILLAMANT Your pardon, madam, I can stay no longer. – Sir Wilfull grows very powerful. Egh, how he smells! I shall be overcome if I stay. Come, cousin.

[*Exeunt Millamant and Mrs Fainall*]

LADY WISHFORT Smells! He would poison a tallow-chandler and his family. Beastly creature, I know not what to do with him. – Travel, quoth 'a! Ay, travel, travel, get thee gone, get thee but far enough, to the Saracens or the Tartars or the Turks – for thou are not fit to live in a Christian commonwealth, thou beastly pagan.

SIR WILFULL Turks, no; no Turks, aunt: your Turks are infidels, and believe not in the grape. Your Mahometan, your Mussulman, is a dry stinkard – no offence, aunt. My map says that your Turk is not so honest a man as your Christian. – I cannot find by the map that your Mufti is orthodox – whereby it is a plain case, that orthodox is a hard word, aunt, and [*hiccup*] Greek for claret.

[*Sings*]

> To drink is a Christian diversion,
> Unknown to the Turk and the Persian:
> Let Mahometan fools
> Live by heathenish rules,
> And be damned over tea cups and coffee.
>   But let British lads sing,
>   Crown a health to the king,
> And a fig for your Sultan and Sophy.

Ah Tony!
[*Enter Foible, and whispers Lady Wishfort*]
LADY WISHFORT   Sir Rowland impatient? Good lack! what shall I do with this beastly tumbril? – Go lie down and sleep, you sot, or as I'm a person, I'll have you bastinadoed with broom-sticks. Call up the wenches.
[*Exit Foible*]
SIR WILFULL   Ahey! Wenches, where are the wenches?
LADY WISHFORT   Dear cousin Witwoud, get him away, and you will bind me to you inviolably. I have an affair of moment that invades me with some precipitation. – You will oblige me to all futurity.
WITWOUD   Come, knight. – Pox on him, I don't know what to say to him. – Will you go to a cock-match?
SIR WILFULL   With a wench, Tony? Is she a shake-bag, sirrah? Let me bite your cheek for that.
WITWOUD   Horrible! He has a breath like a bagpipe – ay, ay, come, will you march, my Salopian?
SIR WILFULL   Lead on, little Tony – I'll follow thee, my Anthony, my Tantony, sirrah, thou shalt be my Tantony, and I'll be thy pig.

– And a fig for your Sultan and Sophy.

[*Exit singing with Witwoud*]
LADY WISHFORT   This will never do. It will never make a match – at least before he has been abroad.
[*Enter Waitwell, disguised as Sir Rowland*]
Dear Sir Rowland, I am confounded with confusion at the retrospection of my own rudeness, – I have more pardons to ask than the Pope distributes in the year of Jubilee. But I hope where there is likely to be so near an alliance, – we may unbend the severity of decorum – and dispense with a little ceremony.

WAITWELL My impatience madam, is the effect of my transport; and till I have the possession of your adorable person, I am tantalized on a rack, and do but hang, madam, on the tenter of expectation.

LADY WISHFORT You have excess of gallantry, Sir Rowland, and press things to a conclusion with a most prevailing vehemence. – But a day or two for decency of marriage –

WAITWELL For decency of funeral, madam. The delay will break my heart – or if that should fail, I shall be poisoned. My nephew will get an inkling of my designs and poison me, and I would willingly starve him before I die – I would gladly go out of the world with that satisfaction. – That would be some comfort to me, if I could but live so long as to be revenged on that unnatural viper.

LADY WISHFORT Is he so unnatural say you? Truly I would contribute much both to the saving of your life and the accomplishment of your revenge. – Not that I respect myself; though he has been a perfidious wretch to me.

WAITWELL Perfidious to you!

LADY WISHFORT Oh Sir Rowland, the hours that he has died away at my feet, the tears that he has shed, the oaths that he has sworn, the palpitations that he has felt, the trances, and the tremblings, the ardours and the ecstasies, the kneelings and the risings, the heart-heavings and the hand-grippings, the pangs and the pathetic regards of his protesting eyes! Oh, no memory can register.

WAITWELL What, my rival! Is the rebel my rival? A' dies.

LADY WISHFORT No, don't kill him at once Sir Rowland, starve him gradually, inch by inch.

WAITWELL I'll do't. In three weeks he shall be barefoot; in a month out at knees with begging alms. – He shall starve upward and upward, till he has nothing living but his head, and then go out in a stink like a candle's end upon a save-all.

Act IV

LADY WISHFORT   Well, Sir Rowland, you have the way. – You are no novice in the labyrinth of love; you have the clue. – But as I am a person, Sir Rowland, you must not attribute my yielding to any sinister appetite, or indigestion of widowhood; nor impute my complacency to any lethargy of continence. – I hope you do not think me prone to any iteration of nuptials –
WAITWELL   Far be it from me –
LADY WISHFORT   If you do, I protest I must recede – or think that I have made a prostitution of decorums, but in the vehemence of compassion, and to save the life of a person of so much importance –
WAITWELL   I esteem it so –
LADY WISHFORT   Or else you wrong my condescension –
WAITWELL   I do not, I do not –
LADY WISHFORT   Indeed you do.
WAITWELL   I do not, fair shrine of virtue.
LADY WISHFORT   If you think the least scruple of carnality was an ingredient –
WAITWELL   Dear madam, no. You are all camphire and frankincense, all chastity and odour.
LADY WISHFORT   Or that –
   [*Enter Foible*]
FOIBLE   Madam, the dancers are ready, and there's one with a letter, who must deliver it into your own hands.
LADY WISHFORT   Sir Rowland, will you give me leave? Think favourably, judge candidly, and conclude you have found a person who would suffer racks in honour's cause, dear Sir Rowland, and will wait on you incessantly.
   [*Exit*]
WAITWELL   Fie, fie! – What a slavery have I undergone. Spouse, hast thou any cordial? – I want spirits.
FOIBLE   What a washy rogue art thou, to pant thus for a quarter of an hour's lying and swearing to a fine lady!

The Way of the World

WAITWELL   Oh, she is the antidote to desire. Spouse, thou wilt fare the worse for't. – I shall have no appetite to iteration of nuptials this eight-and-forty hours. – By this hand I'd rather be a chairman in the dog-days than act Sir Rowland till this time tomorrow.
   [*Enter Lady Wishfort with a letter*]
LADY WISHFORT   Call in the dancers. – Sir Rowland, we'll sit if you please, and see the entertainment.
   [*Dance*]
Now with your permission Sir Rowland, I will peruse my letter. – I would open it in your presence, because I would not make you uneasy. If it should make you uneasy, I would burn it – speak, if it does – but you may see by the superscription it is like a woman's hand.
FOIBLE [*to him*]   By heaven! Mrs Marwood's, – I know it – my heart aches – get it from her.
WAITWELL   A woman's hand? No, madam, that's no woman's hand; I see that already. That's somebody whose throat must be cut.
LADY WISHFORT   Nay Sir Rowland, since you give me a proof of your passion by your jealousy, I promise you I'll make you a return, by a frank communication. – You shall see it – we'll open it together. – Look you here.
[*Reads*] – *Madam, though unknown to you* (look you there, 'tis from nobody that I know) – *I have that honour for your character, that I think myself obliged to let you know you are abused. He who pretends to be Sir Rowland is a cheat and a rascal* –
Oh heavens! what's this?
FOIBLE   Unfortunate, all's ruined.
WAITWELL   How, how, let me see, let me see – [*reading*] *A rascal, and disguised and suborned for that imposture.* – O villainy, O villainy! – *by the contrivance of* –
LADY WISHFORT   I shall faint, I shall die, I shall die, oh!

Act IV

FOIBLE [*to him*]   Say 'tis your nephew's hand – quickly – his plot, swear, swear it –
WAITWELL   Here's a villain! madam, don't you perceive it, don't you see it?
LADY WISHFORT   Too well, too well! I have seen too much.
WAITWELL   I told you at first I knew the hand. – A woman's hand? The rascal writes a sort of a large hand, your Roman hand. – I saw there was a throat to be cut presently. If he were my son, as he is my nephew, I'd pistol him –
FOIBLE   O treachery! But are you sure, Sir Rowland, it is his writing?
WAITWELL   Sure? Am I here? Do I live? Do I love this pearl of India? I have twenty letters in my pocket from him, in the same character.
LADY WISHFORT   How!
FOIBLE   Oh, what luck it is, Sir Rowland, that you were present at this juncture! This was the business that brought Mr Mirabell disguised to Madam Millamant this afternoon. I thought something was contriving, when he stole by me and would have hid his face.
LADY WISHFORT   How, how! – I heard the villain was in the house indeed, and now I remember, my niece went away abruptly, when Sir Wilfull was to have made his addresses.
FOIBLE   Then, then, madam, Mr Mirabell waited for her in her chamber, but I would not tell your ladyship to discompose you when you were to receive Sir Rowland.
WAITWELL   Enough, his date is short.
FOIBLE   No, good Sir Rowland, don't incur the law.
WAITWELL   Law? I care not for law. I can but die, and 'tis in a good cause. – My lady shall be satisfied of my truth and innocence, though it cost me my life.
LADY WISHFORT   No, dear Sir Rowland, don't fight, if you should be killed I must never show my face, or be hanged. – Oh, consider my reputation, Sir Rowland. – No, you

shan't fight. – I'll go in and examine my niece; I'll make her confess. I conjure you Sir Rowland, by all your love, not to fight.
WAITWELL   I am charmed madam, I obey. But some proof you must let me give you; I'll go for a black box which contains the writings of my whole estate, and deliver that into your hands.
LADY WISHFORT   Ay, dear Sir Rowland, that will be some comfort; bring the black box.
WAITWELL   And may I presume to bring a contract to be signed this night? May I hope so far?
LADY WISHFORT   Bring what you will; but come alive, pray come alive. Oh this is a happy discovery.
WAITWELL   Dead or alive I'll come – and married we will be in spite of treachery; ay, and get an heir that shall defeat the last remaining glimpse of hope in my abandoned nephew. Come, my buxom widow.

> Ere long you shall substantial proof receive
> That I'm an arrant knight –

FOIBLE [*aside*]   Or arrant knave.
   [*Exeunt*]

Act V

Scene continues

[*Lady Wishfort and Foible*]

LADY WISHFORT   Out of my house, out of my house, thou viper, thou serpent, that I have fostered, thou bosom traitress, that I raised from nothing – begone, begone, begone, go, go – that I took from washing of old gauze and weaving of dead hair, with a bleak blue nose, over a chafing-dish of starved embers and dining behind a traverse rag, in a shop no bigger than a bird-cage – go, go, starve again, do, do.

FOIBLE   Dear madam, I'll beg pardon on my knees.

LADY WISHFORT   Away, out, out, go set up for yourself again – do, drive a trade, do, with your three penny-worth of small ware, flaunting upon a pack-thread, under a brandy-seller's bulk, or against a dead wall by a ballad-monger. Go hang out an old frisoneer-gorget, with a yard of yellow colberteen again, do; an old gnawed mask, two rows of pins and a child's fiddle; a glass necklace with the beads broken, and a quilted night-cap with one ear. Go, go, drive a trade – these were your commodities, you treacherous trull, this was your merchandise you dealt in when I took you into my house, placed you next myself, and made you governante of my whole family. You have forgot this, have you, now you have feathered your nest?

FOIBLE   No, no, dear madam. Do but hear me, have but a moment's patience – I'll confess all. Mr Mirabell seduced me; I am not the first that he has wheedled with his dissembling tongue. Your ladyship's own wisdom has been deluded by him, then how should I, a poor ignorant, defend myself? O madam, if you knew but what

The Way of the World

he promised me, and how he assured me your ladyship should come to no damage. – Or else the wealth of the Indies should not have bribed me to conspire against so good, so sweet, so kind a lady as you have been to me.

LADY WISHFORT 'No damage?' What, to betray me, to marry me to a cast servingman; to make me a receptacle, an hospital for a decayed pimp? 'No damage?' O thou frontless impudence, more than a big-bellied actress.

FOIBLE Pray do but hear me madam, he could not marry your ladyship, madam. – No indeed, his marriage was to have been void in law, for he was married to me first, to secure your ladyship. He could not have bedded your ladyship; for if he had consummated with your ladyship, he must have run the risk of the law and been put upon his clergy. – Yes indeed, I enquired of the law in that case before I would meddle or make.

LADY WISHFORT What, then I have been your property, have I? I have been convenient to you it seems, while you were catering for Mirabell; I have been broker for you? What, have you made a passive bawd of me? This exceeds all precedent; I am brought to fine uses, to become a botcher of second-hand marriages between Abigails and Andrews! I'll couple you. Yes, I'll baste you together, you and your Philander. I'll Duke's Place you, as I'm a person. Your turtle is in custody already; you shall coo in the same cage, if there be constable or warrant in the parish.
    [*Exit*]

FOIBLE O that ever I was born! O that I was ever married! – A bride, ay, I shall be a Bridewell bride. Oh!
    [*Enter Mrs Fainall*]

MRS FAINALL Poor Foible, what's the matter?

FOIBLE O madam, my lady's gone for a constable; I shall be had to a justice, and put to Bridewell to beat hemp. Poor Waitwell's gone to prison already.

Act V

MRS FAINALL Have a good heart, Foible; Mirabell's gone to give security for him. This is all Marwood's and my husband's doing.
FOIBLE Yes, yes, I know it, madam; she was in my lady's closet, and overheard all that you said to me before dinner. She sent the letter to my lady, and that missing effect, Mr Fainall laid this plot to arrest Waitwell when he pretended to go for the papers; and in the meantime Mrs Marwood declared all to my lady.
MRS FAINALL Was there no mention made of me in the letter? – My mother does not suspect my being in the confederacy? I fancy Marwood has not told her, though she has told my husband.
FOIBLE Yes, madam, but my lady did not see that part. We stifled the letter before she read so far. Has that mischievous devil told Mr Fainall of your ladyship then?
MRS FAINALL Ay, all's out, my affair with Mirabell, everything discovered. This is the last day of our living together, that's my comfort.
FOIBLE Indeed madam, and so 'tis a comfort if you knew all. – He has been even with your ladyship; which I could have told you long enough since, but I love to keep peace and quietness by my good will; I had rather bring friends together than set 'em at distance. But Mrs Marwood and he are nearer related than ever their parents thought for.
MRS FAINALL Say'st thou so, Foible? Canst thou prove this?
FOIBLE I can take my oath of it, madam; so can Mrs Mincing. We have had many a fair word from Madam Marwood, to conceal something that passed in our chamber one evening when you were at Hyde Park and we were thought to have gone a-walking; but we went up unawares, though we were sworn to secrecy too. Madam Marwood took a book and swore us upon it, but it was but a book of verses and poems. – So as long as it was not a

The Way of the World

Bible oath, we may break it with a safe conscience.

MRS FAINALL This discovery is the most opportune thing I could wish. Now, Mincing?

[*Enter Mincing*]

MINCING My lady would speak with Mrs Foible, mem. Mr Mirabell is with her; he has set your spouse at liberty, Mrs Foible, and would have you hide yourself in my lady's closet till my old lady's anger is abated. Oh, my old lady is in a perilous passion at something Mr Fainall has said. He swears, and my old lady cries. There's a fearful hurricane, I vow. He says, mem, how that he'll have my lady's fortune made over to him, or he'll be divorced.

MRS FAINALL Does your lady and Mirabell know that?

MINCING Yes, mem; they have sent me to see if Sir Wilfull be sober, and to bring him to them. My lady is resolved to have him, I think, rather than lose such a vast sum as six thousand pound. Oh, come Mrs Foible, I hear my old lady.

MRS FAINALL Foible, you must tell Mincing that she must prepare to vouch when I call her.

FOIBLE Yes, yes madam.

MINCING Oh yes, mem, I'll vouch anything for your ladyship's service, be what it will.

[*Exeunt Mincing and Foible*]

[*Enter Lady Wishfort and Mrs Marwood*]

LADY WISHFORT O my dear friend, how can I enumerate the benefits that I have received from your goodness? To you I owe the timely discovery of the false vows of Mirabell; to you the detection of the impostor Sir Rowland. And now you are become an intercessor with my son-in-law, to save the honour of my house, and compound for the frailties of my daughter. Well, friend, you are enough to reconcile me to the bad world, or else I would retire to deserts and solitudes, and feed harmless sheep by groves and purling

Act V

streams. Dear Marwood, let us leave the world, and retire by ourselves and be shepherdesses.

MRS MARWOOD Let us first dispatch the affair in hand, madam; we shall have leisure to think of retirement afterwards. Here is one who is concerned in the treaty.

LADY WISHFORT O daughter, daughter, is it possible thou shouldst be my child, bone of my bone, and flesh of my flesh, and as I may say, another me, and yet transgress the most minute particle of severe virtue? Is it possible you should lean aside to iniquity, who have been cast in the direct mould of virtue? I have not only been a mould but a pattern for you, and a model for you, after you were brought into the world.

MRS FAINALL I don't understand your ladyship.

LADY WISHFORT Not understand? Why, have you not been naught? Have you not been sophisticated? Not understand? Here I am ruined to compound for your caprices and your cuckoldoms. I must pawn my plate and my jewels and ruin my niece, and all little enough –

MRS FAINALL I am wronged and abused, and so are you. 'Tis a false accusation, as false as hell, as false as your friend there, ay, or your friend's friend, my false husband.

MRS MARWOOD My friend, Mrs Fainall? Your husband my friend? What do you mean?

MRS FAINALL I know what I mean madam, and so do you; and so shall the world at a time convenient.

MRS MARWOOD I am sorry to see you so passionate, madam. More temper would look more like innocence. But I have done. I am sorry my zeal to serve your ladyship and family should admit of misconstruction, or make me liable to affronts. You will pardon me, madam, if I meddle no more with an affair in which I am not personally concerned.

LADY WISHFORT O dear friend, I am so ashamed that you

The Way of the World

should meet with such returns – you ought to ask pardon on your knees, ungrateful creature; she deserves more from you than all your life can accomplish. – Oh, don't leave me destitute in this perplexity! No, stick to me, my good genius.

MRS FAINALL   I tell you, madam, you're abused. – Stick to you? Ay, like a leech, to suck your best blood – she'll drop off when she's full. Madam, you shan't pawn a bodkin, nor part with a brass counter in composition for me. I defy 'em all. Let 'em prove their aspersions; I know my own innocence, and dare stand a trial.
  [*Exit*]

LADY WISHFORT   Why, if she should be innocent, if she should be wronged after all, ha? I don't know what to think – and I promise you, her education has been unexceptionable. I may say it; for I chiefly made it my own care to initiate her very infancy in the rudiments of virtue, and to impress upon her tender years a young odium and aversion to the very sight of men. – Ay, friend, she would ha' shrieked if she had but seen a man, till she was in her teens. As I'm a person 'tis true. – She was never suffered to play with a male child, though but in coats; nay, her very babies were of the feminine gender. – Oh, she never looked a man in the face but her own father, or the chaplain, and him we made a shift to put upon her for a woman, by the help of his long garments and his sleek face, till she was going in her fifteen.

MRS MARWOOD   'Twas much she should be deceived so long.

LADY WISHFORT   I warrant you, or she would never have borne to have been catechized by him; and have heard his long lectures against singing and dancing, and such debaucheries, and going to filthy plays, and profane music meetings, where the lewd trebles squeak nothing but bawdy, and the bases roar blasphemy. Oh, she would have swooned at the sight or name of an obscene play-book – and can I think after all this, that my daughter can be naught? What, a whore? And thought it excommunication to set her foot within the door of a play-house. O my dear friend, I can't believe it, no, no. As she says, let him prove it, let him prove it.

MRS MARWOOD   Prove it madam? What, and have your name prostituted in a public court? Yours and your daughter's reputation worried at the bar by a pack of bawling lawyers? To be ushered in with an *Oyez* of scandal, and have your case opened by an old fumbling lecher in a quoif like a man-midwife to bring your daughter's infamy to light; to be a theme for legal punsters and quibblers by the statute, and become a jest against a rule of court, where there is no precedent for a jest in any record, not even in Doomsday Book; to discompose the gravity of the bench, and provoke naughty interrogatories in more naughty law Latin, while the good judge, tickled with the proceeding, simpers under a grey beard, and fidges off and on his cushion as if he had swallowed cantharides, or sat upon cow-itch.

LADY WISHFORT   Oh, 'tis very hard!

MRS MARWOOD   And then to have my young revellers of the Temple take notes, like 'prentices at a conventicle; and after, talk it all over again in commons, or before drawers in an eating-house.

LADY WISHFORT   Worse and worse.

MRS MARWOOD   Nay, this is nothing; if it would end here, 'twere well. But it must after this be consigned by the shorthand writers to the public press; and from thence be transferred to the hands, nay into the throats and lungs of hawkers, with voices more licentious than the loud flounder-man's or the woman that cries 'grey peas'. And this you must hear till you are stunned; nay, you must hear nothing else for some days.

LADY WISHFORT   Oh, 'tis insupportable. No, no, dear friend, make it up, make it up; ay, ay, I'll compound. I'll give up all, myself and my all, my niece and her all, – anything, everything for composition.

MRS MARWOOD   Nay madam, I advise nothing, I only lay before you as a friend the inconveniencies which perhaps you have overseen. Here comes Mr Fainall. If he will be satisfied to huddle up all in silence, I shall be glad. You must think I would rather congratulate than condole with you.

[*Enter Fainall*]

LADY WISHFORT   Ay, ay, I do not doubt it, dear Marwood; no, no, I do not doubt it.

FAINALL   Well, madam, I have suffered myself to be overcome by the importunity of this lady your friend, and am content you shall enjoy your own proper estate during life, on condition you oblige yourself never to marry, under such penalty as I think convenient.

LADY WISHFORT   Never to marry?

FAINALL   No more Sir Rowlands – the next imposture may not be so timely detected.

MRS MARWOOD   That condition, I dare answer, my lady will consent to without difficulty; she has already but too much experienced the perfidiousness of men. Besides, madam, when we retire to our pastoral solitude, we shall bid adieu to all other thoughts.

LADY WISHFORT   Ay, that's true; but in case of necessity, as of health, or some such emergency –

FAINALL   Oh, if you are prescribed marriage, you shall be considered; I will only reserve to myself the power to choose for you. If your physic be wholesome, it matters not who is your apothecary. Next, my wife shall settle on me the remainder of her fortune not made over already, and for her maintenance depend entirely on my discretion.

LADY WISHFORT This is most inhumanly savage, exceeding the barbarity of a Muscovite husband.

FAINALL I learned it from his Czarish majesty's retinue, in a winter evening's conference over brandy and pepper, amongst other secrets of matrimony and policy, as they are at present practised in the Northern hemisphere. But this must be agreed unto, and that positively. Lastly, I will be endowed, in right of my wife, with that six thousand pound which is the moiety of Mrs Millamant's fortune in your possession; and which she has forfeited (as will appear by the last will and testament of your deceased husband, Sir Jonathan Wishfort) by her disobedience in contracting herself against your consent or knowledge, and by refusing the offered match with Sir Wilfull Witwoud, which you, like a careful aunt, had provided for her.

LADY WISHFORT My nephew was *non compos*, and could not make his addresses.

FAINALL I come to make demands. – I'll hear no objections.

LADY WISHFORT You will grant me time to consider.

FAINALL Yes, while the instrument is drawing, to which you must set your hand till more sufficient deeds can be perfected; which I will take care shall be done with all possible speed. In the meanwhile, I will go for the said instrument, and till my return, you may balance this matter in your own discretion.

[*Exit Fainall*]

LADY WISHFORT This insolence is beyond all precedent, all parallel; must I be subject to this merciless villain?

MRS MARWOOD 'Tis severe indeed, madam, that you should smart for your daughter's wantonness.

LADY WISHFORT 'Twas against my consent that she married

The Way of the World

this barbarian, but she would have him, though her year was not out. – Ah! her first husband, my son Languish, would not have carried it thus. Well, that was my choice, this is hers; she is matched now with a witness. I shall be mad; dear friend, is there no comfort for me? Must I live to be confiscated at this rebel rate? – Here come two more of my Egyptian plagues too.

[*Enter Millamant and Sir Wilfull*]

SIR WILFULL   Aunt, your servant.

LADY WISHFORT   Out caterpillar, call not me aunt; I know thee not.

SIR WILFULL   I confess I have been a little in disguise, as they say. – 'S'heart! and I'm sorry for't. What would you have? I hope I committed no offence, aunt, – and if I did, I am willing to make satisfaction; and what can a man say fairer? If I have broke anything, I'll pay for't, an it cost a pound. And so let that content for what's past, and make no more words. For what's to come, to pleasure you I'm willing to marry my cousin. So pray let's all be friends, she and I are agreed upon the matter before a witness.

LADY WISHFORT   How's this, dear niece? Have I any comfort? Can this be true?

MILLAMANT   I am content to be a sacrifice to your repose, madam; and to convince you that I had no hand in the plot, as you were misinformed, I have laid my commands on Mirabell to come in person, and be a witness that I give my hand to this flower of knighthood; and for the contract that passed between Mirabell and me, I have obliged him to make a resignation of it, in your ladyship's presence. He is without, and waits your leave for admittance.

LADY WISHFORT   Well, I'll swear I am something revived at this testimony of your obedience; but I cannot admit that traitor. – I fear I cannot fortify myself to support his appearance. He is as terrible to me as a Gorgon; if I see

Act V

him, I fear I shall turn to stone, petrify incessantly.
MILLAMANT If you disoblige him, he may resent your refusal and insist upon the contract still. Then 'tis the last time he will be offensive to you.
LADY WISHFORT Are you sure it will be the last time? – If I were sure of that. – Shall I never see him again?
MILLAMANT Sir Wilfull, you and he are to travel together, are you not?
SIR WILFULL 'S'heart, the gentleman's a civil gentleman, aunt; let him come in. Why, we are sworn brothers and fellow travellers. We are to be Pylades and Orestes, he and I. He is to be my interpreter in foreign parts. He has been overseas already; and with proviso that I marry my cousin will cross 'em once again, only to bear me company. – 'S'heart, I'll call him in – an I set on't once, he shall come in; and see who'll hinder him.
 [*Exit*]
MRS MARWOOD This is precious fooling, if it would pass, but I'll know the bottom of it.
LADY WISHFORT O dear Marwood, you are not going?
MRS MARWOOD Not far, madam; I'll return immediately.
 [*Exit*]
 [*Re-enter Sir Wilfull and Mirabell*]
SIR WILFULL Look up man, I'll stand by you; 'sbud an she do frown, she can't kill you; besides, hearkee, she dare not frown desperately, because her face is none of her own; 's'heart, an she should, her forehead would wrinkle like the coat of a cream-cheese, but mum for that, fellow traveller.
MIRABELL If a deep sense of the many injuries I have offered to so good a lady, with a sincere remorse, and a hearty contrition, can but obtain the least glance of compassion I am too happy. – Ah madam, there was a time – but let it be forgotten. I confess I have deservedly forfeited the

The Way of the World

high place I once held, of sighing at your feet; nay, kill me
not by turning from me in disdain, I come not to plead for
favour; nay, not for pardon. I am a suppliant only for your
pity. – I am going where I never shall behold you more –
SIR WILFULL   How, fellow traveller! You shall go by yourself
then.
MIRABELL   Let me be pitied first, and afterwards forgotten
– I ask no more.
SIR WILFULL   By'r Lady, a very reasonable request, and will
cost you nothing, aunt. – Come, come, forgive and forget,
aunt, why you must, an you are a Christian.
MIRABELL   Consider, madam, in reality you could not
receive much prejudice; it was an innocent device;
though I confess it had a face of guiltiness. It was at most
an artifice which love contrived, and errors which love
produces have ever been accounted venial. At least think
it is punishment enough that I have lost what in my heart
I hold most dear, that to your cruel indignation I have
offered up this beauty, and with her my peace and quiet;
nay, all my hopes of future comfort.
SIR WILFULL   An he does not move me, would I might
never be o' the Quorum. An it were not as good a deed
as to drink, to give her to him again, I would I might
never take shipping. Aunt, if you don't forgive quickly,
I shall melt, I can tell you that. My contract went no
further than a little mouth-glue, and that's hardly dry;
one doleful sigh more from my fellow traveller, and 'tis
dissolved.
LADY WISHFORT   Well, nephew, upon your account – ah,
he has a false insinuating tongue! Well, sir, I will stifle my
just resentment at my nephew's request. I will endeavour
what I can to forget, but on proviso that you resign the
contract with my niece immediately.
MIRABELL   It is in writing, and with papers of concern; but I

Act V

have sent my servant for it, and will deliver it to you, with all acknowledgments for your transcendent goodness.

LADY WISHFORT [apart] Oh, he has witchcraft in his eyes and tongue. When I did not see him, I could have bribed a villain to his assassination; but his appearance rakes the embers which have so long lain smothered in my breast.

[Enter Fainall and Mrs Marwood]

FAINALL Your date of deliberation, madam, is expired. Here is the instrument; are you prepared to sign?

LADY WISHFORT If I were prepared, I am not empowered. My niece exerts a lawful claim, having matched herself by my direction to Sir Wilfull.

FAINALL That sham is too gross to pass on me, though 'tis imposed on you, madam.

MILLAMANT Sir, I have given my consent.

MIRABELL And, sir, I have resigned my pretensions.

SIR WILFULL And, sir, I assert my right; and will maintain it in defiance of you, sir, and of your instrument. 'S'heart an you talk of an instrument, sir, I have an old fox by my thigh shall hack your instrument of ram vellum to shreds, sir. It shall not be sufficient for a mittimus or a tailor's measure. Therefore withdraw your instrument, sir, or by'r Lady, I shall draw mine.

LADY WISHFORT Hold nephew, hold.

MILLAMANT Good Sir Wilfull, respite your valour.

FAINALL Indeed? Are you provided of a guard, with your single Beefeater there? But I'm prepared for you, and insist upon my first proposal. You shall submit your own estate to my management, and absolutely make over my wife's to my sole use, as pursuant to the purport and tenor of this other covenant. [To Millamant] I suppose, madam, your consent is not requisite in this case; nor, Mr Mirabell, your resignation; nor, Sir Wilfull, your right. – You may draw your fox if you please, sir, and make a bear-garden flourish somewhere else, for here it will not avail. This, my Lady Wishfort, must be subscribed, or your darling daughter's turned adrift, like a leaky hulk to sink or swim, as she and the current of this lewd town can agree.

LADY WISHFORT   Is there no means, no remedy, to stop my ruin? Ungrateful wretch! dost thou not owe thy being, thy subsistence, to my daughter's fortune?

FAINALL   I'll answer you when I have the rest of it in my possession.

MIRABELL   But that you would not accept of a remedy from my hands – I own I have not deserved you should owe any obligation to me; or else perhaps I could advise –

LADY WISHFORT   Oh what? what? To save me and my child from ruin, from want, I'll forgive all that's past; nay I'll consent to anything to come, to be delivered from this tyranny.

MIRABELL   Ay, madam; but that is too late, my reward is intercepted. You have disposed of her who only could have made me a compensation for all my services. But be it as it may, I am resolved I'll serve you; you shall not be wronged in this savage manner.

LADY WISHFORT   How! Dear Mr Mirabell, can you be so generous at last? But it is not possible. Hearkee, I'll break my nephew's match; you shall have my niece yet, and all her fortune, if you can but save me from this imminent danger.

MIRABELL   Will you? I take you at your word. I ask no more. I must have leave for two criminals to appear.

LADY WISHFORT   Ay, ay, anybody, anybody.

MIRABELL   Foible is one, and a penitent.

[*Enter Mrs Fainall, Foible, and Mincing*]

MRS MARWOOD   [*To Fainall*]   O my shame! [*Mirabell and Lady Wishfort go to Mrs Fainall and Foible*] These corrupt things are bought and brought hither to expose me.

FAINALL   If it must all come out, why let 'em know it, 'tis but the way of the world. That shall not urge me to relinquish or abate one tittle of my terms; no, I will insist the more.
FOIBLE   Yes indeed, madam; I'll take my Bible oath of it.
MINCING   And so will I, mem.
LADY WISHFORT   O Marwood, Marwood, art thou false? My friend deceive me? Hast thou been a wicked accomplice with that profligate man?
MRS MARWOOD   Have you so much ingratitude and injustice, to give credit against your friend to the aspersions of two such mercenary trulls?
MINCING   'Mercenary', mem? I scorn your words. 'Tis true we found you and Mr Fainall in the blue garret; by the same token, you swore us to secrecy upon Messalina's poems. 'Mercenary?' No, if we would have been mercenary, we should have held our tongues; you would have bribed us sufficiently.
FAINALL   Go, you are an insignificant thing. Well, what are you the better for this? Is this Mr Mirabell's expedient? I'll be put off no longer. – You thing, that was a wife, shall smart for this. I will not leave thee wherewithal to hide thy shame; your body shall be naked as your reputation.
MRS FAINALL   I despise you and defy your malice. You have aspersed me wrongfully. – I have proved your falsehood. Go you and your treacherous – I will not name it, but starve together – perish.
FAINALL   Not while you are worth a groat, indeed my dear. Madam, I'll be fooled no longer.
LADY WISHFORT   Ah Mr Mirabell, this is small comfort, the detection of this affair.
MIRABELL   Oh, in good time. – Your leave for the other offender and penitent to appear, madam.
   [*Enter Waitwell with a box of writings*]

The Way of the World

LADY WISHFORT   Oh, Sir Rowland! – Well, rascal?
WAITWELL   What your ladyship pleases. I have brought the black box at last, madam.
MIRABELL   Give it me. Madam, you remember your promise.
LADY WISHFORT   Ay, dear sir.
MIRABELL   Where are the gentlemen?
WAITWELL   At hand sir, rubbing their eyes; just risen from sleep.
FAINALL   'Sdeath, what's this to me? I'll not wait your private concerns.
   [*Enter Petulant and Witwoud*]
PETULANT   How now? What's the matter? Whose hand's out?
WITWOUD   Heyday! what, are you all got together, like players at the end of the last act?
MIRABELL   You may remember, gentlemen, I once requested your hands as witnesses to a certain parchment.
WITWOUD   Ay, I do, my hand I remember. – Petulant set his mark.
MIRABELL   You wrong him, his name is fairly written, as shall appear. You do not remember, gentlemen, anything of what that parchment contained?
   [*Undoing the box*]
WITWOUD   No.
PETULANT   Not I. I writ. I read nothing.
MIRABELL   Very well; now you shall know. Madam, your promise.
LADY WISHFORT   Ay, ay, sir, upon my honour.
MIRABELL   Mr Fainall, it is now time that you should know that your lady, while she was at her own disposal, and before you had by your insinuations wheedled her out of a pretended settlement of the greatest part of her fortune –
FAINALL   Sir! Pretended!

Act V

MIRABELL   Yes, sir. I say that this lady while a widow, having it seems received some cautions respecting your inconstancy and tyranny of temper, which from her own partial opinion and fondness of you, she could never have suspected – she did, I say, by the wholesome advice of friends and of sages learned in the laws of this land, deliver this same as her act and deed to me in trust, and to the uses within mentioned. You may read if you please [*holding out the parchment*] though perhaps what is inscribed on the back may serve your occasions.

FAINALL   Very likely, sir. What's here? Damnation! [*Reads*] *A deed of conveyance of the whole estate real of Arabella Languish, widow, in trust to Edward Mirabell.* Confusion!

MIRABELL   Even so, sir; 'tis the way of the world, sir, of the widows of the world. I suppose this deed may bear an elder date than what you have obtained from your lady.

FAINALL   Perfidious fiend! Then thus I'll be revenged. [*Offers to run at Mrs Fainall*]

SIR WILFULL   Hold, sir, now you may make your beargarden flourish somewhere else, sir.

FAINALL   Mirabell, you shall hear of this, sir; be sure you shall. Let me pass, oaf!
   [*Exit*]

MRS FAINALL   Madam, you seem to stifle your resentment; you had better give it vent.

MRS MARWOOD   Yes, it shall have vent – and to your confusion, or I'll perish in the attempt.
   [*Exit*]

LADY WISHFORT   O daughter, daughter, 'tis plain thou hast inherited thy mother's prudence.

MRS FAINALL   Thank Mr Mirabell, a cautious friend, to whose advice all is owing.

LADY WISHFORT   Well, Mr Mirabell, you have kept your promise, and I must perform mine. First, I pardon for your

The Way of the World

sake, Sir Rowland there, and Foible. The next thing is to break the matter to my nephew – and how to do that –
MIRABELL   For that, madam, give yourself no trouble; let me have your consent. Sir Wilfull is my friend; he has had compassion upon lovers and generously engaged a volunteer in this action, for our service, and now designs to prosecute his travels.
SIR WILFULL   'S'heart aunt, I have no mind to marry. My cousin's a fine lady, and the gentleman loves her and she loves him, and they deserve one another; my resolution is to see foreign parts. I have set on't – and when I'm set on't, I must do't. And if these two gentlemen would travel too, I think they may be spared.
PETULANT   For my part, I say little; – I think things are best off or on.
WITWOUD   Egad I understand nothing of the matter – I'm in a maze yet, like a dog in a dancing school.
LADY WISHFORT   Well sir, take her, and with her all the joy I can give you.
MILLAMANT   Why does not the man take me? Would you have me give myself to you over again.
MIRABELL   Ay, and over and over again; for I would have you as often as possibly I can. [*Kisses her hand*] Well, heaven grant I love you not too well, that's all my fear.
SIR WILFULL   'S'heart, you'll have him time enough to toy after you're married; or if you will toy now, let us have a dance in the meantime, that we who are not lovers may have some other employment besides looking on.
MIRABELL   With all my heart, dear Sir Wilfull. What shall we do for music?
FOIBLE   Oh, sir, some that were provided for Sir Rowland's entertainment are yet within call.
   [*A dance*]
LADY WISHFORT   As I am a person I can hold out no longer.

I have wasted my spirits so today already that I am ready to sink under the fatigue; and I cannot but have some fears upon me yet that my son Fainall will pursue some desperate course.

MIRABELL Madam, disquiet not yourself on that account. To my knowledge his circumstances are such, he must of force comply. For my part, I will contribute all that in me lies to a reunion. [*To Mrs Fainall*] In the meantime, madam, let me before these witnesses restore to you this deed of trust. It may be a means, well managed, to make you live easily together.

> From hence let those be warned, who mean to wed,
> Lest mutual falsehood stain the bridal bed;
> For each deceiver to his cost may find,
> That marriage frauds too oft are paid in kind.

[*Exeunt omnes*]

Epilogue

Spoken by Mrs Bracegirdle

After our epilogue this crowd dismisses,
I'm thinking how this play'll be pulled to pieces.
But pray consider ere you doom its fall,
How hard a thing 'twould be to please you all.
There are some critics so with spleen diseased, 5
They scarcely come inclining to be pleased;
And sure he must have more than mortal skill,
Who pleases anyone against his will.
Then, all bad poets we are sure are foes,
And how their number's swelled the town well knows; 10
In shoals I've marked 'em judging in the pit;
Though they're on no pretence for judgment fit,
But that they have been damned for want of wit.
Since when, they, by their own offences taught,
Set up for spies on plays, and finding fault. 15
Others there are whose malice we'd prevent;
Such who watch plays with scurrilous intent
To mark out who by *characters* are meant.
And though no perfect likeness they can trace,
Yet each pretends to know the copied face. 20
These with false glosses feed their own ill nature,
And turn to libel, what was meant a satire.
May such malicious fops this fortune find,
To think themselves alone the fools designed;
If any are so arrogantly vain, 25
To think they singly can support a scene,
And furnish fool enough to entertain.
For well the learned and the judicious know,
That satire scorns to stoop so meanly low
As any one abstracted fop to shew. 30

Epilogue

For, as when painters form a matchless face,
They from each fair one catch some differerent grace,
And shining features in one portrait blend,
To which no single beauty must pretend;
So poets oft do in one piece expose   35
Whole *belles assemblées* of coquettes and beaux.

Notes

Technical terms used in these notes are defined in the Glossary, page 224
sd = stage direction

Dedication

Congreve dedicates his play to Ralph, Earl of Montagu, a Whig supporter and patron of the arts whose main residence was Boughton House, Northamptonshire. An 'epistle dedicatory' such as this was an opportunity for a playwright to flatter a powerful, well-connected figure whose patronage he sought to cultivate.

Congreve expresses surprise that the play had some success, as it was not designed to appeal to popular taste. Appalled by what passes for amusing characters in contemporary comedies, he says he had set out to create more subtle types by contrasting *affected* or *false* (line 31) wits with *Truewits* (40). He expresses impatience that the audience, so busy finding fault, had not paid sufficient attention to distinguish between the two.

He implies a comparison between himself and the Roman playwright Terence, whose reputation also needed the protection of a powerful patron. Like Terence, he feels misunderstood by those in the audience too ignorant to appreciate him. He names comic dramatists and philosophers who succeeded each other in a prestigious heritage reaching back to Aristotle, thus identifying himself with the great writers of antiquity.

If he has achieved excellence in writing dialogue, Congreve says, he is indebted to Montagu and the company he kept in the summer of 1699 at Boughton, where Congreve had been an attentive observer of high society. He compares *many* at this gathering to *a Scipio or a Lelius*, with whom Terence conversed (90). If Congreve's own *turn of style* (81) is lacking it is the fault of the playwright, not Montagu's friends at Boughton.

123

Notes

Congreve plays the role of the humble, unworthy servant throughout the Dedication. He ends by recommending poetry to Montagu as worthy of his patronage.

- 2 **arraign** accuse.
- 7 **prefer** offer, recommend.
- 8 **perusal** reading, examination.
  imputation accusation.
- 9 **sufficiency** (confidence in) ability, competence.
  abide withstand.
- 22 **divert** amuse.
- 29 **incorrigible** not capable of reform.
- 40 **Truewit** a character in Ben Jonson's play *Epicoene* (1609).
- 42 **epistle** letter.
- 48 **prostituted** ill-used and degraded.
  poet term used to refer to playwrights in the sixteenth to eighteenth centuries.
- 49 **promiscuously** without discrimination.
  levels brings down to the same level. The reputation of *poets* is so poor that it degrades all those who write.
- 50 **Terence** a Roman playwright (195/185–159 BCE).
- 51 **a Scipio and a Lelius** Scipio Aemilianus (185–129 BCE) was a Roman general and politician of great intellect and culture, who was a patron of Terence; Gaius Laelius (dates unrecorded) was a general and statesman, friend of Scipio.
- 58 **Plautus** Roman playwright (c. 254–184 BCE), famous for his comedies.
- 59 **Horace** leading Augustan poet, famous for his odes and satires (65–8 BCE).
- 65 **Menander** Greek comic dramatist (c. 341/2– c. 290 BCE).
- 69 **Theophrastus** Greek philosopher and disciple of Aristotle (c. 371– c. 287 BCE).
- 71 **Aristotle** Greek philosopher (384–322 BCE). His work on dramatic and literary theory, *Poetics* (c. 335 BCE), was highly influential in the development of the western dramatic tradition.
- 82 **corrigible** capable of being corrected.
- 102 **reciprocal** of mutual benefit to both sides.
- 103 **propitious** favourably disposed.
- 104 **prerogative** power and right.

Prologue

Prologues were a far more important feature of the theatre experience than they are today, especially on the first night. They provided a context for the performance, and acknowledged the power of the audience to make or break a new play. This one touches upon the precarious fortunes of playwrights. Congreve adopts a defensive tone, treating those in the audience who might be hostile with gentle irony.

Of all society's fools, the speaker of the Prologue says, playwrights *fare the worst* (2) since they depend entirely on *Fortune* (3) – the vagaries of public opinion, which makes and then forsakes them. The common run of fools fare better, since *Fortune* nurtures them like *cuckoo eggs* (7), leaving no time to tend to her more worthy offspring.

Playwrights find London a seductive place, especially when their first efforts meet with some praise. Thereafter, each new play risks losing their hard-won reputation. The speaker says the playwright has previously found favour here, but would not dream of presuming on past reputation to gain present approval.

He will accept criticism, however harsh, as long as it is deserved. The speaker is modest about the play's merits, claiming it has *Some plot, new thought* and *humour* (29–30). He ironically suggests that satire, the great corrector of social morals, isn't needed in such a *reformed* (32) place as London. His aim is solely to *please* (33), not to *instruct* (34), and should any fool be ridiculed in the play, his like will not be found in this audience.

The Prologue is written in heroic couplets (see Glossary), as was traditional for the time. It was spoken by the actor Thomas Betterton (1635–1710).

   1–4 Notice the alliteration on 'f' sounds, pleasing to the ear.
     7 **cuckoo eggs** Cuckoos lay their eggs in the nests of other birds.
     8 **changeling** child that has been swapped at birth.
    11 **bubbles** fools, dupes, such as those easily cheated at cards. Gambling imagery is dominant here.
    12 **stakes** money gambled at cards.

125

Notes

13 **hazards** risks; also a pun (see Glossary), as hazard is the name of a card game.
15 **buttered** flattered.
19 **admit resumption** be capable of being withdrawn.
20 **Parnassus** mountain north of Delphi in Greece, sacred to the nine Muses who inspire the arts. A *seat* in *Parnassus* is therefore the right of a successful poet.
21 **forfeited estate** confiscated property. He is risking his valuable reputation as a successful playwright.
25 **on mature deliberation** after lengthy and careful thought.
32 **so reformed a town** This ironic phrase may refer to Jeremy Collier's campaign against the theatre (see page 12).
35 **knave** cheat; also a pun, as it is the name of the lowest court card in the pack (the jack).
expose This suggests the action of turning over a card to reveal its value.

The Characters of the Play

Look at the list of characters in *The Way of the World*. Can you decide on the roles these characters will take by considering what their names suggest to you? What conventions was Congreve following in naming his characters? See Interpretations page 176.

Act I

Two rivals discuss a cabal that threatens a love match (lines 1–106)

Every line of dialogue in the play's opening exchange helps to unfold the intrigue; there is very little embellishment, and much ambiguity.

Two gentlemen and wits, Mirabell and Fainall, have been gambling in a London *chocolate-house*. They appear well acquainted but rather cold towards one other. There is evidently an undertow of rivalry and they are looking to score points. They refer to six of

Act I

the play's characters within one minute of speaking, five of them by name. The audience face an intricate set of relationships and situations, to be digested at speed.

We learn that Mirabell's love interest, Millamant, is Fainall's *cousin* (18) because he is married to her first cousin. Witwoud and Petulant, a pair of false wits, are rival suitors to Millamant. On the previous evening, they attended a *cabal night* (49) with Mirabell, Lady Wishfort (Fainall's mother-in-law), Millamant, Mrs Fainall and Mrs Marwood. The group contrived to make Mirabell feel unwelcome and he departed in a very disgruntled mood.

One half of Millamant's fortune will be forfeit if she marries without her aunt Lady Wishfort's consent. The aunt is most unlikely to approve of Mirabell because she lately discovered that he had been paying her *sham addresses* (63) to disguise his pursuit of Millamant. This imposture has been exposed by Mrs Marwood, as revenge because Mirabell rejected her advances.

We are given succinct indications of character; Fainall is intent upon *refining his pleasures* (12), Millamant sometimes behaves in a way that would *tempt the patience of a Stoic* (19), Lady Wishfort is given to sudden *invectives* (34), Mrs Marwood will not *easily forgive* (83), Mirabell is *a gallant man* (90), while Witwoud and Petulant are both easy targets for the gentlemen's wit.

Fainall, jealous of Mirabell's relationships with women, is the more probing of the two in the conversation. However, it is Mirabell who outwits him by suggesting that Mrs Marwood, supposed friend of Mrs Fainall, is Fainall's lover (96–99). Fainall feels the heat of this and withdraws to an adjoining room to find Witwoud and Petulant.

- 1 sd **chocolate-house** These were fashionable meeting places for gentlemen.
- 6–7 **The coldness... winner** This is a perverse aphorism (see Glossary) as only the mean-spirited would agree with it. To Fainall, success at cards and success at seduction are similar aims.
- 15–16 **grave... gay** Mirabell makes witty use of antithesis (opposites) and alliteration.
- 18 **humours** moods (see Glossary).

Notes

- 19 **Stoic** a follower of the ancient Greek philosopher Zeno (c. 334– c. 262 BCE), someone who believed in exercising self-control and being indifferent to pain or pleasure.
- 20 **coxcomb** vain, foolish fellow.
- 23 **evil genius** person with malign power over another's fate.
- 27 **Mrs** This is a respectful abbreviation of the title 'mistress', used for both married and single women.
- 30 **the vapours** feelings of faintness, nervousness or depression.
- 33 **taciturnity** silence, lack of speech.
- 38 **She reddened** This is the first of several references to natural emotions that cannot be disguised. See also II.68, 78–9, 140–41, III.47–8, 272.
- 42–3 **be under the necessity of such a resignation** have to comply in this way (with the wishes of her aunt).
- 45 **approbation** consent. This information is key to the plot.
- 49 **cabal** small, powerful clique that meets in secret (French).
- 55–7 **one man... enrolled members** Note the implication that the fops Witwoud and Petulant are each worth only half a real man.
- 61 **ratafia** nut-flavoured liqueur.
- 66 **the state of nature** Fainall has a perverse view of nature: he claims that dissembling or pretence will make relationships more natural.
- 70 **lampoon** gossipy poem for public distribution.
- 74 **dropsy** disease in which the body swells with excess fluid. Did Mirabell mean to ridicule or flatter Lady Wishfort with this behaviour? Does the probability that she will feel flattered excuse his motives, whatever they are?
- 78 **my virtue forbad me** Can Mirabell really claim to have been virtuous? Later we are told that Lady Wishfort *is the antidote to desire* (IV.530).
- 79 **your friend, or your wife's friend** Mirabell's correction is pointed; he knows Mrs Marwood and Fainall are lovers.
- 83 **omissions** failures (i.e. to make love to them).
- 86–7 **apt to interpret a woman's good manners to her prejudice** i.e. inclined to assume that any woman showing polite interest in him is sexually attracted to him.
- 90 **gallant** honourable towards women.
- 93–9 **Yet you speak... your wife** Note the way Mirabell picks up Fainall's words and imitates his phrasing. He substitutes *distrust*

Act I

for *indifference* and *concern* for *negligence*, and he turns *affected* into its negative form.
106 **canonical** hours between 8 am and noon when marriages could legally take place.

Mirabell contrives a new plot to win Millamant (107–76)

All that is revealed here of Mirabell's plot is that it involves a hasty marriage. He is more interested in securing the *certificate* (120) to prove it is legally binding than in the emotional state of the newlyweds. Mention of a *tailor* and *new liveries* (122–3) suggests that someone by the name of *Waitwell* (122) is to be disguised as an aristocrat.

Mirabell's commanding tone implies that the newlyweds are servants, and intriguingly they belong to different establishments; the groom is Mirabell's servant and the bride is from a lady's household (Lady Wishfort's). Mirabell sends word that the newlyweds should meet him *at one o'clock by Rosamond's Pond* (128–9).

Fainall returns to find Mirabell's mood much improved. He continues to probe Mirabell's feelings about Millamant, this time with more success. The audience learn that Mirabell's love for Millamant is sincere even if he is exasperated by her *affectations* (157) and *insolence* (160). They can recognize that this is the play's 'gay couple' (see Glossary).

- 111 **Pancras** St Pancras Church was outside the city of London, so marriages could be performed without a licence.
- 116 **Duke's Place** location of St James's Church, Aldgate, which offered the same marriage service.
- 123 **liveries** servants' uniform, which indicated the family they worked for.
- 126 **consummation** sexual union of newlyweds.
- 127 **Dame Partlet** This nickname for Foible casts her as the hen, the wife of the proud cockerel Chanticleer, in Chaucer's *Nun's Priest's Tale* from *The Canterbury Tales* (written at the end of the fourteenth century).

Notes

- 128 **Rosamond's Pond** This was a lovers' meeting place in St James's Park.
- 146 **understanding** intelligence and discernment.
- 150 **complaisance** desire to please.
- 152–5 **For a passionate lover... too passionate a lover** Note the witty chiasmus (see Glossary).
- 157 **become her** This is a pun meaning 'suit her well' as well as 'are part of her nature'.
  affectations pretences, insincerities, flights of fancy.
- 173 **are your own man again** will be free of your infatuation.

We meet two false wits, and two unwelcome arrivals are announced (177–531)

A messenger arrives seeking Witwoud, as there is a letter for him from Sir Wilfull Witwoud, his half-brother and Lady Wishfort's nephew. Sir Wilfull is coming to London to prepare for a European tour. Mirabell and Fainall find common ground as they make condescending remarks at the expense of the Witwoud brothers. Much of what follows is about establishing a hierarchy of wit among the male characters.

Witwoud enters and reveals that he is dreading his half-brother's arrival, considering him a fool. He is also sulking because he has lost at cards to his friend Petulant. In Petulant's absence, the three gentlemen discuss his demerits as a wit. They are interrupted by the Coachman who brings news of *Three gentlewomen* (339) wishing to speak to Petulant. Witwoud explains that the women are in fact prostitutes hired by Petulant to travel around town and call on him in public places. This is to enhance his reputation as a ladies' man.

Petulant joins them, ostentatiously dismissing the women without seeing them. This may be because there is insufficient audience for such a meeting or simply, as his name suggests, that he is being petulant.

Fainall mischievously claims that Petulant has dismissed the women in order to pursue his courtship of Millamant. Mirabell expresses anger that Petulant should persist in this. Petulant retorts

Act I

that others should really be the target of Mirabell's anger. He repeats a rumour that an uncle of Mirabell's, lately come to town and lodging near Lady Wishfort, might well marry and have an heir, thus disinheriting Mirabell.

Mirabell implies the *truth* (429) of this rumour, demanding to know whether Petulant heard it at the cabal night. Speaking to Fainall, Witwoud confirms this and adds that the uncle might marry Millamant, making Mirabell the loser of not one but two fortunes. We cannot read the effect of this rumour on Mirabell but we should note that he is satisfied enough to close the topic and propose a walk in St James's Park before dinner, intending to meet the ladies there.

207, 208 **knight-errant, squire** A medieval *knight-errant* travelled in search of adventure, often with a young *squire* who assisted him.

209–10 **like a medlar grafted on a crab** The *medlar* and the *crab* are two types of fruit that could not originate from the same tree. The medlar is eaten when it begins to decay, hence it will *melt in your mouth*, and is *all pulp*; crab apples are sour (*set your teeth on edge*) and hard, *all core* (210–12).

216–17 **the monster in *The Tempest*** Caliban was befriended and offered intoxicating drink by Stephano and Trinculo in Shakespeare's play *The Tempest*, II.ii (1610–11).

220 **his memory fails him** i.e. Witwoud repeats the witticisms of others, if he can remember them.

221 **commonplace of comparisons** This would be a notebook in which Witwoud notes down similes that he can use to show off his wit.

225 **exceptious** liable to take offence.

226 **raillery** teasing, witty conversation.

241–2 **panegyric in a funeral sermon** praise of the deceased spoken at a funeral.

242 **commendatory verses** poems that flatter the person to whom they are sent. In this case both sender and receiver are poets, so the language would be intense.

248 **half a fool** Mirabell is implying that Witwoud is a complete one, while apparently saying the opposite.

249 *le drôle!* witty fellow (French).

Notes

- 254 **foreign and domestic** This suggests the sections of a newspaper. It would be unusual for Fainall as *a man of pleasure and the town* (253) to be close to his wife; what seems close to home is likely to be remote from his interests.
- 273 **spleen** bad temper, being out of sorts.
- 278 **repartee** witty and spontaneous verbal contests.
- 284 **breed debates** cause arguments.
- 293 **bum-baily** bailiff who hounds debtors to get them to pay.
- 314 **decay of parts** deterioration of the intellect.
- 316 **positive** opinionated.
- 336 **porter** doorkeeper.
- 344 **cinnamon-water** drink made from cinnamon, sugar, spirits and hot water, believed to help the digestion.
- 345 **strumpets** prostitutes.
- 346 **bawd** procurer of prostitutes for clients.
- 351 **trulls** prostitutes.
- 360–64 **slip, whip, trip, clap, slap** These monosyllables convey the humour and speed of Petulant's tricks through the use of rhyme and onomatopoeia (see Glossary).
- 364 **hackney-coach** coach for public hire.
- 373 **'Sbud** an oath, a contraction of 'God's blood'.
- 376 **Pox on 'em** *Pox* is slang for syphilis, so the phrase is a curse.
- 379 **let it pass** This phrase was commonly used during the game of whist. See also *Pass on* (395) and other phrases connected with card-playing at II.407, III.622, 642, V.501–2.
- 385 **rub off** clear off.
- 389 **Sultana queens** wives or favourite mistresses of sultans. A sultan was the sovereign of a Muslim country such as Turkey.
- 390 **Roxolanas** the name of a Turkish sultana in *The Siege of Rhodes* (1656) by William Davenant.
- 397 **caterwauling** making a noise like a cat in heat.
  conventicle secret religious meeting of believers who did not follow the teachings and practices of the Anglican church.
- 405 **trundle** go in a lumbering fashion.
- 406 **paint** cosmetics.
- 407 **This continence is all dissembled** this self-control is all pretence.
- 421 **your interpreter** Witwoud has said that he likes to *explain* Petulant's *meaning*, see 324–6.

422–3 **you have an uncle** This is an important plot point. Mirabell, we discover later, has falsely spread the word that he has an uncle in town, and is keen to ensure the news reaches the Wishfort household.
443 **whiting** white fish, of the cod family.
443–4 **of orient** from the East.
444 **Mercury** the planet nearest the sun. Its unusual orbit means it is visible for only about two hours before or after sunset.
453 **Pshaw!** This is an expression of contempt.
459 **uncertain** unpredictable.
465 **demme** This is an affected way of saying 'damn me'.
466 **Cleopatra** queen of Egypt, who lived 69–30 BCE and gained a reputation as a *femme fatale*.
474 **a Quaker hates a parrot** Parrots can repeat swear words and these would offend Quakers, who had very strict Christian principles.
474–5 **a fishmonger hates a hard frost** It is difficult to fish successfully through ice.
476–7 **items of such a treaty being in embryo** signs that such an arrangement (i.e. for the uncle to marry Millamant) was being considered.
479 **fobbed** cheated, foiled.
482 **humorist** person of moods or whims.
485 **quintessence** essential part.
489 ***tête à tête*** face to face, in private (French).
497 **the Mall** a fashionable walk in St James's Park.
514 **ribaldry** vulgar joking.
528–9 **plead the error… your practice** excuse what you do by claiming you make decisions based on poor judgement.

Act II

Two ladies pretend to share confidences (1–107)

The scene moves to St James's Park, where Mrs Fainall and Mrs Marwood are taking a stroll. Appearances suggest they are friends and may continue so, as long as Mrs Fainall remains unaware that Mrs Marwood is her husband's mistress. This unpleasant truth hangs

Notes

ironically over the whole exchange.

They discuss emotions, men and sexual politics. We are aware, by their urbane manner and their tactic of matching each other sentiment for sentiment, that they are fencing. Language disguises their feelings but their blushes give them away. Against men's inconstancy, Mrs Fainall proposes a sisterhood of self-sufficiency. Mrs Marwood prefers to take her pleasures as opportunities arise, even though love is fleeting.

Mrs Fainall is quick to point out that Mrs Marwood's *aversion to mankind* (18–19) is contradictory, a pose she has assumed to please Lady Wishfort. Mrs Marwood's response is as variable as her emotional state; she confesses to being a secret *libertine* (29) and pledges to *despise* and *forget* (46–7) all men. She invites Mrs Fainall to admit that she hates her husband, and the reply, *Most transcendently* (37), is no doubt gratifying to a mistress's conscience.

When talk turns to marriage as a means of revenge on men, Mirabell's name causes both women to change complexion. Each probes the other for the cause; both claim to hate him, but we later learn that as the cast-off mistress, Mrs Fainall has in fact reached an accommodation with him. Mrs Marwood says she finds him *insufferably proud* (73), which we can take as evidence that he has rejected her advances. Mrs Fainall passes off her *flush* (79) as a dislike of meeting her husband, who now joins them, accompanied by Mirabell.

The spouses greet each other with a deadly politeness that hardly conceals their mutual loathing. Mrs Fainall invites Mirabell to walk with her. She intends to find out more about the undertow of feelings that led to his dismissal from the cabal night.

    3 **averse**   strongly disinclined.
 20 **free**   frank.
 21 **discourses**   discussions.
 27 **lawful tyrant**   What does this oxymoron (see Glossary) suggest about Mrs Marwood's situation?
 29 **profess**   claim to be.

Act II

      libertine   person with loose morals, who pursues pleasure (see Glossary.
- 35 **inveterately**   constantly.
- 37 **transcendently**   supremely, exceedingly.
- 38 **meritoriously**   praiseworthily.
- 48–9 **an Amazon, a Penthesilea**   In Greek mythology, *Penthesilea* was a warrior queen of the Amazons who fought for the Trojans against the Greeks.
- 57 **cuckold**   husband of an unfaithful wife. Such a man was traditionally a laughing stock, whose forehead would grow horns as a sign of his humiliation.
- 94 **mortification**   deep shame.
- 98–9 **a pleasant relation**   something interesting you were relating.

The relationship between Fainall and Mrs Marwood is clarified (108–251)

We now enter a world where certainty cannot be achieved by asking a question and besides, the motivation behind a question is not as clear as it seems. Fainall reveals that he believes both his wife and Mrs Marwood are pretending an aversion to Mirabell while harbouring love for him. Not to lose face, he claims to have turned a blind eye to his wife's pursuit of Mirabell so that she would not notice his affair with Mrs Marwood. Aiming for the high moral ground in the relationship with his mistress, he cites her betrayal of Mirabell to Lady Wishfort as the revenge of a scorned woman.

Mrs Marwood's defence – that she acted out of friendship to Lady Wishfort – provides Fainall with the easy jibe that she is also a 'friend' of his wife. The quarrel escalates into a passionate argument and Mrs Marwood threatens to disclose their affair to Mrs Fainall. She claims that Fainall has compromised her reputation and spent her money.

Fainall coolly reminds her that his secrecy has safeguarded her honour, and as for her wealth, they have spent it on pleasures *we both have shared* (202). Had she not exposed Mirabell, Millamant might have married him and the *moiety of her fortune* (206–7) that Lady Wishfort controls (we later learn this amounts to the large sum of £6,000) would have been withheld; this would have reverted to

Notes

Fainall in due course through his wife's inheritance, and then could have been spent on his mistress.

To this there is no answer, only further recriminations. Fainall weakens first and attempts to rein in Mrs Marwood's passions, suggesting that she should wear a mask to conceal her tears as he sees Mirabell and Mrs Fainall returning.

- 110 **Ay!**   yes. What would Mrs Marwood's tone be here?
- 115 **Alexander**   Alexander the Great, King of Macedonia (356–323 BCE). His conquests took him as far as India.
- 129 **insensible**   unaware, or not susceptible.
- 160 **credulous**   easily fooled.
- 175 **inviolate**   protected.
- 197 **fame**   reputation.
- 199 **indigent**   impoverished.
- 201 **prodigality**   generosity.
- 206 **had**   would have.
  moiety   half.
- 211 **Death**   This is a curse, short for 'God's death'. See also '*Sdeath* (249).
- 215–16 **to bustle... this world**   This phrase recalls the words of the villainous king in Shakespeare's *Richard III* (1592): 'God take King Edward to his mercy/ And leave the world for me to bustle in' (I.i.151–2).
- 222 **asperse**   falsely accuse.
- 227–8 **Break my hands... get loose**   This is one of two instances of Fainall being involved in potential violence against women; see also V.538.
- 250 **mask**   Mrs Marwood is the only woman in the play who wears a mask. These were worn by prostitutes as well as ladies in the seventeenth century, and were not fully respectable attire, since their purpose was often to conceal the woman's identity.

Trusting friends replace wrangling lovers, revealing more of Mirabell's plot (252–321)

Mirabell and Mrs Fainall also have secrets to discuss, but the mood between them is calm and rational. We learn that Mirabell persuaded

Act II

her to marry Fainall to save her reputation. She had confided her fear of becoming pregnant and this was her lover's solution, one that society would accept.

Mirabell has shown respect by confiding in her the precise details of his plot and trusting her not to use the knowledge against him. He confirms that he has invented the uncle that Petulant and Witwoud gossiped about in Act I. Mirabell's servant Waitwell will impersonate him, and pretend to court Lady Wishfort. Waitwell's marriage to Lady Wishfort's *woman* (288), Foible, is a safeguard against Lady Wishfort entering into a genuine marriage contract with the bogus 'uncle'. Once Lady Wishfort discovers that she has contracted herself to a social inferior, Mirabell will produce the pre-existing marriage certificate and offer to release her in return for Millamant's hand and fortune. Mirabell is also behind Foible's suggestion that Lady Wishfort can disguise her designs on the 'uncle' by pretending to promote a match between him and Millamant.

257 **prudence** moderation.
268 **consequence** i.e. pregnancy.
271 **lavish of his morals** loose living.
  interested self-serving.
278 **you know your remedy** This is a cryptic remark. Does it refer to the *deed of trust* that we learn about at the end of Act V? It is unlikely to mean divorce, which became possible for the wealthy after 1670; divorce proceedings could only be filed by a husband against an adulterous wife and *that idol, reputation* (267) would be ruined by the scandal.
295 **like Mosca in *The Fox*** In the final act of Ben Jonson's play *Volpone, or The Fox* (1607), Volpone's servant Mosca gains the upper hand in their plots and tries to exact *terms* (296) in return for saving him from justice.
306 **carry it more privately** i.e. conceal her designs on the 'uncle'.
318 **green sickness** chlorosis, a chronic disorder caused by lack of iron, once common in adolescent girls.

Notes

A battle of wit ensues as Millamant and Mirabell meet (322–485)

Millamant arrives, pursued by her suitor Witwoud, and followed by her servant Mincing. Mirabell's implied comparison with Dalila's entrance in John Milton's *Samson Agonistes* (1671) provides ironic humour. Millamant is not really as grand and imposing as Mirabell claims. She is nervous and flustered; her entourage is embarrassing for a society beauty. Each remark by Mrs Fainall (blunt and honest) and Mirabell (bemused and then ironic) brings her quickly down to earth.

There is an exchange of wit between the lovers that suggests their courtship has reached an impasse. Mrs Fainall assists Mirabell by drawing Witwoud away. Without an onstage audience, their tone becomes more earnest.

Mirabell reprimands Millamant for refusing to speak with him at the cabal night; her excuse is that she was *engaged* with others (430). These others Mirabell deems fools, scorning her for wasting time on them. Although fully aware of his love, Millamant does not like to be criticized and tells Mirabell, playfully or not, that she won't *have* (448) him. On parting, she reveals that she is aware of Foible's marriage and the attendant plot.

322–4 **Here she comes... fools for tenders** This passage may have been inspired by Milton's *Samson Agonistes* (lines 710–21, see headnote), in which Dalila's entrance is compared to that of a 'stately ship'.
323 **streamers** ribbons.
shoal swarm (of fish).
324 **tenders** small ships attending a large vessel.
325 **sculler** person rowing a small boat (i.e. Witwoud).
328 **the *beau monde*** fashionable society (French).
329 **perukes** periwigs. These became fashionable for gentlemen from 1660. What effect is achieved by Mirabell's use of metonymy, a figure of speech in which attributes (such as periwigs) are used to represent the men themselves?
334 **favourite in disgrace** rejected courtier or politician.

Act II

- 336 **truce with your similitudes** can we agree to calling off your similes.
- 338 **As a physician of a good air** Healthy air means people don't need to employ the doctor.
- 352 Compare Shakespeare's *Hamlet* V.ii.257, in which Osric notes Hamlet's first successful strike at Laertes in the fencing match.
- 356–7 Mincing's speech is affected in an effort to sound refined. See also her pronunciation of *cremp* (370) for 'cramp' and *crips* (373) for 'crisp'.
- 361 **to pin up one's hair** as curling papers.
- 369 **tift** titivated, primped.
- 376 **exceptions** offence.
- 407 **card-matches** cardboard matches; also the holding of a matching pair, or three of a kind, in card games.
- 434 **encumbrance** burden.
- 443 **physics** medicine.
- 444 **assafoetida** an unpleasant-smelling gum resin extracted from the root of the herb ferula. It was used to help with digestive problems.
- 445 **in a course of fools** taking a course of fools (as if they were medicine).
- 450 **distemper** ailment.
- 464 **Sententious** pompously moralizing.
- 465 **like Solomon... old tapestry hanging** Tapestries often portrayed scenes from the Bible. Millamant is referring to the famous story of the judgement made by King Solomon when two women claimed to be the mother of the same baby (see I Kings 3:16–28). In a tapestry the king's wisdom is static and silenced, like Mirabell's wit before her own.
- 474 **watch-light** long-burning night candle.
- 480 **like to speed** likely to succeed.
- 483 **unless she should tell me herself** Clearly, Foible has told Millamant (see 525).

Mirabell briefs Waitwell and Foible and prepares his trap (486–555)

Alone on stage, Mirabell's monologue expresses what a man feels when he cannot help loving a whimsical and contradictory woman.

Notes

His reverie is interrupted by the servants. Mirabell's fictitious uncle now has a name, *Sir Rowland* (515). Foible has told Lady Wishfort that she expects to show Sir Rowland her *picture*, a miniature portrait (516). She intends to report back that he has fallen passionately in love with her beauty and longs to meet her.

Mirabell rewards Foible with money and reminds the couple that he has promised them a secure and well-stocked farm should the plot succeed. Foible catches sight of the masked Mrs Marwood and fears that she will report their rendezvous to Lady Wishfort. She determines to return home quickly to prevent this. Waitwell is left to ponder what marriage and disguise will do to his sense of self.

- 498 **turtles**   turtle doves, love birds.
  billing   cooing.
- 500 **Sirrah**   This is a variant of 'sir' that suggests the person addressed is inferior.
- 503 **solacing in lawful delights**   enjoying making love. This is *lawful* since they are now married.
- 504–6 **have instructed her... a prosperous way**   These remarks carry a sexual innuendo.
- 508 **las**   alas.
- 509 **inquietudes**   agitations, anxieties.
- 522 This is another of Waitwell's sexual innuendoes.
- 528 **diligence**   careful effort, attention to detail.
- 531 As her husband, Waitwell expects Foible to give him her earnings.
- 537 **at her toilet**   dressing, getting ready to be seen.
- 541 **B'w'y**   God be with you.
- 543 **preferment**   rise to an improved status (as a married woman).
- 547 **attended**   waited upon by servants.

Act III

We meet Lady Wishfort, the character at the centre of Mirabell's plot (1–174)

Lady Wishfort's house provides the setting for the remaining three

Act III

acts. She is dressing in the hope of receiving the supposed Sir Rowland, but her colour is fading and Foible has locked the cosmetics away. To console herself, Lady Wishfort calls for the cherry-brandy, only to have to hide the bottle when Mrs Marwood arrives.

Mrs Marwood tells her that she has seen Foible talking to Mirabell in the park. Lady Wishfort's first concern is that Mirabell might discover Foible's mission, which is to show her portrait to Sir Rowland. Foible is heard arriving, and Lady Wishfort ushers Mrs Marwood into the closet so that the servant can be questioned more freely.

Foible describes Sir Rowland as being utterly besotted with the portrait, but Lady Wishfort is first concerned to reprimand her for meeting Mirabell. Foible claims that all she did was defend her employer against Mirabell's gross insults. This goads Lady Wishfort into hoping for a hasty marriage in order to disinherit him.

Lady Wishfort must now repair her makeup to resemble her portrait. Her thoughts move swiftly to the question of whether Sir Rowland will be *brisk* (168) in his love-making so that she can secure him while maintaining her reputation for decorum.

- 4 **veracity** truth.
- 5 **the red** cosmetics to colour her cheeks red.
- 6 **errant** wayward.
  as I'm a person We quickly hear Lady Wishfort use her favourite phrase, which is a claim to possess individuality and substance. Contrast this with her habit of belittling others by names that call their humanity into doubt: *changeling, puppet, wooden thing* (14–16), *Beastly creature* (IV.416), *viper, serpent* (V.2), *caterpillar* (301).
- 8 **mopus** stupid person.
- 9 **ratifia** a variant of *ratafia* (see I.61 and Note).
- 12 **Spanish paper** paper impregnated with red powder, imported from Spain.
- 15 **bobbins** Carrying thread in lace-making, bobbins are in constant motion.

Notes

- 22 **Mrs Qualmsick, the curate's wife** Presumably, she seems constantly sick because of her frequent pregnancies (she's *always breeding*).
- 34 **tapster** person serving ale.
- 36 **Maritornes the Asturian in *Don Quixote*** a partially sighted serving girl from the Asturian region of northern Spain, in the novel *Don Quixote* (1605 and 1615), by Miguel de Cervantes.
- 41–2 **in *dishabilie*** partly dressed (French).
- 43 **a lost thing** This is ironic, as Foible is both missing and lost to Lady Wishfort's cause.
- 60 **closet** small private room.
- 63 **Quarles** Francis Quarles (1592–1644), highly respected religious poet.
  Prynne William Prynne, Puritan author of *Histriomastix* (1632), in which he attacked the immorality of the stage.
- 63–4 ***Short View of the Stage*** See page 12.
- 64 **Bunyan's works** Puritan John Bunyan wrote *The Pilgrim's Progress* (1678). His *Works* were published in 1692.
- 91 **catering** acting as an accomplice to wrongdoing.
- 91–2 **ferreting for some disbanded officer** seeking out a discharged soldier.
- 92–3 **Half-pay is but thin subsistence** the officer's army pension would not be much to live on.
- 94–5 **come down pretty deep** stoop pretty low.
- 95 **superannuated** too old (for finding a husband).
- 96 **Ods** God's.
- 98 **drawer** waiter who draws ale.
- 99 **Robin** typical name for a waiter.
  Locket's a fashionable restaurant at Charing Cross.
- 110 **frippery** cast-off clothing. This suggests something that has passed through many hands. In the seventeenth century, prostitutes were referred to as men's clothing, so the insult is very strong. See also II.289.
  handle you tackle you (with sexual innuendo).
- 118 **Incontinently** immediately.
- 124 **tatterdemalion** wretch dressed in rags and tatters. Lady Wishfort returns the insult of being called *frippery* (110).
- 125 **Long Lane penthouse** Long Lane near Smithfield had secondhand clothes shops.

Act III

　　gibbet-thief thief hanged on the gallows.
125–6 **slander-mouthed railer** one who ruins others' reputations with lies.
　126 **prodigal** wastrel, someone who has spent his inheritance foolishly (like the prodigal son in the Bible story, see Luke 15:11–32).
　127 **the million lottery** a lottery scheme sponsored by the government in 1694 to raise a million pounds.
127–8 **the whole court upon a birthday** Courtiers were required to wear expensive new clothes on the king's birthday.
　130 **Ludgate** debtors' prison in Blackfriars.
131–2 Prisoners dangled *mittens* through the grates of Ludgate prison to beg for money from passers-by walking below them.
　136 **economy of face** suitable looks.
　142 **flayed** skinned.
147–8 **Your picture must sit for you, madam** your portrait must pose as a model for your makeup.
　151 **importunate** pressing, demanding.
　152 **decorums** rules of proper behaviour.
　157 **coy** shy.
　163 **wants features** lacks good looks.
　168 **brisk** forward, lively.
　171 **apprehension** idea.

Mrs Marwood overhears more and sows the seeds of a counter plot (175–263)

Mrs Fainall catches up with Foible and reveals that she knows the plot in every detail, which she recounts without realizing that the *devil Marwood* (176) is eavesdropping. Foible makes further unwitting revelations to Mrs Marwood by updating Mrs Fainall on the latest developments. The women leave, but not before Foible has unknowingly wounded Mrs Marwood by voicing the opinion that Mirabell *can't abide her* (209–10).

Mrs Marwood's suspicions of an affair between Mirabell and Mrs Fainall are confirmed by what she has heard. She shows a disdainful surprise at her rival's generosity. She dwells on the insults to her name and character, hinting at vengeance.

Notes

Lady Wishfort enters, full of apologies for neglecting Mrs Marwood in the closet. We are reminded of the imminent arrival of Sir Wilfull. Mrs Marwood mischievously suggests that he ought to marry Millamant, an idea Lady Wishfort soon adopts.

- 189 **former good correspondence**   This is a tactful way of referring to Mrs Fainall's affair with Mirabell.
- 204 **a Welsh maidenhead**   the virginity of a Welsh woman. This remark promoting an insulting stereotype about Welsh women was presumably amusing to an English audience.
- 209 **month's mind**   strong desire (for Mirabell).
- 215 **Mrs Engine**   Mrs Marwood now appreciates Foible's central part as a vital tool in Mirabell's plot.
- 217 *passe-partout*   master key (French).
- 223 **procure for him**   i.e. assist Mirabell in his plan to marry Millamant, with the connotation of finding a prostitute for a client.
- 227 **driveller**   foolish talker.
- 231 **without**   unless.
- 238 **the day of projection**   when an alchemist calculates the time is ripe to complete his process of turning base metal into gold. Does she mean that Lady Wishfort is base metal seeking to transform herself into gold?
- 244–5 **olio of affairs**   variety of complicated concerns.

Two rivals square up to each other, with victory to Millamant (264–415)

Witwoud and Petulant are announced and Sir Wilfull is expected soon. Mrs Marwood, dispatched to entertain them, encounters Millamant and Mincing. Millamant is in an agitated state, for which she blames being courted by fools. Mrs Marwood remarks that the fools are a cover to hide Mirabell's courtship. She attacks Millamant's right to privacy by imagining female bodies with secrets so gross they cannot be disguised. Millamant remarks on Mrs Marwood's bad humour and sends Mincing to ask the gentlemen to join them.

Millamant's rapid speech and laughter reveal her anxiety to claim Mirabell's affections for herself in defiance of Mrs Marwood's

Act III

attack. Both may claim to hate him, but Mirabell remains faithful to Millamant whatever she professes. Mrs Marwood counters with a general threat that Millamant will not long be making a *merry note* (350). At this provocation, Millamant calls for a song.

While the gentlemen are delayed, the audience hear a song about the competitiveness of love. The sentiments, designed to goad Mrs Marwood, refer to the *glory* (366) of having captured the heart of one *For whom inferior beauties sighed in vain* (367). The entrance of Witwoud and Petulant breaks the tension and Millamant finds an opportunity to depart.

- 281 **fit**   fought.
- 287–8 **doily stuff**   light woollen fabric.
- 291–2 *drap-du-Berry*   woollen fabric from Berry, a province in central France.
- 299 **blind**   disguise.
- 304–5 **Mrs Primly's great belly... her hips**   The name *Primly* suggests a fastidious and moralizing person; she attempts to conceal her pregnancy by tight lacing of her corsets. The displaced fat shows on her hips.
- 306 **Strammel**   The name suggests an unattractive person.
- 307–8 **Rhenish-wine tea**   Rhenish wine (from the Rhine region of Germany) was drunk in place of tea in an attempt to promote weight loss.
- 308 **be comprehended**   fit. Despite her efforts to slim down, Lady Strammel's face will still not fit behind a mask.
- 310 **discarded toast**   Gentlemen would drink the health of famous beauties in a *toast*, until they were no longer young or fashionable.
- 320 **mitigate**   control, reduce.
- 324 **enjoined it him**   required him.
- 327 **so particular... on the other**   i.e. so attentive to Millamant and so indifferent to Mrs Marwood.
- 344 **sybil**   prophetess who reads people's minds and can see into the future (in ancient Greek legend).
- 354 **to comb**   i.e. to comb their wigs.
- 359 sd **Mr John Eccles**   a composer (1668–1735) who wrote the music for many songs in contemporary plays.

Notes

      Mrs Hodgson   Mary Hodgson, a popular singer of the day.
- 366 **swain**   youth.
- 376 **treble and bass**   In musical composition, *treble* is the higher, more dominant sound, *bass* the lower and softer.
- 381 **battledores**   racquets used in the game of battledore and shuttlecock (similar to badminton).
- 388–9 **proof presumptive**   proof based on assumptions rather than hard evidence.
- 396 **parts**   natural wit. There is also a bawdy pun, as *parts* may suggest sexual organs.
- 410 **Ordinary**   prison chaplain. He would choose a *psalm* for condemned prisoners before their hanging.
- 412–13 **a man may do it without book**   One can die (like the condemned man) or make love (like the bridegroom) without reference to learning.

Town fops goad their country visitor, with mixed results (416–596)

Sir Wilfull enters, and rather than greet his half-brother civilly, Witwoud sets Petulant on to goad him. Mrs Marwood intervenes, encouraging the two men to acknowledge one other. Witwoud claims it is not fashionable *to know relations in town* (509). Sir Wilfull is heartily sorry at the change he sees in his brother, recalling how much less foolish he seemed when he was an *attorney's clerk* (528–9). Petulant seizes on this revelation about Witwoud's past to ridicule him.

Sir Wilfull greets Lady Wishfort and Fainall. He is polite but still smarting from the attentions of too many false wits. Mincing announces that dinner is served, and Lady Wishfort invites her guests to dine.

- 416 **Bartlemew and his fair**   Bartholomew Fair was held annually on 24 August at Smithfield.
- 421 **the Revolution**   the Glorious Revolution of 1688 (see page 9).
- 448 **Oons**   God's wounds.

Act III

        starling   These were regarded as stupid birds, only able to mimic other birds' song.
463   **smoke him**   draw him out in order to ridicule him.
480   **'Slife**   God's life.
487   **write myself**   sign myself.
490   **by'r lady**   by Our Lady (the Virgin Mary).
491   **'S'heart**   God's heart.
492   **the Rekin**   the Wrekin, a hill in Shropshire.
494   **becravatted, and beperiwigged**   wearing a cravat (an elaborate neck tie) and full-length wig.
496   **Odso**   by God.
499   **flapdragon**   a dish in which flaming brandy-soaked raisins were extinguished by putting them in the mouth; something worthless.
499–500   **a hare's foot, and a hare's scut**   The foot and tail of hares could not be eaten; Sir Wilfull thinks very little of the welcome he is receiving.
504   **Inns o' Court**   colleges where lawyers trained and law was practised.
507   **Salop**   Shropshire.
508   **Shrewsbury cake**   cake with a biscuit-like consistency.
509   **modish**   fashionable.
510   **lubberly**   clumsy.
        slabber   slobber.
511   **call of serjeants**   ceremony in which new barristers were admitted to the bar.
517   **subpoena**   legal document summoning someone to court.
519–20   **Rat me**   may God rot me.
521   **tale of a cock and a bull**   unlikely tale.
523   **were out of your time**   had completed your legal training.
524–5   **Furnival's Inn**   one of the Inns of Court.
526   **gazettes**   sheets giving the latest news, for local distribution.
527   ***Dawk's Letter***   newsletter popular in rural districts.
        weekly bill   report of all the deaths in London.
545   **weather-cock**   This name suggests that Witwoud changes direction according to the winds (of fashion).
548–9   **If an how... taxes abate**   Catholic countries such as France were prepared to go to war with England to restore James II

Notes

to the throne. Taxes were raised to pay for military campaigns abroad.
556 **lingo** language(s).
564–5 **Dutch skipper from a whale-fishing** i.e. the opposite of a *refined* person.
580 **rallier** one who teases and mocks others to show his wit.
582 **to choose** by choice.

Fainall and Mrs Marwood develop a counter plot (597–694)

Fainall and Mrs Marwood had placed themselves apart at line 583, giving her time to brief him. It is now revealed that Fainall's pride is deeply wounded by his wife's affair and continued support of her ex-lover's interests. Mrs Marwood points out that he now has the opportunity to part from his wife. She then suggests a lucrative plan.

She tells Fainall to reveal his wife's affair to Lady Wishfort, her mother, and threaten to publicly abandon her. She predicts that Lady Wishfort will offer much to save her daughter's reputation, including the *moiety* of Millamant's fortune. If this new plot is to work, Mrs Marwood's suggestion that Millamant should marry Sir Wilfull would be a distraction, and she apologizes for making it.

Fainall determines to get Sir Wilfull too drunk to be a serious suitor. Mrs Marwood then offers to compose a letter *from an unknown hand* and have it delivered to Lady Wishfort when *that rascal who is to act Sir Rowland is with her* (669–71). Mrs Marwood wishes to play down her role because Foible *knows some passages* (674) of her past behaviour. Should the plot fail, Fainall will still take the *best part* of his wife's *estate* through *a deed of settlement* (678–9) in his possession. He promises to abandon his wife and lavish the fortune on Mrs Marwood.

596 sd **Manent** they remain (Latin). This stage direction is used when most characters leave the stage.
597 **rank** corrupt.
599–600 **the way of the world** Fainall sees the ugly reality beneath the appearance of his relationship with his wife. Mirabell has also

148

Act III

seen this but, unlike Fainall, he has been able to exploit it to his own ends. See also V.458, 535.

600–601 **anticipated cuckold, a cuckold in embryo** He was deceived before he was even married.

602 **satyr** half-man, half-goat, with horns (a creature from ancient Greek mythology).
citizen's child illegitimate child born to a merchant's wife and her lover. Such a liaison was a common joke in comedies of the period.

606 **scurvy** contemptible.

612 **fond** foolish.

616 **deputy-lieutenant's hall** county official's reception hall (where stags' heads were commonly displayed as hunting trophies).

617 **cap of maintenance** one of the symbolic objects carried before the king at the state opening of Parliament. In heraldry, it is a cap with two horn-like points. The word *maintenance* is a pun, suggesting that Mrs Fainall's affair may be a means of blackmailing Lady Wishfort to gain an income.

618 **away with** put up with.

622 **Pam** the jack of clubs, the highest trump card in the game of loo.

630 **composition** agreement, arrangement.

641 **drink like a Dane** Danes had a reputation for heavy drinking.

642 **I'll set his hand in** I'll get him drinking, or I'll deal with his hand whatever the game we play.

665 **branches** This is a pun on the idea of the cuckold's horns.

672 **incendiary** trouble-maker, provocateur.

674 **passages** facts, events. Foible has evidence that would disclose their affair.

675 **mine** trap.

677–8 **turn my wife to grass** cast my wife aside (as a farmer would put an old animal out to graze).

678–9 **deed of settlement of the best part of her estate** legal document that signs over the majority of her wealth.

688 **corrupt to superstition** be diminished to a state of clinging to myths.

689 **badge** sign of membership.

690 **order** fellowship, institution.

Notes

Act IV

Lady Wishfort and Millamant encounter contrasting suitors (1–143)

Lady Wishfort's house is putting on its best face for the arrival of Sir Rowland. As his coach is heard, she finds time to inquire whether Sir Wilfull has proposed to Millamant. Fainall's plan seems to be working, as Foible reports that he is *set in to drinking* (36). Lady Wishfort decides to *send him to* Millamant (38) and leaves, instructing Foible not to leave her alone too long with Sir Rowland.

Foible finds Millamant and Mrs Fainall together, so she asks which suitor to admit – Sir Wilfull or Mirabell. After much uncertainty, Millamant decides she will see Mirabell. Mrs Fainall resists Millamant's attempt to foist Sir Wilfull upon her. When he arrives she mischievously encourages his suit to Millamant and leaves, locking them in the room together.

Alone with Millamant, Sir Wilfull attempts some genteel courtship in a half-hearted manner. She is aloof, contrary and condescending. When she offers him a door by which to escape, he readily takes it.

- 3 **sconces** wall brackets to hold candles.
- 5 **postilion** servant who rides one of the horses drawing a carriage.
- 5–6 **fill up the equipage** make up the full complement (of servants).
- 7 **pullvilled** sprinkled with scented powder.
- 29 **levée** getting up (French).
- 50–51 These are the opening lines of an untitled poem by Sir John Suckling (1609–42).
- 61 This is the first line of *The Story of Phoebus and Daphne, Applied*, by Edmund Waller (1606–87). See also 144–5.
- 66 **proxy** substitute, stand-in.
- 73 **break my mind** reveal what I think.
- 92–3 These are the first two lines of *Song* by Suckling. See also 95, 97–8.

150

94 **Anan** pardon. (This is his pronunciation of 'anon'.)
100 **suckling** unweaned child or animal.
101 **stripling** youth.
102 **ruder than Gothic** more crude or unsophisticated than the medieval or primitive.
119 ***l'etourdie*** stupid fool (French).
129–30 **spare... speed** proverbial saying: if you don't speak up you won't make progress.

The proviso scene seals the love match (144–457)

Mirabell replaces Sir Wilfull, completing the couplet Millamant is reciting with perfect poise; she will not dispatch him so easily. So begins the play's famous proviso scene, in which the lovers negotiate the terms and conditions for what they hope will be a lifelong happy union.

Almost imperceptibly, Millamant shifts from regretting the loss of her independence to stating her terms. She wishes to keep many personal liberties and to ensure they do not become a humdrum couple growing indifferent towards each other.

Mirabell asks Millamant not to adopt a female confidante, one who might encourage intrigue. She should avoid cosmetics and other female paraphernalia; and when pregnant, not lace her corsets too tightly and risk harming his child. At the tea-table she should indulge in harmless gossip. As she begins to protest, Mirabell speaks over her and calls for a contract to be agreed.

Mrs Fainall arrives and urges Millamant to accept Mirabell, which she does at last. Mrs Fainall tells Mirabell to escape down the back stairs because Lady Wishfort is approaching. She describes Sir Rowland as nearing success with his suit. However, Sir Wilfull is drunk and threatening to fight Petulant. Mirabell departs and Witwoud enters, with Petulant close on his heels, both the worse for drink. They trade insults. The audience can just make out that the drunken brawling is part of Fainall's plot to prevent Sir Wilfull from proposing to Millamant.

Lady Wishfort arrives accompanied by Sir Wilfull. She remonstrates with him but he is quite out of control. He becomes

Notes

increasingly persistent and vulgar in his pursuit of Millamant, giving her the excuse to escape, accompanied by Mrs Fainall. Foible whispers to Lady Wishfort that she is keeping Sir Rowland waiting. At her request, Witwoud agrees to take charge of Sir Wilfull so that she can turn her attention to Sir Rowland.

- 144–5 See line 61 and Note.
- 163 **grace** God-like power to bestow something valuable.
- 166–7 **independent on the bounty** without being dependent on the generosity.
- 169 **pedantic** schoolmaster-like.
- 170 **pragmatical** complacent.
- 174 **after grace** i.e. after the marriage ceremony.
- 178 **indolent** idle.
- 179 *douceurs* pleasures.
  sommeils du matin lying in bed slumbering, late into the morning.
- 188 **cant** hypocritical language.
- 192 **Hyde Park** place for fashionable people to promenade.
- 193 **chariot** four-wheeled light carriage.
- 211 **inviolate** absolutely private.
- 215 **These articles subscribed** provided that these rules are agreed.
- 218 **bill of fare** menu (of requests).
- 224 *Inprimis* first of all (legal term).
  covenant require, stipulate.
- 228 **decoy-duck** person acting as cover (for a relationship with an admirer).
- 235 **article** lay it down as a condition.
- 236 **passes current** keeps its value.
- 238 **vizards** masks.
- 240–41 **hog's bones... roasted cat** He names fantastical ingredients that might be supposed to be used in cosmetics.
- 244 **atlases** satin fabric made in the East.
- 251–2 **sugar-loaf** Sugar was moulded into oblong shapes.
- 253 **crooked billet** bent stick.
- 260 **prerogative** right.
- 262–4 **orange-brandy... ratifia** These are drinks based on brandy, variously flavoured.

Act IV

- 264 **clary** herb drink made with wine and honey, and flavoured with ginger and pepper.
- 265 **cowslip wine, poppy-water** these were thought to have a sedative effect.
  dormitives substances that cause sleep, sedatives.
- 267 **tractable** biddable.
- 309 **lubber** country bumpkin.
- 315 **pieced** enlarged with extra material.
  unsized camlet garment made of fabric that would shrink on washing if it were not treated with size, which would stiffen it. If it shrank, extra panels were sewn into it.
- 316–17 **noli prosequi** This is a Latin term used to end legal proceedings.
  - 323 **whim it about** spin.
  - 328 **folios** large books with pages made of full-size sheets of paper folded in half.
  - 329 **decimo sexto** the size of a small book in which each page is a sixteenth of a full sheet of paper.
  Lacedemonian Spartan, from Laconia, a region of Greece. Spartans were people of few words and great bravery.
  - 330 **epitomizer** someone who sums up or encapsulates.
- 332–3 He is someone who peddles *phrases* in borrowed snatches so small that if they were fabric, they could be made into *pincushions*.
  - 335 **shorthand** written abbreviations and symbols.
  - 336 **figure** metaphor.
  - 337 **Baldwin** the name of the ass in *Reynard the Fox*, a series of medieval tales.
- 337–8 **A gemini of asses... four of you** Gemini (the twins) is a Zodiac sign. If a pair of asses were split in two, they would make four Witwouds.
  - 339 **mustard-seed** This is a symbol of spiciness.
  - 343 **radish** salad vegetable that is reputed to cause belching and indigestion.
  - 347 **enow** enough.
  - 349 **pair of castanets** small, wooden, cup-shaped musical instruments that are clicked together between the fingers.
- 352–3 **make less matters conclude premises** make small issues the grounds for full arguments.
  - 355 **face** This implies both Millamant's looks and her reputation.

Notes

- 357 **wood-louse** segmented insect that curls into a ball when touched.
- 367–8 **at years of discretion** i.e. an adult.
- 368 **rantipole rate** reckless fashion.
- 372 **borachio** drunkard (from Spanish).
- 377 **grutch** begrudge.
- 380 **laugh in my face** i.e. bubbles up.
- 384 **bumper** glass of wine filled to the brim.
- 391 *In vino veritas* wine makes one speak the truth (Latin).
- 399 **Apollo** in Greek mythology, the god of the sun.
- 403 **pimple** friend.
  soaker drunk.
- 404 **Antipodes** region on the other side of the world.
- 410–11 **keep her own counsel... nine months' end** keep silent for now and cry out in nine months' time (i.e. while giving birth).
- 415–16 **tallow-chandler** maker of tallow candles (a foul-smelling process).
- 417 **quoth'a** says he.
- 418, 419 **Saracens, Tartars, Turks** At the time of the Crusades (between the eleventh and fifteenth centuries) *Saracen* was a term widely used to mean Muslim. *Tartars* and *Turks* were ethnic tribes from central Asia renowned for being fierce warriors.
- 422 **infidels, and believe not in the grape** non-Christians, non-believers in wine (Sir Wilfull's true religion).
- 422, 423 **Mahometan, Mussulman** followers of the prophet Muhammad.
- 425 **Mufti** Muslim cleric and expert in religious law.
- 426–7 **orthodox... Greek for claret** The Greek Orthodox Church is Christian; Sir Wilfull seems to be implying that language is all nonsense, and it's drink that's important.
- 435 **Sophy** name of a dynasty of rulers in Persia.
- 438 **tumbril** farmer's cart used for carrying dung.
- 439 **bastinadoed** beaten, especially on the soles of the feet.
- 443 **inviolably** in a way that cannot be broken.
- 444 **invades me with some precipitation** is so pressing that I have to act quickly. For Lady Wishfort's extraordinary use of language, see also 459, 469–70, 502–4, 507, 515, 525. Some of Lady Wishfort's expressions are almost malapropisms (see Glossary); some are merely affected and inappropriate usage.
- 448 **shake-bag** large and feisty cock (ready for a fight).

Act IV

450 **like a bagpipe** i.e. wheezy and noisy.
451 **Salopian** someone from Shropshire.
453-4 **Tantony... thy pig** The smallest pig in the litter was often called Tantony, associated with St Anthony (because he was sometimes said to have been a swineherd).

The gulling of Lady Wishfort by 'Sir Rowland' resumes (458–534)

Drunkenness and foolery have interrupted this bizarre courtship. The supposed Sir Rowland (Waitwell in disguise) is in a hurry to secure the contract of marriage and urges haste to prevent Mirabell from poisoning him. Lady Wishfort is concerned not to appear as sexually eager as she is feeling. She discloses Mirabell's pretended courtship of her, and Sir Rowland offers to murder him painfully and slowly. Foible announces that the dancers arranged for Sir Rowland's entertainment are ready, and that someone has a letter to deliver to Lady Wishfort in person.

Waitwell snatches a moment with Foible out of role, while Lady Wishfort attends to the dancers. We see the pressure he has been under in courting this repellent woman.

458-9 **at the retrospection of my own rudeness** when I think back on how I have neglected you.
460 **year of Jubilee** The Pope can pardon sin during a *Jubilee* year of Christian celebrations. There was a Jubilee in 1700.
465 **transport** ecstasy.
466 **rack** torture device.
467 **on the tenter of expectation** on tenterhooks, in suspense.
474 **starve him** i.e. by disinheriting him.
481 **perfidious** faithless, treacherous.
490 **A' dies** he shall die.
494 **alms** charity in the form of food or money.
497 **save-all** device to burn candle-ends.
503 **lethargy of continence** lack of (sexual) self-control.
504 **iteration of nuptials** repetition of marriage rites.
507 **prostitution of decorums** degradation or abuse of correct behaviour.

Notes

- 511 **condescension** kindness, generosity.
- 515 **scruple of carnality** tiny amount of sexual desire.
- 517 **camphire** camphor, thought to reduce sexual urges.
- 518 **frankincense** gum resin, used for burning as incense, especially in religious ceremonies.
- 527 **cordial** reviving drink.
- 530 **antidote** cure. Note the irony, as Lady Wishfort has laboured to make herself irresistible.
- 533 **chairman in the dog-days** porter carrying people in a sedan chair in the hottest days of summer.

Mrs Marwood's letter is read, and there are consequences (535–615)

As the dancing begins Lady Wishfort reads the letter. Foible recognizes the handwriting as Mrs Marwood's and signals to Waitwell to wrest the letter away. They are too late and Lady Wishfort becomes hysterical at the revelation that Sir Rowland is a fake. Foible urges Waitwell to persuade her that Mirabell is the author of the letter.

Foible reveals that Mirabell entered Lady Wishfort's house that afternoon to meet Millamant. Waitwell, still in role as Sir Rowland, offers to kill Mirabell and be hanged for it. Lady Wishfort does not wish to lose her lover or her reputation. Sir Rowland offers to fetch his *black box* (600) containing the legal documents pertaining to his estate. This will surely prove his worth in both senses. He asks permission to bring the marriage contract, too. Mirabell's plot is edging nearer to a successful conclusion and there is even talk of producing an heir to foil all the evil nephew's plans once and for all.

- 541 **superscription** handwritten address.
- 559 *suborned* bribed.
- 568–9 **Roman hand** clear, rounded style of handwriting.

Act V

Lady Wishfort takes her revenge, unaware that Fainall is her real enemy (1–76)

Lady Wishfort has evidently discovered the truth about 'Sir Rowland' before the Act begins, as she turns her fury on Foible, ordering her from the house. We learn that Waitwell is in prison and that if she has a say in the matter, Foible will soon be joining him. She departs to find a constable.

Mrs Fainall joins Foible, bringing reassuring news that Mirabell has gone to bail out Waitwell. Foible tells her that Mrs Marwood overheard everything from her hiding place in the closet. When Mrs Marwood's letter failed to implicate Waitwell, Fainall had him imprisoned. Mrs Marwood has since revealed the whole 'Sir Rowland' plot to Lady Wishfort. Mrs Fainall is reassured by Foible that although she was named in the letter, it was snatched away before Lady Wishfort could read that far.

- 4 **gauze** thin, transparent silk fabric.
- 5 **weaving of dead hair** i.e. making wigs.
  blue nose i.e. blue with cold.
- 6 **chafing-dish** dish that held charcoal for heating.
- 7 **traverse rag** curtain used to divide a living area from a working space.
- 12 **small ware** items of little value.
  flaunting upon a pack-thread displayed by hanging on a rope.
- 13 **bulk** stall.
  dead blank.
- 13–14 **ballad-monger** seller of street songs.
- 14 **frisoneer-gorget** coarse woollen cloth used to cover a woman's neck and breast.
- 15 **colberteen** cheap French lace.
- 21 **governante** housekeeper.
- 30–31 **wealth of the Indies** The East and West Indies were famous for silks, spices and other luxurious imports.
- 34 **cast** sacked, dismissed.

Notes

- 35 **decayed pimp** ageing procurer of prostitutes.
- 36 **frontless** without shame.
  big-bellied pregnant, but bold enough to appear on stage.
- 42–3 **put upon his clergy** forced to plead 'benefit of clergy'. A convicted criminal who could prove his ability to read could escape hanging for a first offence. This was a relic of times when clergymen were among the few people who could read, and the clergy were subject only to their own courts of law. The practice was not formally abolished until 1827.
- 47 **broker** agent.
- 48 **passive** i.e. unaware of the role.
- 50 **botcher** fixer.
- 50–51 **Abigails and Andrews** These are typical servants' names.
- 51 **baste** stitch.
- 52 **Philander** The name suggests a sexual philanderer, someone having many affairs.
  Duke's Place See I.116 and Note.
- 56 **Bridewell** women's prison located between Fleet Street and the Thames.
- 59 **beat hemp** Prisoners in Bridewell were put to hard labour such as beating fibres of hemp, a plant used to make oil, wax, rope, and cloth.
- 62 **give security** offer money to vouch for him and secure his release.
- 66–7 **missing effect** failing to achieve its intended result.
- 72 **confederacy** conspiracy.

Foible discloses the Fainall-Marwood affair and a counter attack begins (77–185)

On hearing that Mrs Marwood has betrayed Mrs Fainall's affair with Mirabell to her husband, Foible reveals to Mrs Fainall that her husband and Mrs Marwood are lovers and, what is more, that she and Mincing could swear to it. She relates how the servants once surprised the adulterous pair in an upstairs chamber when Mrs Fainall was out in Hyde Park. Mrs Marwood made them swear to secrecy, but they took an oath on a book of poems rather than the Bible, so Foible feels it isn't binding.

Act V

Mincing interrupts them to say that Millamant wishes to speak to Foible. She informs them that Mirabell has set Waitwell free, and that Fainall is with Lady Wishfort demanding Millamant's money, and threatening to divorce her daughter if he does not get it.

Millamant and Mirabell, knowing of Fainall's move, have sent for Sir Wilfull, claiming that Millamant will marry him in obedience to Lady Wishfort, in order to keep her fortune. Mrs Fainall bids Foible tell Mincing that she must prepare to be a witness to the Fainall-Marwood affair when the moment comes. Both servants readily agree.

Lady Wishfort praises Mrs Marwood for acting as intermediary in her negotiations with Fainall. Mrs Fainall defends her honour and at her suggestion that Fainall and Mrs Marwood are the real villains, Mrs Marwood feigns offence and offers to withdraw. Mrs Fainall insists she is innocent and departs. Lady Wishfort is unsure who to believe, and recalls her daughter's exceptionally chaste upbringing.

- 121 **intercessor** person who pleads on someone's behalf (usually a priest, praying for someone's soul).
- 122 **compound for** achieve a settlement over.
- 125 **groves** small clearings in a wood. Lady Wishfort uses images common in pastoral poetry, which idealized country life.
- 141 **naught** wicked, immoral.
  sophisticated corrupted.
- 143 **caprices** whims
  cuckoldoms adulteries.
- 153 **temper** moderation.
- 166 **leech** bloodsucking worm used in medicine to take blood from patients.
- 167 **bodkin** needle (trifling object).
- 168 **brass counter** worthless imitation coin, such as used in card games.
  composition settlement, restitution.
- 169 **aspersions** damaging accusations.
- 174 **unexceptionable** exemplary.
- 180 **though but in coats** even though he wore long clothes (like a baby).

Notes

    181 **babies**   dolls.

183–4 **made a shift to put upon her for a woman**   contrived to pass off as a woman in front of her.

    185 **going in her fifteen**   approaching 15.

Fainall and Mrs Marwood make a counter move (186–299)

Lady Wishfort calls for proof of the charges against her daughter. In response Mrs Marwood paints a terrifying picture of how a court of law and the press might handle the affair. Lady Wishfort, in fear for her reputation, decides to part with all her wealth, and Millamant's too.

Fainall joins them and introduces fresh terms. Lady Wishfort may continue to live in comfort during her lifetime as long as she does not marry, and Mrs Fainall is to settle upon him all her remaining fortune. He also justifies his claim to Millamant's money; she has, he says, disobeyed Lady Wishfort by refusing Sir Wilfull and agreeing to marry Mirabell. Fainall leaves to fetch a document for Lady Wishfort to sign.

She is left to bewail her daughter's behaviour. We learn that Mrs Fainall's first husband was chosen by her mother, and she feels that the second (Fainall) was her daughter's folly, but we know there is more to that story.

    189 **catechized**   taught religious doctrine and values.

    196 **excommunication**   expulsion from the Church, and risk of damnation.

    202 **worried**   mauled, savaged (like a hunted animal).

    203 ***Oyez***   'Hear ye', the call of a court officer at the start of proceedings.

    205 **quoif**   white lawyer's cap.
           infamy   shame.

206–7 **legal punsters and quibblers by the statute**   lawyers who pick on fine points of the law for debate.

    207 **jest**   subject of ridicule.

Act V

- 209 **Doomsday Book** the record of a survey of land and property rights carried out in 1085–6, during the reign of William the Conqueror.
  discompose the gravity disturb the solemnity.
- 210 **naughty interrogatories** wicked, degrading questions.
- 212 **fidges** fidgets.
- 213 **cantharides** dried Spanish beetle, used as a diuretic and an aphrodisiac.
- 214 **cow-itch** cowage, a plant covered in stinging hairs.
- 216–17 **revellers of the Temple** students of law, enjoying a good time.
- 217 **'prentices at a conventicle** Apprentices were required to keep notes of sermons they attended for their masters.
- 218 **in commons** in the dining hall.
- 226 **flounder-man** seller of flounders (flat fish).
  cries shouts out (offering to sell).
- 259 **apothecary** supplier of medical cures.
- 263 **Muscovite** i.e. cruel (Russians were reputed to be wife beaters).
- 264 **his Czarish majesty's retinue** The Russian Czar Peter the Great's courtiers accompanied him on a visit to England in 1698. They stayed as guests of the king at Sayes Court, Deptford for three months and did considerable damage to the house and gardens.
- 278 ***non compos*** *non compos mentis*, not in his right mind (Latin), i.e. drunk.
- 282 **the instrument is drawing** the legal agreement is being prepared. There is also a pun on the drawing of a sword.
- 283 **set your hand** sign.
- 293–4 **her year was not out** A year's mourning was normal for the loss of a husband.
- 294 **Languish** This is an aptronym (see Glossary) suggesting lethargy.
- 296 **she is matched now with a witness** she has met her match now and no mistake.
- 298 **be confiscated at this rebel rate** have my property taken from me at a rate as high as that demanded of traitors.
- 299 **Egyptian plagues** See the Bible, Exodus 7:14–11:10 for the ten plagues suffered by the Pharaoh of Egypt.

Notes

The Mirabell-Millamant camp take a calculated risk (300–453)

Millamant enters, accompanied by a sober and contrite Sir Wilfull. The pair say they have agreed to marry, with Mirabell as witness. Millamant has required Mirabell to appear in person to give up his claim to her in front of Lady Wishfort. Sir Wilfull and Mirabell are to travel together after the wedding. With this show of obedience, the pair trust that Lady Wishfort will tolerate Mirabell's presence. Mrs Marwood is highly suspicious and leaves to make some enquiries.

Mirabell makes a fulsome and parodic (see Glossary) apology to Lady Wishfort. She accepts, provided that he hands over a signed document releasing Millamant from their agreement to marry. Mirabell has sent his servant for the document, which he says is held *with papers of concern* (390).

Fainall enters with Mrs Marwood, bringing his document for Lady Wishfort to sign, but there have been developments: Lady Wishfort can no longer sign away Millamant's *moiety* as the young woman has agreed to marry Sir Wilfull. Fainall dismisses this as a sham, much to the protestations of the assembled parties, but in any case still pursues his wife's money and Lady Wishfort's estate. In despair, Lady Wishfort calls for someone to save her and Mirabell steps forward, offering to assist her without reward. Lady Wishfort responds by promising him Millamant and *all her fortune* (447–8) if he can deliver her from Fainall's clutches.

- 303 **in disguise**   not myself, i.e. drunk.
- 314 **be a sacrifice to your repose**   give up my desires to ensure your peace of mind.
- 325 **Gorgon**   in Greek mythology, a female monster who could turn to stone anyone who looked at her.
- 328 **Then**   also, moreover.
- 336 **Pylades and Orestes**   in Greek legend, loyal friends and travelling companions.
- 350 **mum for**   say nothing about.
- 359 **suppliant**   pleader (with a religious connotation).
- 367 **an**   if.

Act V

369 **receive much prejudice** be harmed too much.
372 **venial** less serious, easily forgiven.
378 **o' the Quorum** a Justice of the Peace.
382 **mouth-glue** glue that becomes sticky when moistened by the tongue; i.e. the contract is only a spoken agreement.
398 **instrument** legal document.
408 **fox** sword.
409 **ram vellum** parchment made of sheep's hide.
410 **mittimus** arrest warrant.
410–11 **tailor's measure** tape measure.
414 **respite your valour** contain your bravery.
416 **Beefeater** guard in the Tower of London.
419–20 **as pursuant to the purport and tenor of this other covenant** in compliance with the meaning and conditions of this other agreement.
423 **bear-garden** Bear-baiting was a popular entertainment and spectators could be rowdy, fighting among themselves.
426 **hulk** ship.

Lowly witnesses, false wits and legal documents decide the outcome (454–600)

Foible, Mincing and Mrs Fainall are given leave to appear before Lady Wishfort. It takes only a few whispered words for Lady Wishfort to learn the truth about Mrs Marwood. Fainall turns his anger on his wife, but she is defiant. Lady Wishfort fears this revelation is not going to be enough to defeat Fainall, and Mirabell begs leave to call a final witness. Waitwell enters, carrying the *black box* (492). Petulant and Witwoud are also at hand, having slept off their drunkenness.

Mirabell prompts them to recall that they once witnessed a document for him. He explains that when Mrs Fainall was widowed and could act independently, she entrusted him with her entire fortune by signing a *deed... in trust* (528). Its earlier date invalidates Fainall's document. In a fury he turns on his wife, who is defended by Sir Wilfull. Fainall and Mrs Marwood leave separately in haste and fury.

Notes

All the players with the exception of these two villains are assembled for the play's final scene. There is the making of amends, and pleasure all round as Lady Wishfort forgives Waitwell and Foible. Sir Wilfull's agreement to marry Millamant is revealed as a pretence, and he confirms his travel plans. He invites Witwoud and Petulant to join him, but cannot get a sensible response from either.

Lady Wishfort gives her blessing to the match between Mirabell and Millamant. Sir Wilfull calls for a dance. The celebration is halted by Lady Wishfort, who airs one last concern – that Fainall's violence has yet to spend itself. Mirabell reasons that Fainall is now so short of funds he will have to be better behaved towards his wife. In handing over the *deed of trust* (595) to Mrs Fainall he hopes to empower mother and daughter to live more easily with the play's villain.

458 **the way of the world** Fainall is again late in recognizing that the discrepancy between appearance and reality, typical of high society, is about to be exposed. See III.599–600 and 535 below.
465 **profligate** wasteful.
468 **mercenary** She implies they have been paid to speak against her.
471 **Messalina's poems** Mincing may mean a miscellany (unrelated collection) of poems. The Roman Empress Messalina (who died in 48 CE) was the wife of the Emperor Claudius, and had a reputation for greed, cruelty and sexual depravity.
484 **groat** coin of small value.
490 What do you think is Lady Wishfort's tone in the first half of this line? What about the second half?
501–2 **Whose hand's out?** who's losing at cards? The answer is Fainall, who has no more trumps to play.
503–4 What is the effect of this remark?
508 **mark** This implies that Petulant cannot write.
534 **Confusion** This is Fainall's moment of anagnorisis (see Glossary), when he suddenly discovers the truth of his situation.
535 **the way of the world** Mirabell has the last word with this telling phrase (it has been twice spoken by Fainall). Again the phrase refers to the discrepancy between appearances and an

underlying reality, one that Mirabell has mastered. See III.599–600 and 458 above.
539–40 **make your bear-garden flourish somewhere else**   See 423–4.

Epilogue

The epilogue was spoken by Anne Bracegirdle. She looks ahead to how critics will attack the play and bids them remember how hard it is to please everyone. Bad writers and disaffected critics, hostile to a play, can usually be found crowding out the pit. Some believe the characters are meant to represent real people and spend their efforts trying to name them. By their ill will, they threaten to turn satire into libel. She trusts those critics recognize themselves as contributing to the depiction of fools. The truth is that the characters are a blend of many people observed by the playwright.

- 17 **scurrilous**   mischievous.
- 20 **copied face**   i.e. person on whom a character is based.
- 21 **glosses**   interpretations.
- 22 **libel**   false, damaging representation.
- 30 **abstracted**   particular.
- 36 *belles assemblées*   distinguished gatherings (French).
  coquettes and beaux   young, flirtatious women and handsome men of the town.

Interpretations

Restoration comedy

Restoration comedy was written and performed from about 1660 to 1710. Its fortunes were closely aligned to the nation's political struggles, as it celebrated the values of the Stuart court. Its finest achievements came in the 1670s with *The Country Wife* (1675) by William Wycherley, and *The Man of Mode* (1676) by George Etherege.

The figure of the 'rake' hero (see Glossary page 224) was an invention of Restoration comedy. The type reflected positively on the court, where rakish behaviour (seductive, witty, and arrogant) was much admired. Mirabell and Fainall are variations on the rake figure adapted for the post-1688 worldview (see page 9).

Cynicism, satire, sexual explicitness and intricate plots were important features of Restoration comedy. These popular plays sustained a topical commentary on class, desire and the marriage market. Some made comic intrigue their focus, while for others it was greed, gulling (see Glossary) and adultery. A mixing of styles was common; scenes of sophisticated sparring between young lovers might be juxtaposed to burlesque (see Glossary) subplots featuring amorous old fools. The Puritans, who had helped bring Oliver Cromwell to power after the Civil War in 1653, were now on the losing side, making them easy prey. They were the butt of many jokes; see, for example, Aphra Behn's creation Blunt in *The Rover* (1677).

'Comedy of manners' plays were a popular sub-genre of Restoration comedy. They depicted the fashionable, sophisticated codes of behaviour of the aristocracy. Appearance and the maintenance of reputation were all; truth and morality came a long way behind. Plots typically hinged on characters driven by lust and greed whose goal was to negotiate the most lucrative deal in the marriage market. Their moral disorder was disguised by their cleverness with language and their powers to seduce.

These plays featured two character types: attractive young aristocrats who manipulated the codes of fashionable behaviour; and their rivals, middle-class pretenders who wished to appear fashionable and worldly but were exposed as fools operating out of their depth.

The plots often featured two pairs of contrasting lovers. There was the 'gay couple', like Mirabell and Millamant, who would banter and tease their way to a choice of marriage partner. Playwrights explored the complexities of commitment through such characters, while the audience enjoyed the spectacle of pleasure deferred. In contrast was the faithful but unexciting pair whose path to marriage was hindered by outside forces. Whatever the lovers' journey, the plots usually ended with a celebration of marriage.

Restoration comedy was generally clear in its understanding of right and wrong behaviour. Congreve, however, is more uncertain and ambiguous, as his nuanced use of these conventions shows.

From the mid-1690s onwards, playwrights like him were setting a softer, more tempered tone. Their work now had to appeal to a wider audience, one with more women and a greater social mix. These audiences were more likely to disapprove of cynicism, rakish behaviour and sexual explicitness. Marriage, rather than courtship and adultery, became the focus of intrigue. The plight of Mrs Fainall was quite new, as was Mrs Marwood, with her *month's mind* (III.209). The false wit Sir Wilfull turns out to be kind and sensible, and the arch-schemer Mirabell has a moral conscience.

In *The Way of the World* Congreve masters the conventions of Restoration comedy and subverts them by the use of nuance and by questioning accepted forms and values. He shows his audience just how much scheming, will-power and egotism are needed to defeat the Fainalls and Mrs Marwoods of his world. He introduces a new concern with the problem of experiencing genuine emotion while keeping to the rules of decorum. He fashions this as burlesque in the case of Lady Wishfort, as melodrama with respect to Mrs Marwood, and as psychological realism in Millamant and Mrs Fainall.

Restoration comedy revelled in an awareness of its own theatricality. Congreve also enjoyed the witty conceit (see Glossary) that reality can be theatrical and theatre can be realistic (V.503–504).

Interpretations

Activity

Through a close reading of the play's opening scene (1–104), discuss the ways in which Congreve introduces themes and dramatic conflict in *The Way of the World*.

Discussion

A mock conflict between Mirabell and Fainall in the form of a game of cards has just ended as the play begins. Fainall has enjoyed a winning run; Mirabell concedes that he is *a fortunate man* (1) and submissively offers to *play on to entertain* him (3). By the end of the play and after a real conflict of interests where important values are at stake, the situation will be totally reversed. Fainall's luck and wealth will have run out, and Mirabell will have asserted his power over all the players.

In the opening exchange we see that Fainall's win is neither as conclusive nor as satisfying as he would like, and within the complex reasons for this there are clues to the play's intrigue, and his eventual defeat at the hands of Mirabell. Well might he ask: *Have we done?* (2). Mirabell's answer, *What you please* (3), implies that the action cannot be over until Fainall's unbridled appetite and will are defeated; that is going to *entertain* (3) us rather than him.

Fainall's offer to give Mirabell his *revenge another time* (4) will be remembered later in the play when his urbane use of the hyperbole *revenge* (see Glossary) comes to signify something far closer to its literal meaning. The audience will also have to wait to appreciate the irony of the moral reversals he describes – that a man who is a good loser is not worth beating, and a woman who does not value the loss of her *reputation* (10) is not worth seducing. Fainall will be the worst of losers, and well worth beating; and he will discover that his wife had already lost her reputation when she came to him as a bride.

Revenge, play, gamester, fortune, reputation, cabal, breed, honour – with these words Congreve signposts the play's themes. What isn't disclosed is just as interesting. Mirabell hides his trump card, the *deed of trust* (V.595). Fainall cannot win outright because Mirabell has been entrusted with *Pam* (III.622, see Note page 149) – Mrs Fainall's allegiance and fortune, safeguarded in law.

Gambling and playing will be Congreve's metaphors for the way the world works when love, inheritance and Whig ideals play for the

168

Restoration comedy

highest stakes. All the characters are players: some play a solo hand like Millamant; some like Fainall and Mrs Marwood play doubles; some switch partners like Lady Wishfort; and it takes a team effort to outface the villains in Act V. In the play's closing moments Petulant asks: *Whose hand's out?* (V.501–502) and Witwoud observes: *are you all got together, like players at the end of the last act?* (503–504). They are discovered *rubbing their eyes; just risen from sleep* (497–498) as if awaking from a dream, the illusion that has been the play's time on the stage.

Oaths, witnesses, parchments, wills and black boxes – all are reassuring signs that the law is working, and are absent from the opening scene. In the right hands, the law will work like providence to modify the random and detrimental effects of gambling. Its disclosure as a key force in the drama will be gradual but unstoppable.

Fainall attempts to read Mirabell's behaviour (5–6, 13–14, 17–21, 81–84, 90–95) in order to probe his emotions and stir up discontent about love and money. He sets the style for the way characters will interact with each other. It is an unsettling, intimidating way to operate, but essential in establishing the upper hand in a society where people mask their true feelings.

In Mirabell's description of the ageing Lady Wishfort (58–78), Congreve offers us a classic type from Restoration comedy. She heads a cabal of women and *publishes her detestation of mankind* (59–60). In the course of the play Congreve returns to this theme, and women as dissimilar as Mrs Fainall and Mrs Marwood contribute to it. They all entertain a fantasy – albeit unstable, deniable and sometimes ridiculous – of female solidarity as a refuge from a male-dominated world (II.1–49, V.123–130).

The opening scene tells us this drama will be played out between a small, select group of people, connected by acquaintance, class, marriage, blood and desire. Friendship is not a player. We get an unusually detailed glimpse of a set of circumstances that are highly relevant to the coming action, but not presented on stage. The *cabal night* (49), Mrs Marwood's disclosure of Mirabell's *sham addresses* (63) to Lady Wishfort, Mirabell's snubbing by Millamant and the cabal (27–39), Sir Jonathan Wishfort's will (44–45), Mirabell's rejection of Mrs Marwood's advances (81–89), and the card game itself – all these events have preceded the start of the play.

Interpretations

Eighteenth-century engraving showing 'coffee-house politicians' discussing the latest events

Spectacle and intimacy: Inside a 'tennis court theatre'

The Way of the World had its première at Lincoln's Inn Fields in a building that was once Lisle's Tennis Court. It had opened for real tennis (an earlier form of the modern game) in 1656. After refurbishment it served as a theatre from 1695 to 1705, and three of Congreve's five plays were staged there. By 1714 the building had been demolished. Today an extension of the Royal College of Surgeons, built in 1848, occupies the site. Restoration theatres that had been tennis courts were small and intimate inside. Here are some facts and figures about them.
- They could accommodate an audience of between 400 and 600 people.

Spectacle and intimacy: Inside a 'tennis court theatre'

- The interior measured about 75 by 30 feet, the stage was 34 by 20 feet and had a proscenium arch. The forestage, where most of the acting took place, jutted out from the curtain line by about 20 feet into the pit. There were access doors for the actors on either side.
- Most scene-shifting took place behind the proscenium arch.
- The central seating area, the pit, was filled with backless benches and surrounded on three sides by stepped seating.
- There was a gallery level offering the cheapest seats.
- In this small space, actors could project their voices easily, paying attention to variety and range of tone. This encouraged them to deliver their lines faster than would be the practice in modern theatre.
- The stage and auditorium were brightly lit by candles and lamps hanging in chandeliers from the ceiling and walls.
- Plays usually ran for between eight and ten performances, with profits from the third night going to the playwright.

Scenic effects representing the *chocolate-house*, *St James's Park* and *Lady Wishfort's House* would have been painted on flats, wings and backdrops. Machines were used to move the flats into place along three or four grooves on either side of the stage floor. The wings were arranged on the slant, and fixed in position. From the auditorium they appeared to recede upstage towards a vanishing point, creating an illusion of depth. By closing the space between the moveable flats, a shallower stage space could be created.

Actors did not walk out of their imaginary location once their dialogue had ended. A pair of flats could be moved to reveal another pair behind, to relocate them where they stood. This may have happened to take Mirabell from the promenades in *St James's Park* to *Rosamond's Pond* (II.497–501) and Lady Wishfort from her drunken guests to the seduction couch in her dressing room (IV.458). The spaces between flats were large enough to allow room for furniture such as her dressing table (III.1 sd) and *couch* (IV.23).

Flexible settings meant that Congreve could divide his acts into many short scenes without slowing the pace. A simple technique

Interpretations

he uses is to time exits to coincide with entrances (II.251, III.64, 174, 214, 269, IV.41, V.116, 345). Three acts of the play may be set in *Lady Wishfort's House* but the impression is one of multiple rooms with easy access between them – a true reflection of upper-class houses of the period.

Congreve makes good use of a large acting space that could easily have accommodated the play's dances (IV.536, V.584). Characters are discussed before and as they appear (I.207–230, 274–371) and he provides dialogue to accompany their walk to the forestage (II.78–86, 321–326). He often requires characters to be on stage together but grouped separately, a device essential for intrigue (I.450–483, III.421–449, 583–596, V.455–463).

Congreve's characters are unencumbered by props: cards, money, a bottle of brandy, a china cup, a letter, a black box and two parchments make the full complement. Sir Wilfull's *country riding habit* and *boots* (III.421 sd, 589) are the only significant costume requirement. All gentlemen characters would have worn swords (V.408–12, 538).

For ambitious young actors, a substantial period of training was needed. Most parts required them to play aristocrats, which meant intensive training in elocution, deportment and fashionable manners. In the late seventeenth century, the upper classes identified themselves by strict codes of etiquette, which had to be mastered to make the play world believable to the audience. *The Way of the World* requires familiarity with hats, fans and periwigs. There are many encounters where extravagant bows and curtseys need to be convincing: see II.87–94, III.566–575, IV.94–96, 140–142, V.344–345, 352.

An acting style that was considered realistic was used for comedies, although a modern audience would not recognize it as such. Today, we value naturalism and psychological realism in actors. The Restoration audience expected a varied but prescribed use of voice, gesture and movement. Actors out on the forestage were subject to the intense scrutiny of the pit. The scene between Fainall and Mrs Marwood in which he imprisons her hands and she dares him to *Break* them (II.227), vowing she would *leave 'em to get loose* (228), may well have been outside their experience of comedy.

Who were Congreve's audience?

By 1700 theatre had become a wholly commercial enterprise, no longer patronized by the court. King William had a passion for military campaigns; Queen Mary was rather reclusive and inclined to disapprove of acting. They showed little interest in theatre except for wishing to control its potential for profanity and vice.

City merchants, their wives and servants, a substantial middle class and a vocal group of critics now outnumbered the aristocracy at the theatre. Some had strong Puritan loyalties and it was easy to trigger their suspicions of theatre's power to corrupt. Theatre admission charges were high relative to income, but that did not deter Londoners from making theatre a popular leisure pursuit.

Plays needed to appeal to this broad audience and make a profit. Performances began between five and six in the evening, to accommodate people who worked for a living. Interludes with farcical afterpieces (see Glossary), singing, dancing, acrobatics and pantomime were gradually added to the bill to cater for wide tastes and short attention spans.

To be considered a commercial success, a play needed to achieve full houses for just ten consecutive performances; a change of programme was then expected. The repertoire always needed new plays, but they were rarely successful if they strayed too far from what the audience knew and liked.

Audiences were highly opinionated and conservative in their tastes; they relished the familiar, the tried and tested. They knew the repertoire, the actors and the best parts. They were not bored by predictable plots and stereotyped characters – greater familiarity meant a greater level of spectator pleasure. Night scenes of danger and threat, chases, mistaken identity, songs, letters and exhibitions of sword-play were all well-loved and warmly anticipated pleasures.

Congreve employs very few of these diversions in *The Way of the World*. His stage directions make little specific use of asides (III.79, 480, IV.615, V.393), although there is potential for more in performance (see, for example, II.325, III.34–36, 448–449, IV.102).

Interpretations

Audiences loved this simple technique, where characters addressed them directly from the forestage, taking them into their confidence. Congreve chose to probe and unsettle his audience rather than give too much away. His play demanded active listening, reflection and interpretation. This would have demanded much of an audience who came to the theatre to see and be seen and who valued socializing with others, including the actors, above attending to the play.

Activity

In what ways might seeing *The Way of the World* for the first time pose a particular challenge?

Discussion

The Way of the World was, to take the pessimistic view, a failure that marked the end of Congreve's career as a playwright. It is now considered his masterpiece but is rarely performed, and is still considered a challenge for directors, actors and audiences. Why is this?
- Does Congreve deliberately disorientate us at the start of the play? His fragmentary clues and hints are insufficient to make firm judgements about the characters (I.11–12, 46–47, 65–66, 78–80, 85–89, 144–146). He expects us to retain disparate pieces of the jigsaw without showing how they fit together. He denies his audience a main source of pleasure – a privileged position in relation to the plot.
- The attentiveness of the audience might not be high at the start of the play, yet important information is delivered in the opening minutes. The Wishfort family tree is complicated, and those wishing to graft themselves to it have complex motives. The necessary exposition can be tedious and undramatic. Consider how Fainall might deliver these lines: *he is half-brother to this Witwoud by a former wife, who was sister to my Lady Wishfort, my wife's mother* (I.188–190). Is Congreve parodying the rules of exposition and wittily drawing attention to the burdens of the technique? Are the precise details of the characters' relationships really necessary to appreciate the play's themes and concerns?

Who were Congreve's audience?

- The action begins *in media res* (Latin for 'in the middle of things'). In exchange for the momentary excitement this brings, Congreve has to provide a considerable 'back story' (see Glossary). We hear about recent events that are so rich and varied they are in danger of stealing the show: *sham addresses* to a rich widow, a will with conditions unfavourable to love, a vengeful woman, adultery, strange behaviour at a cabal night, a Duke's Place marriage. Is this what we would really like to see in order to entertain us? If so, Congreve would have to write a much longer play, and besides, melodrama is not central to his concerns.
- Audiences are usually quick to align themselves with a play's hero and to follow his progress. How easy is it for them to decide where to invest their loyalties? Are the clues too subtle to pick up? No character is immediately likeable. Mirabell is not named until line 90, and the consequences of his rakish past may be too evident to allow him to be the play's moral beacon. As Fainall and Mirabell, Congreve cast the actors Thomas Betterton and John Verbruggen (see pages 178 and 183) against type, adding to the uncertainty. Is there too long a delay before the entrances of Millamant (who represents beauty, verve, and whimsy), Lady Wishfort (a humours character, burlesque) and Sir Wilfull (benevolent country fool)? These three enliven the play considerably.
- Is there too little action in the first four acts and too much in Act V?

The play also has plot points that may be considered stumbling blocks, or alternatively may pass successfully in performance.
- Is Mirabell's pretence to be Lady Wishfort's lover just a contrivance to prolong comic mishap? It is hardly worthy of his clever, strategic mind and involves a degree of farce out of keeping with his character. Exposure is inevitable if his ruse is to succeed, yet exposure means failure. Is there an inbuilt lack of logic here that does not ring true?
- There is a gap separating the circumstances at the end of Act IV from those at the beginning of Act V. This requires yet more catching up from an audience who would be expecting a smooth dénouement (see Glossary) at this point. Once more, dramatic

Interpretations

> events happen off stage and have to be related through dialogue (V.60–79, 98–110).
>
> - By V.107 it is clear that Mirabell is aware of Fainall's plot against Lady Wishfort. Why doesn't he show his trump card at that point? Is it that he relishes showmanship (V.352–364, 390–392, 450–453, 488–537) and values his performance above putting everyone at ease? In practical terms, the play could otherwise end too soon. But might an audience feel his *black box* was all a sleight of hand too far? Does it weaken the play's overall design to need a *deus ex machina* (see Glossary) to bring closure?

Sources and literary references for *The Way of the World*

Congreve had an excellent classical education. He translated the Roman playwrights Plautus and Terence, admiring their comedy of manners style. Their plays featured elaborate plots and stock characters, notably gullible masters duped by trickster servants. Greedy legacy-hunters, family disputes and generational conflict were common themes. Congreve considered them worth emulating when he began to write for the London stage.

He was also influenced by the Elizabethans, whose plays – though adapted and bowdlerized – were never out of the repertory. Congreve's use of the theory of humours (dominant traits of personality, see Glossary) to define characters – such as Lady Wishfort's lust and Fainall's hypocrisy – is indebted to plays such as Ben Jonson's *Every Man in his Humour* (1598). Jonson used aptronyms (see Glossary) to name his characters, a simple technique that Congreve adopted in *The Way of the World*. Lady Wishfort, Sir Wilfull and Witwoud all have antecedents in Jonson's plays, but Congreve gave them greater complexity and humanity. Shakespeare's gay couple (see Glossary) Benedick and Beatrice, in *Much Ado About Nothing* (1598), were much admired and imitated in Restoration comedy, and may have been a source for Mirabell and Millamant (see Appendix 3 page 233).

Sources and literary references for The Way of the World

Irish playwright Thomas Southerne (1660–1746) was one of Congreve's friends and mentors. His comedy *The Maid's Last Prayer* (1693) may have been influential. Southerne also uses the gambling metaphor, and offers a serious portrayal of the plight of women trapped in unsatisfactory marriages to rakes. His plots expose the unequal relationship between husbands and wives, and he satirizes the moral decay of contemporary society.

The French playwright Molière (1622–1673) was much admired and imitated for his comedy of manners style. He developed characters that were more complex and subtle than was thought possible for the genre. He also broke new ground by using comedy to satirize the ruling classes. Congreve's risky decision to delay the first appearance of major women characters may have been suggested by Molière's similar strategy in *Le Misanthrope* (1666).

The proviso scene has been traced to a variety of English and French sources by Kathleen M. Lynch in *The Social Mode of Restoration Comedy* (1926). The idea was first used by Dryden in *Secret Love, or The Maiden Queen* (1667).

Poets Edmund Waller and Sir John Suckling (see Notes to IV.50–51, 61, 92–93) toy with opposing views of how to play the game of love; Millamant recites fragments of their poems to test her suitors. Sir Wilfull fails Millamant outright, but Mirabell, by completing the quotation *Like Daphne she as lovely and as coy* (IV.145), shows that he is worthy of her. He completes her line as well as he complements her character, showing a sensitive understanding of how the poem speaks to her predicament.

Congreve expected his audience to know Waller's poem *The Story of Phoebus and Daphne, Applied*. He presents Millamant as a cultured, educated woman gripped by a dilemma about love. Waller borrowed his narrative from the Roman poet Ovid's *Metamorphoses*. Ovid dramatized power relationships between the sexes by telling stories of male gods in sexual pursuit of unwilling nymphs and girls. They pay a high price for being the object of male lust: against their will, they are transformed, transfixed and renamed as the only means of escape.

Waller's poem implies a comparison between the mythical Apollo

Interpretations

and Daphne, and Thyrsis and Sacharissa, a contemporary couple. Pursuit rather than love is at the centre of their relationships. Daphne is concerned to guard her virginity; Sacharissa remains indifferent to her pursuer's love. Waller notes that because the rejected Thyrsis sang of his love, his song attracted admiration. The song does not resolve the problem of unrequited love but allows Thyrsis to find some sort of consolation elsewhere.

Millamant hopes for a better outcome than this for herself. She contrives to keep Mirabell so interested in the chase that he does not take consolation in the arms of the likes of Mrs Marwood, who heeds his 'song' more readily. She loves him and intends to accept him, but constructs the chase as a bargaining tool to win concessions for herself and time to contemplate the loss of her independence.

The sentiments in Suckling's *Song, I prithee spare me, gentle boy* (IV.92) may be lost on Sir Wilfull, but an audience familiar with the poem would have found it very informative of Millamant's state of mind. She has a heart that is, in the words of the song, 'grown/ Sullen and wise', which 'flies only where't can kill'. This is just as well, as men 'scarce say grace... but seek another place'.

The other poem of Suckling's that Millamant cites, *There never yet was woman made* (IV.50), is an exploration, quite cynical and resigned in tone, of the sexually possessive nature of love. It has explicit sexual imagery, using the metaphor of bees and flowers to represent men and women: 'the gallant elsewhere loads his thigh', and 'One lights, one tastes, gets in, gets out'. We can understand Millamant's concerns that sexual desire, once satisfied, might be fleeting, and women will fare the worse for it.

Casting and characters

Mirabell

John Verbruggen, famous for playing fine gentlemen, wits and rakes, created the role of Mirabell. An energetic, well-built actor, he had a good voice and an open, natural style. He was often given prologues to speak, which is an indication of his popularity with audiences. He and Thomas Betterton (see page 183) played opposite each other many times and were rivals on and off stage.

Mirabell, whose name suggests 'wonder' or 'miracle', has a major impact on the house of Wishfort. He humiliates the mother, pursues the heiress, seduces and marries off the daughter, and outwits the son-in-law. Yet each of these actions has another side and can be read in a positive light. His authority and self-confidence make him attractive and influential to everyone in the play, whether they are of high or low status. Does he use these advantages well, exercising power responsibly as a hero should? He certainly puts his reading of character to good effect. He plays on all Lady Wishfort's weaknesses – lust, vanity, hypocrisy, fear of scandal – in the trap he sets for her. Perhaps he foresees that Fainall will turn villain and so protects his ex-mistress, her relatives, and ultimately his own assets, against him.

Characters flock to his aid when his plots falter: Foible and Mincing testify to Mrs Marwood's adultery (V.454–465); Sir Wilfull selflessly pretends to have secured Millamant's hand in marriage (309–310); together, Sir Wilfull and Millamant persuade Lady Wishfort to allow Mirabell to enter the place where key events are unfolding (321–341). The trust that others place in him finds its most solemn, resonant expression when Mirabell recalls how Mrs Fainall acted upon *the wholesome advice of friends and of sages learned in the laws of this land* (526–527). With these words, in a moment of great theatricality, he produces the *deed of trust*.

After featuring strongly in Acts I and II Mirabell is absent from Act III, plays only the proviso scene in Act IV and re-appears to deliver the *coup de grâce* (decisive stroke) in the final act. However, numerous comments and anecdotes about him remind the audience of his continuing influence – see, for example, III.46–48, 76–134, 183–210, 229–236, 299–371, 610–616.

Mirabell is Congreve's hero for the new age, his answer to the Stuart court's love of *élan* (vigour and style). As a true wit he is incisive and worldly but also concerned with sobriety and proper

Interpretations

behaviour (I.77–78, 85–89, 140–143, 522–531, II.317–320, 435–438, 461–463, 531–534). He is consistently well mannered, tactful and composed. He knows more about the ways of the world than any other character and works to advance the interests of all who are deserving of his protection.

For more discussion of Mirabell see pages 168, 181, 185–186.

Millamant

Anne Bracegirdle created the role of Millamant, which quickly became a coveted star part.

Millamant, whose name means 'a thousand loves', is always on the move and continually flustered as she is pursued by a medley of suitors. She encourages the attentions of the false wits to disguise her love for Mirabell. She cannot turn down Sir Wilfull without forfeiting half of her fortune, so she must deter him from proposing without declining his company. Equally, she needs to encourage Mirabell's interest but delay his proposal. She needs time to consider what is (in the seventeenth century) by far the most momentous decision of any woman's life.

She is actively – frantically, even – engrossed in the prospect of marriage in a world where cynical, negative views of the institution are commonplace (I.111–117, 171–173, 250–263, II.53–64, 87–97, 108–116, 211–216, 254–256, 350–351, III.603–606). She has created a feminine persona that is coquettish, whimsical and illogical (II.358–373) to disguise her intelligence and seriousness. Her destiny as a beautiful heiress is to marry, produce children, grow old and die (384–405). She is not daunted by these life stages as she is busy securing the best journey for herself – one that will allow her some personal freedoms.

Millamant's broken sentences, indecisiveness, cruelty and sudden flights can be understood in terms of the perverse circumstances of her life (II.354–355, 376–379, 454–456, 469–476, III.273–279, IV.273–279). She is rich yet economically dependent, she is an orphan in the power of an aunt, her cousin is her lover's ex-mistress, her aunt's closest friend is jealous and hostile. She allows herself some revenge

William Hogarth's depiction of marriage negotiations in *The Marriage Settlement*, c. 1743

and can be teasing and even spiteful to her rivals (II.398–399, 422, III.342–371, IV.62–64, 273–286).

For more discussion of Millamant see pages 193–194.

Activity

What is at stake in the proviso scene?

Discussion

The proviso scene is framed by Sir Wilfull's and Petulant's farcical proposals to Millamant (IV.126–139, 325–327). It begins with a reference to the problematic Apollo and Daphne myth and ends with the long-suffering Mrs Fainall witnessing the lovers' commitment formally (270–272) and emotionally (303–304). Mirabell thinks Millamant has locked the door and interprets this as he pleases, but it is actually Mrs Fainall's doing. By these means, Congreve presents this as a moment of hope in an imperfect world.

Mirabell is the more realistic of the lovers when he declares that an honourable chase must always give way to matrimony, and that its

Interpretations

pleasures cannot be sustained indefinitely without diminishment. He freely anticipates the sexual pleasures marriage will bring (172–174, 182), but what is in store for Millamant? She is fond of the freedom and privacy of *solitude, contemplation,* and *morning thoughts, agreeable wakings, indolent slumbers* (176–178). She wishes to safeguard her domestic space: her *bed* (181), *dressing-room, closet,* and *tea-table,* where she requires the power to grant permission to approach and a knock before entering (210–215). We have seen Millamant flustered and besieged in public places and can sympathize with her needs. She may also believe that distancing herself from her husband might help to maintain her mystique when courtship gives way to marriage.

She expects freedom of association, correspondence and discourse, without being guided, supervised and censored by a husband. Congreve is making clear connections here between private and political rights, but note how far Mirabell modifies her demands.

Millamant's dislike of the pet names associated with married love is her way of escaping social definition. She shows her contempt for the city's obsession with the form over the content of relationships, which is most apparent in the Fainalls' public greeting (II.87–90). She won't keep up appearances to prop up her reputation.

When Mirabell speaks, he adds a legal framework (224, 235, 242, 244). He fears the female cabal – the secrecy, game-playing and masking that the powerless resort to. He expresses a masculine impatience with women's trivia, especially cosmetics. But he shows a serious concern with masking here; he connects it with presenting a face to the world using trickery, something he associates with women and fops (see Glossary).

There is nothing more personal to a woman's body than pregnancy and birth. Many characters make comically grotesque references to the subject (I.61–62, 73–75, III.21–23, 303–305, IV.408–411, V.36), but only Mirabell marries the grotesque with the real. His observation that a woman could *make me the father to a crooked billet* (252–253) is a striking reminder of the play's argument that personal freedoms should be modified by responsibility to others and ultimately the state. The image of the male child in the womb is one of confinement, dependence and freedom from social classification. In a state of nature he is in danger of being damaged by irresponsible behaviour and self-interest before he is even born. But what is there for Millamant when *breeding* replaces sexual pleasure? The word suggests serial periods of confinement wearing loose garments. Without the customary *strait-lacing*, she would be unable to go out into society.

Mirabell has more to say, introducing the language of politics, nationhood and war. Congreve sees that the personal struggle to live a full and honest married life is bound up with good governance and a strong national identity. Mirabell adds several provisos to Millamant's request to reign over her tea-table. He frames the domestic world in terms of *dominion, province, prerogative, auxiliaries, native* and *foreign* (253–262) because its practices and values should be at one with those of the nation. He believes that a woman overstepping the mark into a man's realm is as alien to English ways as *foreign forces* (261–262) on English soil. He directs his wit away from urbane generalizations to practical things that really matter. This probing of the realities of married life by wit was something new in comedy.

Millamant interrupts Mirabell several times, but rather ineffectually, coquettishly picking away at the margins (234, 246, 249, 268–269). She is a little too concerned with decorum; does she miss the chance to contest the onslaught? Why doesn't she object to the strong vocabulary of prohibition in his speech: *denounce, exceed not, restrain yourself, on no account, I banish, I allow* (250–266)? Or does she think he is parodying the domestic tyrant, who turns out to have dominion only over masks, fans and ratifia? The important thing to consider is not so much his manner as the detail of what he agrees to and what he forbids. He is wary of her powers of discourse, for example, and demands that she confine her conversation to trivial matters associated with women.

He is witty, but she is earnest, having more to lose. Both use amplification (see Glossary) but with different effects. She adds significant detail to clarify what she wants (202–215); he embellishes his speech with rhetorical flourishes (224–233).

She will curb her whimsy and keep her beauty for him alone; he will curb his tendency to dominate. They agree upon a contract in which each gives up power over the other and modifies individual rights in order to put unity in marriage first.

Fainall

Thomas Betterton, renowned for playing tragic heroes, created the role of Fainall. His acting style was less open, more artful than

Interpretations

Verbruggen's, as the part required. He had been a favourite actor of Charles II but by 1700 his star was waning. Was he deliberately cast as the play's great loser?

Fainall's name suggests he 'feigns all' or that he 'fain would desire all'. He is an arch-deceiver with an appetite for risk, seduction and high spending.

The Fainalls' marriage exemplifies all that is wrong with the institution. Each married for hidden motives; each is fully aware of the other's hatred and contempt. The affectation in the couple's behaviour as they strive to keep up appearances borders on farce (II.80–97). Are his scenes with Mrs Marwood too melodramatic to be sincere (II.151–152, 218–251)? The two argue passionately, but are they passionately in love? They are well matched, as each is driven by appetite and envy; they are unhappy and suspicious of each other, as deception is corrosive of trust.

Thomas Betterton, in a mezzotint version of a portrait by Sir Godfrey Kneller

Casting and characters

Fainall is driven to test the loyalty of others because he is a jealous and dishonest man himself. He probes Mirabell, Mrs Marwood and Mrs Fainall for signs of weakness or disloyalty. He lacks self-control while attempting to control others. He can only sustain his wasteful, indulgent lifestyle by getting his hands on women's fortunes. When he has exhausted seduction and marriage as sources of income, he resorts to threats, blackmail and finally the sword.

Activity

The rake outmoded and the rake reformed: how does Congreve compare Mirabell and Fainall?

Discussion

Congreve recast the rake figure to express his belief in the political muscle and moral vision of the Whig (liberal, see Glossary) project. In the contest between Mirabell and Fainall, the old-style rake is defeated on his own terms by a character working to a new set of values, still strongly masculine in appeal.

By giving Mirabell and Fainall some characteristics in common, Congreve suggests the complex interface between appetite and social responsibility.

- Members of the same social class, they share a taste for gambling and social intrigue.
- Both understand the discrepancy between the private self and the public role, and seek to exploit it.
- They collude in ridiculing false wits (I.182–336).
- Both value wit as an expression of their intellectual and social superiority.
- They expect marriage to bring them wealth and accept that scheming is a fair means to achieve it.
- Both make serious miscalculations in their dealings with women. Mirabell underestimates Lady Wishfort's and Mrs Marwood's desire for revenge. Fainall underestimates his wife's independence of thought and action (III.598–623).
- They accept the rule of law (V.282–287, 536–537).

Interpretations

It is their differences that determine who is the hero.
- Fainall is mercenary and deceitful with women. Mirabell is Millamant's true and constant lover.
- Mirabell is highly attractive to all the women in the play. Fainall is loathed by his wife and distrusted by his lover, to whom he is submissive.
- In witty banter they appear evenly matched, but Mirabell has the last word (I.96–99, 154–155, 213–214, 262–263). He is the deeper thinker and faster at repartee (see Glossary). Fainall's use of antithesis (see Glossary) seems mannered, as if learned by rote (I.6–10, 90–93, 209–212).
- Fainall is passionate in a needy, lustful, unreflecting way (II.224–251). Mirabell accepts the depth of his emotions once he has applied his rational mind to understanding them (I.155–170). He wants in Millamant a real woman, faults included.
- Mirabell wishes to join the Wishfort family through marriage. Fainall plots to raid the family coffers and abandon his duties as husband.
- Fainall brings chaos to the Wishfort household by making the false wits drunk and disorderly. Mirabell defends the Wishfort women and recruits its 'half-men' and country fools to his cause.
- Mirabell never uses physical force. Fainall restrains Mrs Marwood (II.224–228) and attempts to attack his wife (V.538).
- Mirabell is the more rounded character: to Waitwell and Foible, he is both arrogant aristocrat and kind master (I.109–130, II.497–536). Petulant brings out the fighting cavalier side of his character (I.411–413) and Mrs Fainall sees his calculating, pragmatic mind (II.266–278). Only in front of Millamant does his confidence falter; with her, he can be rattled (II.445–449), urbane (IV.145–149), sententious (II.415–417, 461–463) and candid (II.457–458, 467–468, 486–497).
- Mirabell's plot is underpinned by legal documents. It is part of a long-term strategy, solely of his devising and freely endorsed by others. Fainall's plot springs from greed, revenge and low self-worth. He is dominated by Mrs Marwood emotionally and intellectually, and she drives their counter plot (III.627–635, 666–676).

Mrs Fainall

The part of Arabella Fainall was created by Mrs Bowman, an actor who held shares in the new company at Lincoln's Inn Fields. Mrs Fainall is a woman more sinned against than sinning. Her mother, ex-lover, husband, cousin and 'friend' all control or make use of her to some degree. Her nature is mainly passive, but she speaks truth to power at times (II.254–256, 279–280, IV.65–66) and is instrumental in exposing the hypocrisy of Mrs Marwood (V.96–97, 112–113, 453–456).

She shows generosity of spirit in accepting Mirabell's rejection and helps him woo Millamant (II.423–425, III.192), risking her husband's wrath. She is difficult to read in the scenes when she witnesses Millamant's acceptance of Mirabell's offer of marriage (IV.77–85, 273–307), but she rallies in Act V to defend her honour and defy her husband and his mistress (V.145–147, 165–170).

See also pages 194–197.

Mrs Marwood

Congreve wrote the part of Mrs Marwood for the formidable, independent-minded Elizabeth Barry, one of the greatest and most versatile actors of the Restoration period. She had been the mistress of the notorious rake John Wilmot, Earl of Rochester (1647–1680) in the 1670s. By 1700 she was a successful businesswoman, mother of two illegitimate children and unmarried by choice. She would have brought considerable stage presence to the part of Mrs Marwood.

As Mrs Marwood's name suggests, she 'would mar' all if she could; she is an unhappy woman at the mercy of her passions. On occasions, when triggered by some personal slight, she reveals a deeper vision that is full of disgust for the world (II.240–241, III.225–228).

She is quick to seek revenge when threatened (II.193–194), but derives neither happiness nor peace of mind from her actions. She is full of contradictions, fed by dissatisfaction and a lack of moral certainty (compare II.22–25 with 167–170). As Fainall has run through her wealth, she now relies on him for financial support, a dependence she resents.

Interpretations

She is most alive when goading others into action; Lady Wishfort and Fainall both feel the force of her persuasive powers (III.607–636, V.200–228). She does not hesitate to expose others (I.78–80, III.45–46, 302–303, 583 sd, IV.551–560), and when she is herself threatened with exposure, moves to distance herself. A thorough hypocrite, she smoothly claims the high moral ground on the subject of *wantonness* in women (V.152–158, 290–291).

She eventually falls victim to the most humiliating of exposures: caught in the act of adultery by servants she had tried to silence by a farcical oath (V.469–474). The woman who has used the word *hate* more than any other character finally leaves the stage with a desperate-sounding threat, and we hear no more about her.

Lady Wishfort

Elinor Leigh was famous for playing ageing widows in pursuit of lost youth and love. She was a safe choice for the part of Lady Wishfort.

Technically, hers is a minor role but her pivotal position as the victim of both plot strands means that we hear about her long before she appears in Act III (I.23–24, 58–80, II.19, 297–320, 514–541). An actor has considerable scope for interpretation with this part: she can be portrayed as an energetic bully, a hypocritical prude or a pathetic and vulnerable elderly dowager. If she is the widow of a city knight (see Glossary) she would not be noble by birth, while her age and gender make her vulnerable to foolish 'amours'.

Lady Wishfort is a classic blocking character, at whose door several foolish deeds can be placed. She raised her daughter to have neither understanding of nor communication with men – a ridiculous distortion of Puritan values. She refuses to entertain Mirabell as Millamant's suitor because he has offended her vanity. She is easy prey to two blackmail plots, and almost forfeits her family's entire wealth to Fainall. She represents the worst excesses of the Stuart court: living on past glories and obsessed with her own sexual and social potency.

She is the most linguistically versatile and spontaneous of all the characters. Her best speeches blend rich social observation with colloquial directness (III.3–36, IV.17–32, V.1–54). She can evoke the poverty, noise and smell of London life better than anyone. Her language, with its strong emphasis on the figurative (see Glossary), is as excessive as everything else about her. Her lust, anxiously repressed beneath a veneer of decorum, surfaces in unconscious verbal slips (III.96, 161, 166–167, 172–173, IV.443–444, 480–481, 501–561). Her decorous side has highly selective hearing and fails to register the innuendo.

In Act IV her sexual eagerness produces a stream of questionably applied words, the forerunners of malapropisms (444, 459, 469–70, 502–4, 507, 515, 525). They reveal the moral confusion that arises when language is detached from its role of signifying reality. See also pages 201–202.

Activity

Is Lady Wishfort more than simply a humours character in the Jonsonian tradition?

Discussion

Lady Wishfort is Congreve's most recognizable humours character, but if the part is played for sympathy as well as comedy, she can be 'rounded out' considerably.

According to humours theory, Lady Wishfort is a classic sanguine type, associated with the influence of the blood. In proper balance, this should make her youthful and noble, but she is as disordered as her house. The sanguine part of her temperament is so deeply ingrained that it dominates the rest of her character. Her aptronym, Wishfort (wish-for-it), is a sexual innuendo and reminder that she is driven by desire. She is in a permanent state of wishfulness because so much has passed her by: youth, beauty, love, reputation, decorum. Once Congreve has established her traits he can sustain the laughter by varying the situations in which they are expressed.

Her power over others' lives derives from social class, marriage, family ties and the laws of inheritance, rather than natural ability or worthy deeds – she is hardly a figure for the new age. The disorder of her house is suggested by the religious hypocrisy (III.62–64, V.172–197),

Interpretations

eavesdropping (III.215–236), adulterous liaisons (V.88–95), drunken foolery (IV.298–302), and trickster servants it contains. She cannot function without Foible to dress her, paint her face and compose her mind. She is duped by everyone in the play, as she lacks skills in reading character or situation. She is the classic foolish guardian and amorous old woman of comic tradition.

There are convincing human qualities amid this grotesque concoction, however, which soften the laughter and encourage reflection on her plight. She shows ingenuity in using the possibility of pregnancy to consolidate her position in the family (compare I.62 with IV.610–612). She heads a very effective cabal (I.28–62), is gracious to guests (III.566–583) and firm with miscreants (IV.367–376, 415–420, 438–440).

Her most repeated remark is the intriguing *As I'm a person* (III.6, 34, 243, IV.370, 439, 500, V.52, 585). Is she self-aware enough to anxiously proclaim her humanity, to counter her tendency towards the grotesque?

Lady Wishfort is most human when she screeches to a halt and recognizes her own absurdity in *the glass*. Her declaration *I look like an old peeled wall* is breathtakingly candid, matched by her determination to cheat reality by having a *repair* (III.142–143). She is shored up against the pains of reality by her illusions – of youth, beauty and allure. She is both the maker and made, the forger and the deceived. She cannot be accused of affectation because she is not self-knowing enough to perform it.

Whatever her faults, Lady Wishfort is not wicked. We feel sympathy for the way she is ruthlessly manipulated by Fainall and Mrs Marwood as they play upon her fear of public exposure. She becomes a figure of pathos in Act V, finding some dignity as she presides like a magistrate over the disputing sides who covet her fortune.

Witwoud and Petulant

Petulant is a foil for Witwoud and both are foils for the play's true wits. Congreve uses these self-conscious fops to expose the vanity and affectation of the town. They are the sterile end-product of a society that values appearance over substance. They hark back to a former age but their sexual potency, along with their wit, has faded (I.386, 456–457).

Casting and characters

Penelope Keith as Lady Wishfort and Jeremy Swift as Sir Wilfull at the Chichester Festival Theatre, 2012

Mr Bowen had played the Shropshire country fool Sir Joseph Wittol in *The Old Bachelor*, making him an obvious choice for Witwoud. As his name suggests, he 'would be thought a wit' and strives to present himself as one, with limited success. Mr Bowman was cast as Petulant, a false wit with bad-tempered, irritable moods.

The biggest joke against them is that they are only half-men and both are needed to make up the one man Lady Wishfort requires for her cabal (I.53–57). There is a serious side to their pursuit of Millamant; as effeminate fops, though despised by proper gentlemen rivals they are still possible contenders for the hand and fortune of a city heiress. Mirabell disapproves of Millamant's cultivation of fops, not because he is jealous but because they burlesque (caricature) manly competition in the marriage market.

They act indiscriminately, getting Sir Wilfull drunk to assist Fainall and yet apparently mindlessly witnessing the *deed of trust* to Mirabell's advantage. Each has his moment when he is centre stage. Witwoud's comes when his brother reveals his unfashionable Shropshire roots and former life as an *attorney's clerk* (III.513–536).

Interpretations

Petulant's comes when Witwoud gossips about his attempts to create a fashionable persona for himself and the measures he takes to maintain it (I.345–406).

For more on Witwoud and Petulant see pages 206–207.

Sir Wilfull Witwoud

Cave Underhill (1634–c.1710) brought 30 years' experience playing comic types, clowns and rustics to the part of Sir Wilfull. He is reputed to have been larger-than-life, tall and robust with blunt features.

Sir Wilfull's Shropshire and the Wrekin would have represented the unfashionable depths of rural England to the audience. His name suggests that he is wilfully stubborn in his desire to be thought a wit. He is tongue-tied before Millamant, but boorish and vulgar when drunk before Lady Wishfort.

Congreve redeems him in Act V in a number of small but significant ways; it becomes evident that his essential good nature is more valuable than keeping to decorum. He pleads Mirabell's cause before Lady Wishfort and helpfully pretends to be Millamant's suitor. He stands up to Fainall, challenging his threatening behaviour and matching his wit (V.539–540). He suggests a dance of celebration and becomes the benevolent, reconciling senior character at the close of the play.

See also pages 200–201.

Foible and Waitwell

Elizabeth Willis (c.1669–1739) created the role of Foible. She enjoyed a 50-year stage career playing mainly comic parts of 'low humour' (see Glossary). Mr Bright created the role of Waitwell, the servant who lives up to his name. The marriage between Foible and Waitwell seems to be a love match, making Mirabell's manipulation of their personal lives more acceptable.

Foible is employed by one household but her loyalties have been recruited by another. She is quick to react to a fast-changing situation. She is inventive, and actively embellishes or modifies Mirabell's plot along the way (II.514–529, 538–541, III.79–132, IV.291–292, 542–

543, 577–589, V.43–44, 84–85, 461). Foible is intelligent, ironic and devious. She can be witty and manages to speak her mind while maintaining a humble demeanour (III.145–148). Her name suggests both a weapon used in fencing, and a minor flaw of character: she is Mirabell's fencing weapon and Lady Wishfort's weakness.

The law does not make Foible's life easy because her prospects are severely limited by her social class and gender. As is made clear at the beginning of Act V, Lady Wishfort can pluck a servant such as Foible from the dangers of the market-place and just as easily cast her back into its uncertainties. The aristocratic lady offers only unending servitude, whereas collaboration with Mirabell for a fixed time span offers Foible real rewards. Through possession of the well-stocked farm (II.533), Foible can acquire a stake in the country and enjoy the law's protection.

Waitwell's role is mainly to be an agent in Mirabell's plot and purveyor of the *black box*. As 'Sir Rowland' he is a burlesque version of Fainall, the seducer cavalier. He makes a complacent husband, congratulating himself for training Foible (who is really much cleverer), and expecting to be given the rewards she has earned. He is less imaginative than Foible, wondering whether playing a social superior will disrupt his sense of identity (II.547–551).

What women want in *The Way of the World* (and what they get)

The Way of the World features some of the strongest-willed, most scheming women in seventeenth-century comedy. Early in the play we hear that Lady Wishfort has declared her *detestation of mankind* (I.60), and that Millamant uses Mirabell *with... insolence* (160); Mrs Fainall claims to hate men *Heartily* (II.35) and Mrs Marwood to *despise 'em* (45–46). Whatever their motives or candour, women's wish to be independent of men is strongly voiced but ultimately comes to nothing. These women do not care for each other and are not friends. A lack of female bonding, together with social realities,

Interpretations

means they have to depend on men, for better or worse.

The reputations of Mrs Fainall and Mrs Marwood rely on the discretion of the lovers to whom they have entrusted their honour (II.200, 267–270). Millamant's honour is intact because she has cultivated the knack of seeming to know the world while being untainted by it. Language is her defence, precarious as this may seem; she teases, pretends to misunderstand, and fences, and men never master her since *motion, not method is* her *occupation* (II.494).

Millamant's elusiveness is strongly at variance with the hard facts of the law, which work to define her as heiress and eventually wife. She promotes her attractions to men yet evades their attempts to understand her. For her, affectation is a serious means of disguise. Even Mirabell cannot decide whether she is naturally artful or artfully natural (I.156–157), and it is to her advantage to keep him guessing. She will eventually have to accept the *physic* (II.449) of marriage. Her cultivated guises and strategies define her existence only as an object of desire to male suitors, and without change she could harden into a Lady Wishfort caricature.

Knowing that her beauty and 'honour' give her power over men, she intends to wield this power while it lasts, before she becomes *old and ugly* (II.387). She disagrees with Mirabell's view that the relationship between lovers is mutually beneficial. He claims she is only beautiful because he finds her so; she pours scorn on his wish to share her power, seeing it as an attack on her independence.

There are no male heirs to the Wishfort estate, making women the target of fortune-hunters. Lady Wishfort's preferred solution would be to marry and produce an heir, even in middle age. This natural remedy is presented as mere farce compared to the solution the law eventually provides. But the protection of the law comes at a price, and she is forced to accept Mirabell's terms; we are in no doubt that he will stamp his authority on the Wishfort household.

Lady Wishfort's *cabal* is a minor example of female autonomy at the start of the play. Its female members work collaboratively and effectively enough to expel Mirabell, who then warns Fainall against allowing his *wife to be of such a party* (I.136). The cabal deals in what women are supposed to excel in: gossip. Gossip can undermine patriarchy by setting its own rules for creating celebrity and exposing those it dislikes. The reported cabal night, however, is quickly overtaken by events and its importance is short-lived.

Only women blush in *The Way of the World*. It is a natural emotional response they would rather conceal, because others make it their business to read their faces (I.38, II.68, 78–79, 140–141, III.272). Women's strong emotions disturb their social mask, putting them at a disadvantage (II.249–250). But the overriding disadvantage they face is that age is the enemy of beauty, a woman's trusted weapon in the seduction and marriage market. Lady Wishfort's desire to delay or at least disguise the ravages of age on her appearance is clear in her concerns with rouge and face-painting (III.3–7, 134–144).

Mrs Fainall has good reason to be weary of the world; she has abandoned desire by the start of the play, having already *loved without bounds* (II.262–263). We find out most about her in the scene with Mrs Marwood in *St James's Park*. After a series of failed relationships with men she advocates self-sufficiency and sisterhood as a means to happiness. She may be adopting a persona to probe Mrs Marwood, but her arguments are convincing; she describes the way in which abandoned women are made insubstantial and ghost-like because men shun and fly from them (II.6–8). As Alexander Pope writes in *Epistle II. To a Lady* (1743): 'Still round and round the Ghosts of Beauty glide,/ And haunt the places where their Honour died'. This is Mrs Fainall's fate, since there are no sisters trustworthy enough to abandon the world with her.

At the end of the play she has to accept the consequences of her damaged reputation and rely on the support and forgiveness of others. She does escape the standard fate of the disgraced woman in Restoration comedy; it is small comfort, however, that she cannot be married off to the play's dupe as she begins the play already married to its rake.

Mrs Marwood is not suited to passive resignation, and is far too vivid to be ghostly. There is a wicked humour in her regret *that the man so often should outlive the lover* (II.10–11). She intends to take what pleasure she can while still young. Not for her the pastoral retreat that Lady Wishfort longs for when the stresses of society

Interpretations

become intolerable (V.123–127). She submits to love as an emperor and a *lawful tyrant* (II.27), an oxymoron that puts her firmly out of step with the values of 1688. She disguises her 'unfeminine' will by pretending friendship to Lady Wishfort (II.162–164, V.154–156, 233–235, 466–468), which convinces no one. Excessive desire and wilfulness in women was considered ungodly and had to be punished. She becomes increasing silent as her enemies clamour against her, and she leaves the stage empty-handed.

Activity

How fairly does Mirabell treat Mrs Fainall?

Discussion

Consider these points of view:
- Congreve does not influence our judgement directly, and certainly does not suggest that Mirabell should have married Mrs Fainall.
- By the double standards of the time (men were expected to have amours, women to guard their virtue), Mirabell behaves considerately and fairly. Widows were commonly believed to have strong sexual appetites and to be suitable prey for illicit amours. He may not show emotional empathy, but Mirabell remains sensitive to her situation (I.79, 96–99, 134–136, 260–263, II.91, 257, V.522–531).
- Mirabell defends (and disguises?) his libertine behaviour rationally (II.266–278). He points out that he saved Mrs Fainall's reputation by marrying her off to Fainall, because had she become pregnant she would have avoided the stigma of having an illegitimate child. Fainall had many faults, but his *reputation with the town* was good enough to make it believable that she should accept him. Only a cad like Fainall should have been deceived in such a way, but someone worse than Fainall would not have been suitable. There is always the *deed of trust* (V.595) to protect her interests.
- Mirabell's rejection of Mrs Fainall and transference of his affections to Millamant belong to the back story of the play,

which lessens their emotional impact – the audience meet the pair already collaborating in a new kind of partnership. There is no indication that he has broken a promise to marry her, and no character mentions it as an option.
- They are mutually dependent: he guards her secret and the *deed of trust*, while she is *privy to* his *whole design* (II.281–281) and assists him diligently. Is this arrangement entered into freely? Or are they trapped?
- By making Mrs Fainall Mirabell's accomplice, Congreve keeps Millamant free of the taint of scheming. It is acceptable for Mrs Fainall to act hypocritically because she is sexually compromised.
- Mrs Fainall is responsible for her lost honour, making her unworthy to be Mirabell's wife. She cannot claim to live by a moral standard superior to the (male) ways of the world, so she must accept its verdict on her.
- She is disloyal to her mother and husband in her continuing preference for Mirabell.

A dance celebrating love and marriage soon gives way to more serious concerns as the play ends. At the moment when we might expect to see the lovers centre stage, we see Mirabell hand Mrs Fainall the deed *before... witnesses* (594). He speaks of *a reunion* (593) between the Fainalls. This is his solution, not hers; earlier she had confided to Foible that her *comfort* would be to part from her husband (V.78–79). Would a divorced Mrs Fainall be a threat to Mirabell's future happiness and the Wishfort dynasty? How far does his pious warning against *marriage frauds* (V.600) rebound on the pair?

Making drama out of unpromising material: Money and the law

England's mercantile classes conducted lively public debates about money and the law during the 1690s. Congreve saw their potential for drama and placed them centre stage in *The Way of the World*. He makes a convincing case that men and women are together responsible for the fair apportionment of the nation's wealth. In the

Interpretations

right hands, contracts – personal and civil, spoken and written – can guard against criminal behaviour and underpin civilized society. In the absence of religious reference points, does the law play a providential role in the play?

The will of Sir Jonathan Wishfort, with its mean-spirited and uncompromising *moiety* clause on Millamant's inheritance, has lively currency in this drama, casting a long shadow. The *moiety* proves a slippery asset for greedy hands to grasp at. As characters scheme to secure it, their actions sometimes produce unexpected outcomes (II.203–207, 300–302, III.632–639, V.108–110, 230–231, 270–277, 400–401, 446–448). It takes the concerted effort of all the characters, good and bad, to secure it in the end for a love match.

Congreve makes the play very topical by lacing his dialogue with current legal references. Their sheer variety would have intrigued audiences who increasingly encountered the law in their everyday lives (III.412–413, 504, 517, 523, IV.224, 316–317, V.202–219, 282). For props, Congreve turns a commonplace object like the law's *black box* into an instrument of providence. It is first put to work as a ruse to fool Lady Wishfort. The counterfeit Sir Rowland claims it holds *proof* of his identity (IV.599–602). He pays for his deceit by immediate imprisonment. When the box finally appears, it is unveiled by Mirabell with a dramatic flourish. As we gaze upon it there is a lengthy and tense wait for its contents to be revealed (V.489–534). Now, in the right hands, it reveals the truth.

Congreve's villains make criminal use of the law, undermining the value of marriage as a social contract. Fainall marries only *to make lawful prize of a rich widow's wealth* (II.208–209). He will make a mockery of the law, ultimately turning to blackmail until he is outplayed, in both senses of the word, by Mirabell's better *deed* (V.536–537). By contrast, Mirabell will conserve and develop wealth through the birth of sons (IV.245–253) and projects like the well-stocked farm with its lease *made good* (II.533) with which he rewards Foible and Waitwell.

Moieties, marriage certificates and pre-nuptial contracts fuel the farce. Mirabell acquires the servants' marriage *certificate* (I.120–121) at an early stage in the action. Associated with grotesque, illegal unions, such a document is key to the comic intrigue. It is meant to work in tandem with the fraudulent betrothal contract between Lady Wishfort and Sir Rowland. Lady Wishfort's attempt to marry (and defy the law of inheritance by the extreme measure of giving birth at the age of 55) leads her into the danger of being *caught in a contract* (II.297). Both documents are comic foils for the spoken contract negotiated and agreed between Mirabell and Millamant in Act IV (270–272).

The law proves highly adaptable to comic satire when Mrs Marwood terrifies Lady Wishfort into submission. Her speeches about the horrors of appearing in a *public court* (V.200–228) are full of malicious wit and social observation. Her language is racy: *prostituted, fumbling lecher, naughty, licentious*. There is a vulgar portrait of a judge (211–214). It is a picture that might have been illustrated by the eighteenth-century painter and printmaker William Hogarth (see page 181 and Glossary), but it has something a painting cannot offer – a sense of the noisy clamour of scandal: *bawling, Oyez, simpers, talk, throats, lungs, voices, loud, cries*. Her speech exploits the dread of being shamed by the law in a crowded, urban society. The audience would have been aware that Fainall could sue Mirabell for adultery as a preliminary to filing for divorce. The law would uphold his suit and award damages for trespass, since a wife was seen as a man's property. The Wishfort family would suffer humiliation in the court and in the press.

Mrs Marwood deliberately blurs the distinction between a trial court, where high society scandals would be aired, and tales of lower-class criminality appearing in the press. Scandal is depicted as swift and unstoppable in its path from court to the world beyond, falling by stages into the hands of the lowest in the land. But the play's final scene assures us that such unreliable gossip and malicious rumour can be defeated by documents in the *black box*.

Those formally entrusted with carrying out the law do not appear to advantage in the play. Witwoud, the failed *attorney's clerk* (III.528–529), and Sir Wilfull, a Justice of the Peace (V.378), behave immoderately and prove to be bad judges of character and situation. Witwoud has no recollection of what Mirabell asked him to witness

Interpretations

(V.510–512) and Sir Wilfull thinks he can defeat Fainall by the sword (V.408–414).

Lady Wishfort achieves some dignity when Congreve frames the play's deciding scene as a court of law. Her role as head of the household and an ill-used dowager means she must be applied to for mercy. Witnesses are called, items produced, revelations made. A faint sense of religious solemnity invites us to respect the proceedings as Sir Wilfull intercedes for the sinner Mirabell. Lady Wishfort will *forgive all that's past* (437) echoing *The Book of Common Prayer* (1662). Sir Wilfull reminds her that forgiveness is her duty as *a Christian* (366–367). Mirabell's use of words such as *remorse, contrition, compassion, confess, suppliant, pity, venial* contributes to the mood.

Activity

Explore the comic effects of the contrasting of town and country ways in *The Way of the World*.

Discussion

The country squire who comes to town in his riding habit and unfashionable boots was a long-standing joke in Restoration comedy. The gentle buffoonery of Sir Wilfull Witwoud provides some comic relief in a play full of scheming, tense sophisticates. The scene in which he is locked in with Millamant and pressured to propose derives its comedy from the contrast in their speech styles (IV.67–142). She is commanding, haughty, erudite; he is diffident, hesitant, colloquial.

The usual play on differences between town and country ways is aired during Sir Wilfull's first appearance (III.422–596). In the town the gentry rise late and dine later, no one readily recognizes their relatives, and servants tend to be temporary. Country folk are childlike, obstinate and vulgar, but loving when drunk (I.215–217). They are ignorant of city fashions in dress and formal greetings, and of upper-class culture such as poetry.

Sir Wilfull is a plain-speaking man, if a little tongue-tied on occasions and given to heavy drinking, especially when socially out of his depth. The town fops don't have things all their own way, though, and Sir Wilfull mocks their pretensions heartily, using rustic expressions (III.499–501). His drunken song in Act IV is patriotic but insulting to foreigners, especially non-Christians. The gentry cannot bear his rank smell (IV.371, 415–416, 450), and boorish ways (III.591–593), although the audience probably enjoyed the song and endorsed the opinions. He holds his own among the assembled characters because *plain English* serves him better than the *lingo* of the town (III.556, IV.103–105).

Language and style

Writing for performance

Congreve had a fine ear for both the rhythm and authority of upper-class speech and the bluster and guile of fools and servants. His dialogue is precise and structured, but actors can always make it lively and conversational in performance. He captures the cadences (see Glossary) of both ironic and comic phrasing, choosing his words for sound as well as sense. Listen to the sound effects of V.1–22 to appreciate how the arrangement of vowels and consonants, allied to repetition, contribute to the comic excess of Lady Wishfort's speech. The meagre existence of London's poor is conveyed through a rich tapestry of everyday objects that sound grotesque: *chafing-dish, starved embers, traverse rag, frisoneer-gorget, yellow colberteen, old gnawed mask*.

Here and elsewhere Congreve's use of alliteration adds musicality and drama: *bleak blue*; *bigger... bird*; *do, do; do, drive... do; brandy... bulk*; *yard... yellow*; *beads broken*; *treacherous trull*. The harsh consonants assist the actor in expressing assertiveness and disgust. A different use of alliteration is the softer consonantal sounds that convey Mirabell's perplexed state of mind: *mind and mansion*; *whirlwind... windmill... whimsical*; *motion, not method*; *persevere to play*; *fool by the force* (II.487–497).

Congreve guides his actors through dialogue rather than stage directions. See III.273–275, 319–320 and 333 for hints as to how Millamant might use her fan to show how uneasy Mrs Marwood's

Interpretations

scrutiny makes her. In V.352–360, Mirabell's speech suggests that he kneels and gestures while Lady Wishfort turns away *in disdain*.

Lady Wishfort's musings in III.149–174 begin with a series of questions, each of which takes her thoughts forward. Her speech moves rhythmically back and forth, in keeping with her need to temper lust with decorum. Repetitions of key words such as *fail, importunate, advance, handsome* and *decorums* mimic her thought processes – impulsive yet hesitant. Her use of obscure expressions such as *push, forced to advance, break decorums* and *breaking her forms* betray her reluctance to acknowledge the reality of her desires. They build in frequency until we get the obfuscation of *Nothing but importunity can surmount decorums* (172–173). When describing the image she wishes to project with terms such as *tenderness, dyingness* and *swimminess* (160–162) she lapses into whimsy and bad grammar. Her repeated use of the first-person pronoun speaks eloquently of her towering ego.

Lady Wishfort may strive for decorum in her social speech but in private she seems most true to herself when she is repetitive, dogmatic and querulous. Heavily stressed monosyllables express irritation and a need to dominate: *Fetch me the red – the red, do you hear... Look you how this wench stirs!* (III.5–7); *Out of my house, out of my house* (V.1). A scattering of dashes in her speeches suggests indecision. Her scolding of Foible at the beginning of Act V has a coarseness that suggests a bawd taking to task a whore she has made and managed; she even refers to herself as a *receptacle* for a *pimp*, and a *passive bawd* (V.34–35, 48). She believed she had rescued Foible from a life on the streets, but Foible has had the upper hand all along.

Congreve gives the actor playing Lady Wishfort further scope when he presents her rehearsing for her meeting with Sir Rowland (IV.17–32). Her use of the words *figure* and *first impression* invite us to look at her as she practices simple movements: *sit, walk, turn, lie, receive, loll, lean, dangling, jogging, start, rise*. There is a gradual increase in movement and excitement in what is akin to an interior monologue, until the whole is topped by *Hark!* – his coach is heard just as she has sharpened her tools of seduction.

Millamant's first entrance is memorable because the actor,

carrying a fan, can marry speech with gesture and movement. *Long! Lord, have I not made violent haste?* she exclaims (II.345). This disingenuous appeal to the audience prepares them for her contrariness as she moves in stately, leisurely fashion across the stage. Mincing, who provides a sense of reality, has to remind her of why she was late. Instead of offering a rational explanation concerning the reading of letters, Millamant goes off at a tangent, claiming that letters *serve one to pin up one's hair* (361). She repeats the word *letters* five times until she can dismiss them by transforming them into a witty conceit. This is a masterly piece of affectation, a defence of her privacy (where has she been?) and a satire on the pretensions of letter-writers – especially would-be suitors.

When Congreve uses figurative language, the richness of expression and ideas are a gift for the actor (see I.51–52, II.322–326, 464–466, III.141–143, 217–218, 236–238, 613–616, V.165–167, 349–350). To look at a single example more closely, birth imagery is widely used and Congreve's phrasing means it can be expressed with gusto. In III.302–305 and IV.408–411 it is associated with a truth being revealed in the course of time, for which pregnancy is a pertinent analogy (see Glossary). It is used to explore the play's concerns with ageing and inheritance, as in I.73–75 and IV.250–253, while in I.73–75, III.21–23 and 302–305 it also plays with fears that women's bodies may transform into grotesque versions of their former selves.

True and false wits in *The Way of the World*

In the seventeenth century, wit meant more than the ability to make people laugh – affectation, farce and burlesque could do that. It meant using language in an intellectually stimulating and novel way. Such language would be elegant, structured and subtle. The style in which an original idea was expressed could make as much impact as the idea itself. Wit stimulated the mind, and any laughter would be appreciative and knowing rather than infectious.

True wit was unpredictable, spontaneous, sparkling – these were its fanciful aspects. Equally important was its judgemental side, which

Interpretations

was accompanied by restraint, decorum, and cultural insight. Wit was neither exclusively rational nor deeply philosophical; rather, it was seriously playful with words and ideas. Wit in a play was not always dramatic or necessary to the action, and tended to express a sceptical, world-weary point of view.

Congreve uses the full armoury of wit in *The Way of the World*: punning (III.665), double entendre (IV.182), antithesis (I.88–89), paradox (I.155–156), aphorism (I.6–7), similitude (II.330), raillery (II.376–422), repartee (I.209–214), quibbling (IV.328–343), irony (IV.16), epigram (I.149–151) and the conceit (II.317–320). (See the Glossary for any unfamiliar terms.) Successfully witty conceits are measured, nothing is forced or excessive, and the comparisons challenge thought because they are both apt and strange at the same time.

The ability to 'turn a witty phrase' was deeply respected by Congreve and his peers. We can see it at work in Mirabell's and Millamant's sparring over power, love and beauty (II.378–417). They use the kind of language we expect from Fainall and Mrs Marwood: *pain, cruelty, vanity, power, ugly, suffer, ruin, destroy, vain, dies, cheat, mortifies*. But these words are wielded lightly and mockingly as they flirt and play with ideas. There is depth of feeling but it remains concealed, not reducible to the words they play with because Millamant wants to resist being the object of courtly love, knowing it leads to servitude in marriage. Mirabell's teasing remark about *how lost a thing* Millamant would be without a lover is taken up seriously later in the play: *if Mirabell should not make a good husband, I am a lost thing* (IV.303–304). Compare their use of courtship language here to how they speak in the proviso scene.

There is more of judgement than fancy in Mirabell's wit, as he is the guardian of Whig values in the play and the scourge of imposters and fools. The authoritative tone of his conceit about *An old woman's appetite* is an arresting example (II.317–320). First a riddle is set: how can *appetite* and *depraved* apply to both an old woman and a young girl? The answer is then given: both have *green sickness*, a disease that affected girls at puberty, its symptoms being a greenish skin tone and poor appetite. The originality of the conceit lies in the dissimilarity

Language and style

of the comparison. The old woman, it is suggested, is sexual and immoral, while the girl is diseased and unwholesome, yet they are similar in that both are *depraved*.

Green sickness solves the riddle and points the way to the second simile. The words *spring*, *fall* and *bloom* are aptly chosen as the seasons remind us of the brevity of youth and beauty. Greenness is *the faint offer* of a late spring in an old woman's life. Sadly and inevitably, though, the *bloom* it promises is false as it is diseased. Is Mirabell sympathetic to ageing women? Or is he suggesting their desires are unnatural and rightly bound to fail? Compare this conceit with II.461–466 where Millamant accuses him of being sententious. Can you see why she rebukes him?

Fainall and Mrs Marwood are dangerous false wits, using their intellect and verbal skills to disguise their hypocrisy and pursue selfish, mercenary goals. Their language betrays them. Fainall's outburst on hearing of his wife's affair with Mirabell is more venom and sophistry (see Glossary) than wit. See III.601–606, where he struggles to find words to express his feelings. He pictures himself as a horned stag yet also a *snail*, *out-stripped* by a wife. Later he claims that in return for half of Millamant's wealth he could have borne being so big a cuckold that his forehead had *been furnished like a deputy-lieutenant's hall* (615–616). Both are wickedly funny and farcical images.

In 645–658 Fainall deals with humiliation using rational, logical inference, but there is no vitality or conviction to his argument. Words such as *over*, *jade*, *Jealous*, *Weary*, *none* and *lose* set the tone. His phrasing is tedious and plodding because his thought processes are laborious. His use of syllogism (see Glossary) indicates his imperfect reasoning (660–663). When he pauses we are not hanging on his words as we see through the sophistry of his argument.

Mrs Marwood's language is irrational, violent, and coarse, because passion not wit holds sway (619–620). Her speech is full of absolutes and an obsession with baser values: she uses vocabulary such as *eternal*, *ever*, *never*, *hate*, *loathe*, *despise*, *detest*, *abhor*, *false*, *malice*, *vicious*, *baseness*, *violence* and *aversion*. She abuses language by making threats she does not follow through (II.189–198), as anger produces excess in the form of hyperbole (167–170, 174–175, 210,

Andrew Long as Fainall and Deanne Lorette as Mrs Marwood at the Shakespeare Theatre Company, Washington DC, 2008

218–219). When Fainall declares his love, Mrs Marwood loathes *the name of love after such usage* (221) because she cannot trust anything he says. Her vulgar imagination (*have your case opened by an old fumbling lecher*, V.204) is typical of her character and, for the time, shocking in a woman's speech.

The less threatening, but equally false, wits Witwoud, Petulant and Sir Wilfull are exposed as fools by their misuse and abuse of language. False wits speak profusely but cannot sustain a sensible conversation or communicate effectively (III.373–413, IV.318–362). Petulant blurs names (I.385, 494); Witwoud forgets detail (I.266–270). The more they say on a subject, the less they make progress in rational argument.

One of the first signs that Witwoud has become a fop and a fool is a change in the style of his letters home (III.518–522). Sir Wilfull's addresses to Millamant are a triumph of style (gallantry) over substance. They fail as suitors because vulgarities in their speech show they are not worthy (IV.354–356, 392–394, 407–411). Their final words show the mental fog they inhabit: Witwoud *understands nothing of the matter – I'm in a maze yet, like a dog in a dancing school* (V.568–569) and Petulant lapses into confusion: *I say little; – I think things are best off or on* (566–567).

Similitudes were considered very stylish witticisms in Restoration comedy, but had fallen out of fashion by 1700. Witwoud's similes betray the man: they are unoriginal, dull, have too much matter and are too close to the everyday to excite us (I.239–244, II.330–335, III.380–382, IV.312–317). They fail to strike fire, and he delivers them without spontaneity. He also lacks decorum, as he never reads situations but simply wastes language on anyone who happens to be nearby. The situations he encounters are not interesting enough to justify so much verbal attention, nor is what he says illuminating.

Petulant's view that Witwoud is *an annihilator of sense* (IV.331) applies equally well to himself. His mangling of the language is perverse and irritating, particularly to Millamant (III.277–279). In I.373–376, for example, he compares *a professed midwife* to *a professed whoremaster*. The dissimilarity is striking but the similarity – both offer services that a man might call on at any time – is unconvincing and vulgar rather than witty. Petulant's moral disorder is what strikes us, rather than the aptness of the comparison.

False wits abuse language, breaking the correspondence between words and the reality they represent. Their motives are false and in the worst cases, they use wit to disguise their immoral and predatory natures. Congreve expected his audience to be able to distinguish between true and false wits. Was he successful? Even Pope, an admirer of Congreve, found the distinction between Mirabell, Fainall and Witwoud less than clear, leading him to ask: 'Tell me if Congreve's fools are fools indeed?' (*Imitations of Horace*, 1733–1738).

Interpretations

Activity

Identify the patterns that shape a performance of *The Way of the World*.

Discussion

The Way of the World is structured around a broad set of contrasts: loveless and loving unions, youth and age, true and false wits, reformed and unreformed rakes, town and country manners, honesty and deception, passion and reason, spoken and written contracts, criminality and the law.

The cast of characters is small but so closely interrelated that their competing jealousies and loyalties provide enough intrigue to drive the plot. Congreve places juxtaposed (see Glossary) couples and situations in the spotlight in elegant rotation. Each act offers a succession of paired characters, building to a larger grouping and then returning to a pairing, to close with some significant plot development. In Act II Fainall's wife and mistress are juxtaposed; Congreve then switches to pairing lovers and mistresses, disrupting respectability. He revives interest by introducing Lady Wishfort at the start of Act III, using her as the anchor figure to a succession of characters. Her appearance highlights the convergence of the two plots that target her. In classic style, Act IV – which is concerned with three contrasting wooing scenes – ends with the play's climactic scene. Act V uses Lady Wishfort as the anchor character again until Congreve gradually adds more arrivals, increasing the dramatic tension until all are assembled for the dénouement. This is achieved through small dramas of revelation that contribute to the overall pattern, which is concerned with truth, punishment and forgiveness.

The play's concerns about how to achieve respect and harmony in marriage are aired by juxtaposing Mirabell and Millamant with the Fainalls. True and false contracts are compared by juxtaposing Mirabell and Millamant with Lady Wishfort and Sir Rowland. Mirabell's dominance in the plot is suggested by his hand in steering a succession of substitutions: servants for aristocrats, Fainall for himself in marriage, Sir Rowland for himself as ardent lover and his own uncle.

Congreve respects the unities of time and action (see Glossary), but he modifies unity of place by using three London settings.

Language and style

He chose three highly fashionable settings, one exterior in St James's Park and two interiors featuring a chocolate-house and Lady Wishfort's home. In 1700 the chocolate-house was where gentlemen enjoyed mildly intoxicating drinks, gambling and debate. In theatre it replaced the tavern settings of earlier Restoration drama as it was more respectable, if less exciting. St James's Park had made promenading and meetings – social and clandestine – very attractive to London's fashionable classes. It had a formal layout with wide walks and small arbours set amid trees and shrubs. Its reputation for intrigue and questionable goings-on made it perfect for the second act. Congreve's characters promenade as they would have done in the park: assembling, changing partners, separating and spying as they share confidences and hide from view.

Compared to these settings, the private rooms in Lady Wishfort's house were a place where women could host social events and determine what happened. Her closet, a space associated with women's private affairs, works to expose Mirabell's plot, and he is denied access to the house until late in the play.

As we have seen, the action is organized around competing claims for the Wishfort estate, and all plot strands converge on this contest. Anticipation and cohesion are achieved by signposting important events before they happen. We see this when Sir Wilfull arrives (I.179–184 and III.422 sd), Foible shows Lady Wishfort's portrait to Sir Rowland (II.515–519 and III.71–73), Lady Wishfort decides that Sir Wilfull should woo Millamant (III.260–261 and IV.70), Fainall exposes his wife's affair to her mother (III.628 and V.77–79), Fainall decides to get Sir Wilfull drunk (III.641–642 and IV.298), Mrs Marwood writes a letter (III.668–670 and IV.537–538), Sir Wilfull pretends an engagement to Millamant (V.107–110 and 309–310), and the *black box* appears (IV.600 and V.489 sd).

Congreve obeys the unity of time, although events seem very compressed as a result. The characters often refer to time passing, creating a sense of urgency (III.113–114, 201–202, 262–263, 268). We are told it is almost one o'clock at the chocolate-house and Mirabell's meeting with the servants at Rosamond's Pond is to be at one. At the end of the first act, the gentlemen are to visit the Mall; shortly into Act II they arrive, creating the sense that Mrs Fainall and Mrs Marwood have been talking while the gentlemen made their journey. At Rosamond's Pond, Foible says she must hasten back to Lady Wishfort, whom she

Interpretations

has left dressing (II.537–538). Act III opens with Lady Wishfort yet to dress because she needs Foible's help. When Mrs Marwood arrives, she has come fresh from the Mall and confirms that Foible has been *but now* (III.45) in conference with Mirabell. Congreve successfully creates a sense of actions taking place simultaneously. We know that Act IV begins after dinner because Sir Wilfull is drunk (III.641–642, IV.36). In Act IV the meeting between Lady Wishfort and Sir Rowland happens at the same time as the proviso scene (IV.288–292). Dinner is a reference point for many, strongly linked to a sense of time hastening on. It is anticipated as early as Act I (498) and referred to before and after it has happened (III.121, 263–265, 427, 573, 586–587, 592–593, 641–642, V.65–66).

Critical views

The Way of the World was written just before literary and theatre criticism was established. In 1700 a playwright could expect the first published response to his work to take the form of commendatory verses. These were usually penned by critics and wits, and they duly appeared. They were generally fulsome in their praise, marvelling at the youthful Congreve's mastery of the comic form.

Unfortunately for him it was Jeremy Collier's views on drama (see page 12) that had a lasting influence throughout the eighteenth century, persisting into the Victorian period. Even those who admired his strong characters and sparkling wit found Congreve's moral vision questionable or absent. The problem of persuading critics that a comic approach to sexual misdemeanours was justified lasted well into the early twentieth century.

William Hazlitt, in his *Lectures on the English Comic Writers* (1819), broke rank to write the first balanced critique of Congreve's plays. He paid attention to language and style, and to escape the impasse about morality, he suggested that aesthetic values were the way to a non-prejudicial appreciation of the plays. His was a lone voice; the Victorians could not accept what they saw as the flaunting of sexual impropriety. They also disliked the cynical wit, mercenary schemers and artificial dialogue.

Critical views

It was not until the late 1880s that the first serious, academically sound account of Congreve's life and work appeared. Edmund Gosse's *Life of William Congreve* (1888) presented Congreve's comic vision in its proper historical context. It proved to be a turning point in the establishment of Congreve's plays as central to the English canon (see Glossary).

Gosse's pioneering scholarship paved the way for Montague Summers to prepare the first critical edition of the complete works in 1923. Based on the original editions of the plays and poems, it placed the Collier school of thought in its historical context and challenged its prejudices. Readers could at last see what Congreve had originally written before edits, cuts and bowdlerization had distorted his work.

In 1941 John Hodges published *William Congreve, The Man*, bringing excellent scholarship to a wider reading public. His interest lay not in the plays but the life. He presented detailed research on Congreve's relationships with Anne Bracegirdle and Lady Henrietta Godolphin for the first time.

Freed, after 250 years, from the shadow of Collier and supported by excellent biographical and historical research, twentieth-century critics opened up rich and diverse veins of criticism. The 1950s produced good contributions from American scholars. Thomas Fujimura's *The Restoration Comedy of Wit* (1952) offered a thought-provoking analysis of wit, aligning it to the moral underpinning of the plays. He rejected the view that aesthetic concerns can be divorced from moral ones, arguing that Congreve produced serious explorations of real social and political issues.

Norman Holland's *The First Modern Comedies* (1959) shows the conflict between appearance and reality in Congreve's plays. He also examines how Congreve's plays present the conflict between the manners of civilized society and disruptive natural appetites. W.H. Van Voris, in *The Cultivated Stance* (1965), shows why the play's intricate plotting and dramatic dialogue are deserving of critical attention. Peter Holland's *The Ornament of Action* (1979) asks how far Congreve was influenced by theatrical conditions and conventions. Aubrey Williams's *An Approach to Congreve* (1979) offers a modern Christian perspective on the plays, emphasizing moral concerns and

Interpretations

providential elements in the plot. Others have disagreed and taken a Hobbesian view (see pages 11–12), seeing Mirabell as the supreme Machiavel (see Glossary), operating in a self-interested world for his own ends.

More recent debates, such as Richard Braverman's *Capital Relations and The Way of the World* (1985) and Richard W.F. Kroll's *Discourse and Power in The Way of the World* (1986), mostly conducted in journals, have considered how far the play is a political expression of Whig values and how far Congreve's portrayal of women is progressive and sympathetic.

These critics are well worth investigating as you study this wonderful play. All the works referred to, and more, are listed in Further Reading page 220.

Essay Questions

1 Do you find Congreve's satire on ageing women like Lady Wishfort benevolent or malicious?

2 'Competition between Mirabell and Fainall, rather than competition for Millamant, forms the play's central conflict'. Discuss the implications of this statement and say how far you agree with it.

3 'Mirabell is presented with a degree of blindness and he is treated sentimentally at the end' (*The Case Against Congreve*, George Parfitt, 1972). How far do you agree?

4 Discuss theatre critic William Hazlitt's view of Millamant: 'We are not sorry to see her tamed down at last, from her pride of love and beauty, into a wife' (*The Edinburgh Magazine*, 1819).

5 Explore the effectiveness of Witwoud's and Petulant's contribution to the play's presentation of wit.

6 How far is it possible to tell the difference between the expression of real feeling and affectation in the play? Consider Congreve's presentation of Mrs Fainall and Mrs Marwood in your answer.

7 'Congreve does not classify his characters into good and evil types; he represents the world as he finds it.' Discuss.

8 How successful is Congreve in creating distinctive voices to represent character in *The Way of the World*?

9 'His characters are commonly fictitious and artificial, with very little of nature, and not much of life... his personages are a kind of intellectual gladiators; every sentence is to ward or strike' (Samuel Johnson, *Prefaces, Biographical and Critical, to the Works of the English Poets*, 1781). How far do you agree with Johnson's view of characters in the play?

10 Why are risk-taking and gambling important in *The Way of the World*, and how are they represented?

Essay Questions

11 How effectively does Congreve suggest the value of reputation at critical moments in the play?

12 Discuss Congreve's concerns with the relationship between the individual and society in *The Way of the World*.

13 Discuss the use and abuse of the law in *The Way of the World*.

14 'We want breath or attention to follow their repartees; and are so charmed with what everybody says, that we have not leisure to be interested in what anybody does. We are so pleased with each person, that we wish success to all; and our approbation is so occupied, that our passions cannot be engaged' (Horace Walpole, 1776). How far do you agree with this view of the play?

15 'Critics who do not find a moral compass in *The Way of the World* are mistaken; Congreve's moral vision is simply too subtle for some.' Discuss.

16 Discuss Congreve's understanding of what the 'way of the world' is in terms of the relationship between private and public morality.

17 How successfully does Congreve achieve 'the artful solution of the fable' (Dedication 62)? Is there too little action in the first four acts and too much in Act V?

18 'The play is more interesting to read than to see on stage; it is essentially undramatic'. Discuss.

19 What does Congreve achieve by obeying (with minor exceptions) the unities of time, place and action in *The Way of the World*?

20 How might an appreciation of the forms and conventions of Restoration theatre inform your understanding of *The Way of the World*?

Chronology

William Congreve's life

- 1670 Born 24 January in Bardsey, West Yorkshire.
- 1674 Father takes up army post in Youghal, Ireland; his family accompany him.
- 1681 Family settles in Kilkenny, County Kildare, where his father becomes a lieutenant in the Irish army.
- 1682–6 Congreve attends Kilkenny College.
- 1686 Attends Trinity College, Dublin.
- 1688 Political uncertainty causes Congreve's family to return to the family seat at Stretton, Staffordshire.
- 1691 Congreve enrols as a law student at the Middle Temple, London.
- 1692 Publishes *Incognita: or, Love and Duty reconcil'd*.
- 1693 March: Congreve's first play, *The Old Bachelor*, premières at the Theatre Royal, Drury Lane. His second play, *The Double Dealer*, premières in December, also at Drury Lane.
- 1695 April: his third play, *Love for Love*, premières at Lincoln's Inn Fields. He is made commissioner for licensing hackney coaches (until 1705). He faces health problems: fatigue, dyspepsia and gout.
- 1697 February: his fourth play and only tragedy, *The Mourning Bride*, premières at Lincoln's Inn Fields.
- 1698 Collier publishes *A Short View of the Immorality and Profaneness of the English Stage*.
- 1700 March: *The Way of the World* premières at Lincoln's Inn Fields.
- 1701 Writes libretto for the masque *The Judgement of Paris*, and the opera *Semele* (unperformed in his lifetime).
- 1700–2 Appointed Customs Collector at Poole, Dorset.
- 1702–3 Relationship with Anne Bracegirdle, begun in the 1690s, ends.

1705 Retires from any active role in theatre management or writing; appointed Commissioner for Wine Licences (until 1714) and Under-Searcher for Customs in the Pool of London.

1710 Jacob Tonson publishes a collected edition of *The Works of Mr William Congreve* in three volumes. This edition marks the formal end of his writing career. Congreve's eyesight begins to fail owing to cataracts.

1714 By this date he has begun a relationship with Lady Henrietta Godolphin. Appointed to secretaryship of the island of Jamaica.

1723 November: Henrietta gives birth to a daughter, Mary, most likely Congreve's child.

1728 Congreve is badly injured in a carriage accident, from which he never fully recovers.

1729 19 January: dies in his Surrey Street lodgings. He is buried in Westminster Abbey.

Historical, literary and cultural events

1649 Charles I beheaded and the Commonwealth proclaimed.

1653 Cromwell becomes Lord Protector until his death in 1658.

1661 Charles II, restored to the throne in 1660, is crowned, signalling the formal end of the Commonwealth under Oliver Cromwell and his son, Richard.

1674 Formation of two political parties begins in England.

1685 Charles II dies; accession of his brother James II.

1688 June: James's second wife, Queen Mary, gives birth to a (Catholic) son and heir. Prince William of Orange and his wife Mary (daughter of James II) are invited to England to assume the throne. James II deposed and exiled.

1689 22 January: Convention Parliament held. William and Mary are crowned as joint constitutional monarchs in Westminster Abbey.

1690 July: William defeats James II and his army in Ireland at the

Battle of the Boyne.
1691 Society for the Reformation of Manners founded and brings lawsuits against offending playwrights.
1694 Death of Queen Mary.
1696 Lord Chamberlain requires that all plays are licensed and subject to censorship.
1698 Royal proclamation against profanity (swearing, especially showing disrespect to God and religion) on the stage.
1702 William III dies; Queen Anne, Mary's sister, succeeds him.

The Way of the World's performance and publishing history

In 1700, *The Way of the World* premièred at Lincoln's Inn Fields and was published by Jacob Tonson. A second edition followed in 1706.

In 1710, the play was included in Congreve's *The Works of Mr William Congreve*, published by Tonson in three volumes. A second edition appeared in 1717 and a third in 1719–20. Congreve revised the play for *The Works*. He divided the acts into a large number of scenes arranged around exits and entrances. He wanted to create a play text for readers, and dispensed with some performance features.

The play was revived in 1718 with Anne Oldfield (1683–1730) taking the role of Millamant. Robert Wilks (c. 1665–1732) played Mirabell. Both were celebrity actors and there was considerable interest in how they would interpret the parts compared to Bracegirdle and Verbruggen.

In December 1732, theatre manager John Rich (1692–1761) selected *The Way of the World* for his inaugural production at the Theatre Royal, Covent Garden. This revival helped establish the play in the Georgian theatre repertoire, where it was adapted and bowdlerized to suit the prevailing taste for sentimental comedy. It continued to feature at both Drury Lane and Covent Garden until virtually the end of the eighteenth century, being performed well over 200 times.

Chronology

By the early part of the nineteenth century, *The Way of the World* made only rare appearances on the London stage. The trend for cutting and rewriting prevented audiences from experiencing the play as Congreve intended. It had virtually disappeared from view by the second half of the nineteenth century.

In the early twentieth century, the first of a small number of revivals started to appear. These were the work of stage societies with a specialist interest in rarely performed classics. The Mermaid Society staged the play for members only in April 1904.

In 1923, Montague Summers' first complete edition of Congreve's plays appeared, using the original acting quartos. This was an expensive edition that aimed for a limited readership. However, in 1925 Bonamy Dobrée published a new edition for Oxford University Press's 'World's Classics' series in a format and at a price that made the plays more accessible. These remained standard works until 1967, when Herbert Davis published *The Complete Plays of William Congreve*, again based on the original quartos, for the University of Chicago Press.

1924, Nigel Playfair's production of *The Way of the World* at the Lyric Theatre, Hammersmith was a turning point in the play's fortunes. Edith Evans's memorable interpretation of Millamant impressed audiences deeply (see opposite). This production started a trend for presenting Congreve's world as a bizarre one, with fantastical, over-fussy sets, extravagantly detailed costumes and ridiculous wigs. This was an unfortunate development, as the over-complicated visuals detracted from Congreve's strengths, which lay in characterization, dialogue and wit.

The 1940s and 1950s saw infrequent productions that achieved only lukewarm popular and critical success. Congreve was no longer considered 'too strong', but the absence of the forestage, some mannered acting and outlandish productions continued to hamper his appeal. There were some memorable performances: Edith Evans excelled as Lady Wishfort at the Old Vic in 1948, and Sir John Gielgud directed and played Mirabell at the Lyric Theatre, Hammersmith in 1953.

Edith Evans as Millamant and Robert Loraine as Mirabell,
Lyric Theatre, 1924

In recent times, the Chichester Festival Theatre mounted a successful production in traditional costume in spring 2012. Penelope Keith starred as Lady Wishfort and Rachel Kavanaugh directed. By contrast, some critics found the over-the-top high street fashions of Lyndsey Turner's production at the Sheffield Crucible in February 2012 an unnecessary distraction.

Any modern production has to tackle the challenges of articulating Congreve's highly stylized language and finding the right manner of playing. Little can be gained by removing the play from its historical setting, and consequently few attempts have been made to do this.

Further Reading

Editions of Congreve's plays

Herbert Davis (ed.), *The Complete Plays of William Congreve* (University of Chicago Press, 1967)
Donald F. McKenzie (ed.), *The Works of William Congreve*, 3 vols (Oxford University Press, 2011)
Montague Summers (ed.), *The Complete Works of William Congreve*, 4 vols (Nonesuch Press, 1923)

Congreve's life and times

Edmund Gosse, *Life of William Congreve* (Walter Scott, 1888)
John C. Hodges, *William Congreve, The Man: A Biography from New Sources* (Modern Language Association of America, 1941)
Kathleen M. Lynch, *A Congreve Gallery* (Harvard University Press, 1951)
David Thomas, *William Congreve* (Macmillan, 1992)

Critical books: Congreve's theatre

Richard W. Bevis (ed.), *English Drama: Restoration and Eighteenth Century, 1660–1789* (Longman Literature in English Series, 1988)
Thomas H. Fujimura, *The Restoration Comedy of Wit* (Barnes & Noble, 1952)
Harriett Hawkins, *Likenesses of Truth in Elizabethan and Restoration Drama* (Oxford University Press, 1972)
Norman N. Holland, *The First Modern Comedies: The Significance of Etherege, Wycherley and Congreve* (Harvard University Press, 1959)
Peter Holland, *The Ornament of Action: Text and Performance in Restoration Comedy* (Cambridge University Press, 1979)

Elizabeth Howe, *The First English Actresses: Women and Drama 1660–1700* (Cambridge University Press, 1992)

Derek Hughes, *English Drama, 1660–1700* (Oxford: Clarendon Press, 1996)

Donald Kay (ed.), *A Provision of Human Nature: Essays on Fielding and others in honor of Miriam Austin Locke* (University of Alabama Press, 1977)

Robert Markley, *Two-edg'd Weapons: Style and Ideology in the Comedies of Etherege, Wycherley, and Congreve* (Clarendon Press, 1988)

Brian Morris (ed.), *William Congreve* (Mermaid Critical Commentaries, Ernest Benn, 1972)

Deborah Payne Fisk, *The Cambridge Companion to English Restoration Theatre* (Cambridge University Press, 2000)

Gill Perry with Joseph Roach and Shearer West, *The First Actresses: Nell Gwyn to Sarah Siddons* (National Portrait Gallery Publications, 2011)

Katherine M. Quinsey (ed.), *Broken Boundaries: Women and Feminism in Restoration Drama* (University Press of Kentucky, 1966)

J.L. Styan, *Restoration Comedy in Performance* (Cambridge University Press, 1986)

W.H. Van Voris, *The Cultivated Stance: The Designs of Congreve's Plays* (Dolmen Press, 1965)

Aubrey L. Williams, *An Approach to Congreve* (Yale University Press, 1979)

Douglas M. Young, *The Feminist Voices in Restoration Comedy: The Virtuous Women in the Play-worlds of Etherege, Wycherley, and Congreve* (University Press of America, 1997)

Linda Zionkowski and Cynthia Klekar (eds), *The Culture of the Gift in Eighteenth Century England* (Palgrave Macmillan, 2009)

Journal articles: *The Way of the World*

Richard Braverman, *Capital Relations and The Way of the World*, ELH Vol. 52, No. 1 (Spring 1985), pp. 133–158

Frank Capogna, *The Way of the Golden World: Ovidian Myth in*

Further Reading

> *Congreve's The Way of the World,* Adelphi's Journal of Ideas Symposium Vol. XI, Adelphi University Academics, 2011

Robert A. Erickson, *Lady Wishfort and the Will of the World*, Modern Language Quarterly 45 (4), December 1984, pp. 338–349

Jean Gagen, *Congreve's Mirabell and the Ideal of the Gentleman*, PMLA Vol. 79, No. 4 (September 1964), pp. 422–427

Charles H. Hinnant, *Wit, Propriety and Style in The Way of the World*, Studies in English Literature, 1500–1900 Vol. 17, No. 3, Restoration and Eighteenth Century (Summer 1977), pp. 373–386

Anthony Kaufman, *Language and Character in Congreve's The Way of the World*, Texas Studies in Literature and Language Vol. 15, No. 3 (Fall 1973), pp. 411–427

Richard W.F. Kroll, *Discourse and Power in the Way of the World*, ELH Vol. 53, No. 4 (Winter 1986), pp. 727–758

John E. Loftis, *Congreve's Way of the World and Popular Criminal Literature*, Studies in English Literature, 1500–1900 Vol. 36, No. 3, Restoration and Eighteenth Century (Summer 1996), pp. 561–578

James E. Neufeld, *The Indigestion of Widdow-Hood: Blood, Jonson, and The Way of the World*, Modern Philology Vol. 81, No. 3 (February 1984), pp. 233–243

Alan Roper, *Language and Action in The Way of the World, Love's Last Shift, and The Relapse*, ELH Vol. 40, No. 1 (Spring 1973), pp. 44–69

Susan J. Rosowski, *Thematic Development in the Comedies of William Congreve: The Individual in Society*, Studies in English Literature, 1500–1900 Vol. 16, No. 3, Restoration and Eighteenth Century (Summer 1976), pp. 387–406

Arthur H. Scouten and Robert D. Hume, *Restoration Comedy and Its Audiences, 1660–1776*, Yearbook of English Studies Vol. 10 (1980), pp. 45–69

Websites

http://www.cft.org.uk/3357/The-Way-of-the-World/209
Chichester Festival Theatre talk: 'Inside *The Way of the World*',

recorded 16 April 2012; Dr Gilli Bush-Bailey, Reader in Women's Theatre History at Royal Holloway University of London, introduces Congreve's play through a discussion of his portrayal of women

http://www.vam.ac.uk/page/t/theatre-and-performance/
Guide to the Theatre and Performance collections at the Victoria and Albert Museum, London

http://www.npg.org.uk
The National Portrait Gallery, London, with a searchable collection of seventeenth- and eighteenth-century portraits of monarchs, actors and playwrights

http://ffh.films.com/id/8752/The_Restoration_Theater_From_Tennis_Court_to_Playhouse.htm
University of Warwick and Films for the Humanities and Sciences video entitled *The Restoration Theatre: From Tennis Court to Playhouse*

http://www.bbc.co.uk/radio4/features/in-our-time/archive/b/3
Radio 4's *In Our Time*, hosted by Melvyn Bragg, has 45-minute discussions on:
- *The Restoration*: how far the reign of the Stuart kings really was a golden age in England (first broadcast on Radio 4 on 15 February 2001)
- *The Glorious Revolution of 1688*: whether the events that brought William and Mary to the throne were either glorious or revolutionary (first broadcast on Radio 4 on 19 April 2001)

eBooks

Jeremy Collier, A *Short View of the Immorality and Profaneness of the English Stage*, 1698: facsimile (photographed copy of the original edition) available to read at Google Books

William Hazlitt, *Lectures on the English Comic Writers* (Taylor and Hessey, 1819): available to read at Google Books

Glossary

Literary and cultural terms

afterpiece short, humorous one-act play or musical piece which followed the full-length play

amplification technique by which a statement or theme once made is then added to repeatedly, to increase the rhetorical effect

anagnorisis moment of recognition or discovery; a comic anagnorisis occurs when a character suddenly discovers the truth of his or her situation

analogy connection between two things or ideas that have features in common

antithesis literary technique where contrasting ideas or words are placed side by side in clauses or sentences

aphorism principle or truth expressed in a concise and skilful manner, similar to a proverb

aptronym name for a character that provides strong clues to his or her personality type or function in the plot

back story events that have happened to characters before the play begins, which are referred to by them and are necessary to fully understand the plot

benevolent having a belief in the essential goodness of human nature (derived from Latin meaning wishing well for others)

bowdlerization the altering of a writer's work to censor material thought to be vulgar or offensive, especially sexual content

burlesque literary or other work mocking a serious subject by caricaturing it or treating it in a ridiculously inappropriate style

cadence rhythmic flow, especially that which indicates a speech is coming to an end, perhaps by a falling inflection

canon collection of literary works considered by scholars to be of the highest merit and treated as such by students, critics and the general reader

chiasmus pattern in which an expression is divided into two balanced parts, with the second part reversing the elements of the first; for example, if the expression begins with a verb, the second part will end with a verb

conceit form of simile, often extended and elaborate; it can suggest a surprising and witty comparison between two unlike things

dénouement ending or resolution, where plot complications are finally resolved

deus ex machina 'god from the machine' (Latin), a plot device such as the appearance of a character or prop that solves a problem suddenly and surprisingly; it can hasten a play's conclusion, usually with a happy ending

dramaturgy the skill, craft and theory of creating plays

epigram witty or satirical saying, concisely expressed

figurative language language that is not literal and straightforward; it may use similes, metaphors, alliteration or hyperbole, for example

fop a foolish, often effeminate, male character who is obsessed with his appearance

gay couple in comic drama, a pair of clever, witty lovers; they seem to act independently of family and other social constraints, and use verbal sparring to test each other's character and suitability for marriage

gulling making a fool of someone in a ritualistic way; in comedy, the victim is usually a character the audience enjoy seeing humiliated

heroic couplets pairs of ten-syllable rhymed lines, with alternating light and heavy stresses (iambic pentameters)

humours tradition from an ancient medical idea that the balance of four bodily fluids (humours) affects our personality traits and behaviour: people can be predominantly sanguine (happy and sociable), choleric (ambitious), melancholic (thoughtful and inward looking) or phlegmatic (relaxed)

hyperbole figure of speech in which exaggeration is used for effect

irony the effect that occurs when a character says one thing and means another, or says something that can be contrasted with his or her context and a wider significance is uncovered by the audience

juxtaposed placed side by side for contrasting effect

Glossary

low humour the comedy of characters who are neither well bred nor genteel, but often vulgar and farcical

malapropism unintentional misuse of a word by confusing it with one that sounds similar; the word is pronounced correctly but amusingly misapplied (from the French *mal à propos*, ill-suited, inappropriate)

onomatopoeia the effect where a word sounds like the noise or action it represents

oxymoron figure of speech that juxtaposes two apparently contradictory terms

paradox apparently self-contradictory or illogical statement that, when explained, raises surprising and meaningful ideas

parody imitation of a literary style or genre that mocks its conventions, usually by exaggeration and/or exaggerated seriousness

pun play on words that, in a given context, can have more than one meaning

quibbling punning or other types of word play

repartee rapid succession of witty exchanges where each character tries to outdo the other, often by turning an insult against the originator

sentimental comedy the most popular form of comedy throughout the eighteenth century; it featured virtuous characters, fine moral sentiments and emotional platitudes

sophistry skilful but false argument, intended to deceive

syllogism method of argument in logic where two premises (statements of fact) are put forward, and by linking them a speaker can draw a conclusion

unities in drama, the traditional three unities of time, place and action, derived from Aristotle's *Poetics*, that were often adhered to by seventeenth- and eighteenth-century playwrights; the action had to take place in a single location with 24 hours, and be concerned with one main action rather than having many subplots

Historical terms

city knight   one who earned his title (rather than inherited it) as a reward for services to London commerce

Convention Parliament   parliament convened without being summoned by the sovereign

Hanoverian succession   the right of succession to the English and Irish crowns by Sophia Electress of Hanover and her Protestant heirs (she was the granddaughter of James I; nearly all surviving members of the Stuart dynasty were Catholic, but Sophia's son became King George I and started the Hanoverian dynasty in 1714)

Hogarth   William Hogarth (1697–1764), a painter and printmaker, depicted human failings in a satirical and richly detailed manner (see page 181)

Kit-Cat Club   early-eighteenth-century gentlemen's club, based in London; it had strong literary and political affiliations and supported the Whig cause

libertine   self-interested person who is sexually promiscuous and believes in the expression of personal freedom at all costs

Machiavel   after Niccolò Machiavelli (1469–1527), an Italian political thinker and writer; term used to refer to strategists who seek to dominate and control others for their own ends

Puritan   member of a group of English Protestants who in the sixteenth and seventeenth centuries advocated strict religious discipline along with simplification of the ceremonies and creeds of the Church of England; seventeenth-century Puritans were involved in commerce and regarded Parliament and the law as a means to protect their interests

rake   abbreviation of 'rake-hell', used commonly in the seventeenth and eighteenth centuries to describe someone who is immoral, debauched and dissolute

royalist   supporter of government by monarchy; a soldier who fought for Charles I during the English Civil War, also referred to as a cavalier

Glossary

sinecure official, paid position that requires little responsibility or work

theatre patents legal documents drawn up under Charles II that granted a monopoly on performance rights to two London theatres; they form the legal foundations of today's Theatre Royal, Drury Lane and the Royal Opera House, Covent Garden

Tories politicians in opposition to the Whigs; they defended traditional political and social institutions (not to be confused with the modern Conservative party)

Whigs politicians in opposition to the Tories; they were pro-Parliamentarian rather than royalist, and had liberal views

Appendix 1

Congreve's London

Westminster Abbey: 20 Dean's Yard, London SW1P 3PA
Congreve's memorial is near his grave in the south aisle of the nave. It is a marble monument by sculptor Francis Bird consisting of a sarcophagus with scattered books and theatrical masks. There is a large oval medallion in a black marble frame containing a half-length portrait of Congreve. Anne Bracegirdle is buried in the east cloister. Lady Henrietta Godolphin is buried near Congreve but has no monument or gravestone.
Tube: Westminster

St James's Park
The park is the oldest royal park in the capital. It was landscaped in the early years of the seventeenth century under James I. Charles II made significant changes to its design and opened it to the public for the first time. Its centrepiece was a straight canal, lined with avenues of trees.
Tube: St James's Park, Victoria or Westminster

Hyde Park
The park was in existence for hundreds of years before the Restoration period but was developed into a fashionable meeting place by the Stuarts. Charles I created a circular track called the Ring where members of the royal court could drive their carriages. Charles II stocked the park with deer and encircled it with a brick wall; the park had been opened to the public in 1637 and became fashionable for promenades and carriage rides.
Tube: Hyde Park Corner

Appendix 1

Museums and art galleries

The National Portrait Gallery: St Martin's Place, London WC2H 0HE
The second floor has displays of portraits of seventeenth-century royal and cultural figures. Room 10 displays the portraits of Kit-Cat Club members. Sir Godfrey Kneller painted 48 portraits of its members, including Congreve, some of which can be seen here.
Tube: Leicester Square

The Victoria and Albert Museum: Cromwell Road, London SW7 2RL
Theatre and Performance galleries opened in 2009.
Tube: South Kensington

Appendix 2

Ideas for studying the play in the classroom

1 Research the history of how tennis courts were converted into theatres. Use the information to sketch out a theatre interior, labelling the parts and showing their dimensions.

2 Write a 60–90-second version of the play to familiarize yourself with the plot; present your version to the class. This could take the form of a puppet show, mime, or magazine gossip column.

3 Try 'hot seating'; after reading or acting a scene, students who have taken the main parts could sit on a panel and, keeping in role, answer questions on their motivation, feelings and behaviour.

4 Try gender switching: swap male for female parts and vice versa. Discuss how the scenes play differently.

5 Take on the role of casting director; create a collage featuring actors you would cast for the play.

6 Re-write one of Mirabell's or Lady Wishfort's speeches in modern prose. Consider how important Congreve's style is to the effect of the speech on an audience.

7 Watch a television comedy to familiarize yourselves with the basic techniques of writing good comic dialogue. Compare techniques with those Congreve used.

8 Research aspects of late seventeenth-century society referenced in the play. Suggestions are: marriage, divorce, women's social lives, servants, rakes, chocolate-houses, royal parks, wits, gambling.

Appendix 2

9 Write a sentence for each character summing up their type. Students could choose a character each and bring in a single item of clothing or prop that helps identify that character. Use the items for easy identification of characters while acting scenes from the play.

10 Try voice recognition; select some dialogue that you think reveals contrasts in character through style and expression. Type it into a Word document and ask other students to match the dialogue to the characters, and justify their decisions.

11 Use a diagram to map out the past, present and future relationships between characters. Distinguish between blood, familial, social, friendship and illicit relationships. Consider why some characters are more powerful than others, and don't forget the deceased Sir Jonathan Wishfort.

Appendix 3

Comparative texts

If you have enjoyed Congreve's play and want to learn more, here are some suggestions for wider reading.

The gay couple
One of the best to compare with Mirabell and Millamant is Benedick and Beatrice in Shakespeare's *Much Ado About Nothing* (1598):
- Act I Scene I lines 105–131 (Beatrice: I wonder that you will still be talking.... *to* Beatrice: You always end with a jade's trick. I know you of old)
- Act II Scene I lines 114–255 (Beatrice: Will you not tell me who told you so? *to* Benedick: I cannot endure my Lady Tongue)

Restoration rakes, sexual predation, mismatched marriage and country fools

See *The Country Wife* (1675) by William Wycherley. Act II Scene I introduces the audience to Margery and her new husband Pinchwife. It jokes about the folly of mismatched marriage partners, and town versus country attitudes. This is an earlier Restoration comedy and is more cynical and bawdy than *The Way of the World*. Read other scenes in the play to compare its rake figure Horner with Mirabell and Fainall.

Another good example of a rake figure is Dorimant in *The Man of Mode* (1676) by George Etherege.

Did Congreve influence Sheridan?

A comparison of characters and themes in *The Rivals* (1775) and *The School for Scandal* (1777) by Richard Brinsley Sheridan would help answer this question.

Appendix 3

- From *The Rivals*: Mrs Malaprop's hunt for a husband, domineering tendencies, vanity, and rich and often misapplied vocabulary owe much to Lady Wishfort; see I.ii.180–329 and V.iii.227–241
- From *The School for Scandal*: the cabal, the importance of reputation and avoiding scandal, and the marital disharmony of the Teazles are indebted to Congreve but also modify these themes for a more sentimental age; see I.i., II.i. and III.i.215–332

Satire on cosmetics, women's vanity, grotesque bodies, ageing and gambling

See *The Rape of the Lock* (1717) by Alexander Pope.

- For Pope's satire on the sacred rites that the solemn application of makeup entails for a young beauty preparing to appear in society: Canto I 121–148
- For Pope's satire on gambling: Canto III 25–100
- For Pope's satire on ageing: Canto IV 25–30 and Canto V 15–34
- For grotesque bodies and birth imagery: Canto IV 47–54

Pope's heroine Belinda makes an interesting comparison with Millamant.

See also Sheridan's *The Rivals* and *The School for Scandal*.

- From *The Rivals*: Lydia Languish and her maid use the pages of Fordyce's *Sermons* to curl her hair in a joke that recalls Millamant and Mincing's efforts, I.ii.168–179
- From *The School for Scandal*: jokes about Lady Wishfort's complexion may have influenced Sheridan's depiction of the scandalmongers, II.ii.35–209